The Political Edge

Edited by Chris Carlsson

City Lights Foundation
San Francisco

Book design and Typography: Typesetting Etc., San Francisco
Cover design: www.justicedesign.com
Cover photograph: Chris Carlsson
End sheets: Market Street Railway Mural by Mona Caron, a public mural depicting a 180-degree bird's-eye view of San Francisco's Market Street through different time periods and events in history, ending with a utopian vision. The mural is located at 300 Church St. at 15th St. in San Francisco's Castro district. See more views at www.monacaron.com.

Thanks to David Ho and Marlena Sonn for campaign materials.
Historical photos and maps courtesy Greg Gaar collection and Shaping San Francisco.

Cataloging-in-Publication Data

The political edge / edited by Chris Carlsson
p. cm
    ISBN 1-93140405-4
    1.   San Francisco (Calif.)–Politics and government. 2. Mayors– California– San Francisco– Election. 3. Gonzalez, Matt, 1965–. 4. Political culture– California– San Francisco. 5. San Francisco (Calif.)–Social conditions. 6. San Francisco (Calif.) –Biography.   1. Carlsson, Chris, 1957-

    LC & Dewey shelf numbers are available from the Library of Congress

CITY LIGHTS FOUNDATION is the nonprofit wing of City Lights Books. We believe that the ability to think critically, discern truth, and communicate knowledge is essential to a democratic society. Our goal is to advance deep literacy, which is not only the ability to read and write but to develop the knowledge and skills to consciously shape our lives and the life of our community. City Lights Foundation books are published at the City Lights Bookstore, 261 Columbus Avenue, San Francisco CA 94133. www.citylights.com

THE POLITICAL EDGE

What Is Political?

Chris Carlsson

Anthologies bear the unsustainable burden of trying to be comprehensive. In this case, it's a burden made heavier by widespread confusion in our culture about what is political. This culture commonly associates "political" with elections and governments, candidates and campaigns. Politics is seldom understood as something bound up in the minutiae of our daily lives, in the ways we interact with each other at work and in the streets. This book, taken as a whole, reveals a deeper politics shaping our built environment and our housing options, our sense of community and identity, how we express ourselves, how we move around, what kind of work we do, and yes, how we think about representation. That said, this book originated in the wake of the surprising popular mobilization on behalf of the campaign to elect underdog Matt Gonzalez mayor of San Francisco.

"The personal is political" has traveled a long way over the past generation to land on shopping and entertainment choices. Music, food, fashion, and transit choices have become the arena in which individuals express "dissent." Broadly speaking, alternative subcultures contest social norms on a daily basis. Most alternative culture expressions are reduced to commodities for sale and easily tolerated, while others threaten the status quo. Going beyond the banal politics of consumerism, for example, some challenge scientific expertise and structures of authority while others attack embedded racism and sexism. Others still reject electoral politics as a hollow simulacra of "real politics." But rarely do contemporary radicals join with cultural rebels and neighborhood activists to engage in a local election campaign. This collection analyzes where the emergent political energies came from, and where they're going. Though far from representing all voices and tendencies in San Francisco, this book still covers a number of key groups and themes.

San Francisco has long played the role in the United States of an incubator, a place where cultural and political trends erupt first. It is a city that not only tolerates dissent, but thrives on it. Nevertheless, the city's political establishment is more like the powers-that-be in the rest of the country than not. San Francisco's waves of political revolt and cultural experimentation have barely impacted the actual governance of the city.

In San Francisco we've just endured two mayoral terms of Willie Brown. Once a civil rights and criminal attorney, he became the longest-sitting

Speaker of the Assembly in the infamously corrupt California State Legislature. "Termed out," he was elected San Francisco's mayor in 1995 where his deal-making skills kept the wheels of commerce turning. During his eight years he presided over and encouraged a frenzied real estate boom in a city that boomed and busted dozens of times in its storied history. By the time the real estate market was peaking in 1999, during the dot.com bubble and the lowest commercial and residential vacancy rates in memory, Brown won reelection against an insurgent write-in campaign from the left for the city's Board of Supervisors' then-president Tom Ammiano. Keith Hennessy in "Queerly Shifting Agendas" and Michelle Tea in "Vote Yesterday" recount the hope and expectation that Ammiano would again become the progressive standard-bearer in the recent election. Hennessy's piece unpacks the stark divisions that have emerged in the once-thought-homogenous "gay community." The Ammiano campaign to rid the city of Brown failed, but the political momentum carried over to re-establishing district elections for the Board of Supervisors, electing a new majority of anti-Brown "progressives," and passing a series of referendums to diminish the executive power of the mayor.

Brown endorsed as his successor Gavin Newsom, a young businessman whose career was launched when Brown appointed him first to a city commission, then to a vacant seat on the Board of Supervisors. Newsom was known for his restaurants, wine shops, and real estate investments, many in partnership with the billionaire oil-rich Getty family. Newsom furthered his image as a politician of the elite by launching a ballot proposition cynically named "Care Not Cash" to reallocate general assistance funding away from cash grants to poor people toward "services" that by all objective accounts could not be provided by those funds. A cagey ad campaign for the proposition shrewdly fed the affluents' predisposition to feel victimized; billboards blanketed the city showing middle-class people with cardboard signs decrying having to smell pee or step over sleeping homeless.

Newsom and his wealthy benefactors fully expected him to be elected mayor in a nearly uncontested landslide. Much to their surprise, Board president and Green Party member Matt Gonzalez electrified the same progressive forces that had earlier checked Brown at the ballot box. Gonzalez won thousands more votes on election day in December 2003, but Newsom's vast 5 to1 financial advantage had allowed his campaign to solicit and "bank" a 75% majority of absentee ballots, and win the election at 53%.

Whatever one felt about the election, the excited frenzy that pushed the Gonzalez campaign was hard to miss. Fueled largely by what different writers here refer to as the "alternative culture," a remarkable sense of community and euphoria reproduced itself during the thirty days between the first and second rounds of the election. Josh Wilson starts with a look at "This Magic Moment," the euphoria of collectivity and connectedness that our culture is starving for, and finds—ever so briefly—in election campaigns. Marlena Sonn ("One Small Piece of Gold") and Alli Starr ("From the Streets to Elections") played important leadership roles in the unusual self-expanding grassroots Gonzalez campaign. Michelle Tea ("Vote Yesterday") and Hugh D'Andrade ("Interrupting the Monologue") slogged through the streets and talked to San Franciscans where they could, giving a ground-level view of how the insurgency connected—or didn't—to ordinary citizens. They also embody the experiences of "alt-cult folk" at the activist base of the campaign; some of their deeper aspirations appear too. Michael "Med-o" Whitson ("Engagement and Enragement") and Alejandro Murguía ("Into the Fray") offer contrasting views of the deeper questions surrounding participation, representation, and voting. Whitson argues for a more direct politics that can make "felt" social power become "real," while Murguía underlines the gap between representatives and the represented. David Rosen puts the "alt-cult" into a global context, situating the youthful makers and consumers of music and art within a worldwide restructuring of the culture industry.

San Francisco has always attracted people ready to push the edges of politics, cultural expression, and lifestyle. Erick Lyle describes the indefatigable punk culture in San Francisco in "On the Low Frequencies." From squatting in billiard halls to grazing in dot.com fridges, from covering buildings in public art to joining street protests against war, Lyle has been at the epicenter of an incredibly lively current of revolt. On a parallel track, Mattilda has been an instigator of the no-holds-barred group Gay Shame, shocking gay assimilationists and inspiring everyone who believes that life has much more to offer than another weekend of Pottery Barn shopping ("Furthering the Divide").

Quintin Mecke, a longtime community organizer who helped form the South of Market Anti-Displacement Coalition, takes a look at the planning and land-use legacy of Willie Brown's regime in "McFrisco." In "A Decade of Displacement" James Tracy describes the devastating loss of diversity and shrinking availability of housing for workers and the poor. But he also shows that resilient efforts to counter the power of money and real estate have helped stave off many of the worst-case outcomes that might have been. Housing remains a hotly contested issue in San Francisco, like it is across urban America.

Dr. Ahimsa Sumchai, a physician and neurologist who was born and raised in

San Francisco's public housing, offers an eloquent capsule history of the Bayview-Hunters Point district and details the enormously corrupt scandal unfolding in near silence as the Navy and newly elected Mayor Newsom carry out Willie Brown's "conveyance" of Hunters Point to a private developer ("Put Your Head In It!"). Coalition on Homelessness organizer Bianca Henry ("The Race Card") portrays the harrowing conditions that many residents must survive in Bayview-Hunters Point, San Francisco's remaining black neighborhood, and she shows how Willie Brown, the city's first black mayor betrayed that community.

San Francisco is a world-renowned technology center. Regrettably, this is mostly due to its proximity to Silicon Valley and the heavy use made of computers by the plundering multinationals that call this city home. But Rick Prelinger shows us in "Toward A Copyright-Free Zone" that the Bay Area is also the center of a growing movement of artists, techies, and lawyers seeking to escape the constraints of intellectual property. Right with him, Annalee Newitz gives us a primer in "Digital Politics 101" by introducing us to some of the individuals pushing the edges of techno-politics in ways mostly invisible in the rhythms of representative democracy. Nevertheless, the "hacktivists" and others reshaping the Internet, the media, and our technological practices will eventually be felt throughout society.

Iain Boal's "A City for Idiots" fleshes out the persistent San Francisco tradition of fighting for a human-centered city against a car-centered one. Steven Bodzin wonders "What Does Green Mean?" in San Francisco politics, and argues that a more thoroughgoing green agenda was absent from the recent mayoral campaign precisely because green groups and activists do such a poor job of applying their sensibilities to our everyday lives here in San Francisco. And as if to answer such an admonition, Joel Pomerantz divines the future of water in "San Francisco's Clean Little Secret." He reconnects us to the sloshing abundance below our feet, long forgotten, but yearning to reemerge as part of a more general transformation of our urban infrastructure. Lawrence Ferlinghetti treats us to a brief utopian fable in "Wave of the Future." My own article, "'Jobs' Don't Work," concludes our collection with a rebuttal to the economistic framing of our lives in favor of a semi-utopian call for a new municipal public commons, proposing that time is short for us to reach a lot further than you might imagine.

When the Gonzalez campaign lost, soon followed by his decision to withdraw from running again for supervisor, the wind went out of the sails for many San Franciscans. Something similar happened after Ammiano's 1999 defeat, and after other electoral disappointments in years past. But political experiments continue to germinate here. Cooperative efforts by ordinary citizens to improve life appear in community gardens, public schools, parks, libraries, streets, and in widespread support for neighborhood protection and convivial urban design. Planners and politicians cannot blithely proceed with their monied agendas in San Francisco. Too many people are paying attention. More and more San Franciscans expect so much of life that the old paradigms are starting to give way. The practical contest over the shape of our lives, the incessant drive *to cooperate*—against daunting institutional and social barriers—are the political initiatives that ultimately give me hope.

Perhaps the recent campaign will one day be seen as a harbinger of things to come. Perhaps it will disappear in the mists of blurry memory like so many previous electoral hopes. The world is changing rapidly—politically, economically, and meteorologically. The rhythm of our revolt is quickening, too, even if we haven't won yet. Life can be radically better than this, and sometimes you can taste it. San Francisco offers a surprising number of times and places to savor it.

This Magic Moment
Euphoric Community and the Utopian Impulse

Josh Wilson

It almost sparked, with Gonzalez. For a brief, thrilling moment, the fires blazed hot and bright, and all the disparate utopian dreams suddenly seemed possible: car-free Market Street, an end to the scapegoating of the homeless, arts monies for neighborhoods rather than monolithic institutions, community land trusts to keep housing affordable, universal health care, even a tidal-energy project to get us off fossil fuel addiction!

Up till now, the history of this vision—of a radically re-imagined San Francisco, where the humanitarian rather than economic imperative has the upper hand—has largely been a history of stifled prospects, stillborn dreams, and high hopes that have never amounted to much. You can blame the indifference or outright hostility of the status quo, but you'll be dishonest if you don't also finger the city's amazingly brilliant but chronically fragmented political reformers and urban utopians.

The Gonzalez campaign's unifying power sprang from its affirmation of this vision as not merely beautiful, but inclusive and achievable—a collective, euphoric moment of recognition that, yes, "We can do this!"

There is strength in that moment. It's the same as the aesthetic fugue of an art lover in the gallery; the same moment as when, at the dance party, the music is so good that no one's a stranger anymore; the same boundary-erasing emotion that sweeps over the audience at the rock show, when the band goes pyrotechnic, and all mundane troubles of the world—the bills and romantic conflicts and health insurance nightmares—disappear.

It's the same moment when cruising through Broadway Tunnel among hundreds of other Critical Mass bicyclists, and there are no gunning engines and no choking plumes of exhaust, just bells ringing and people gliding past, hollering, cheering, smiling like an army of blessed liberation, arrived at the nick of time.

Dare I say, it's even the same moment as that sustained suspension of disbelief that can happen at Burning Man, a week into it, sunburnt and dazzled by the monumental, profound, complex, unhinged expressions of human creativity, so far removed from the everyday nine-to-five grind that it seems like another lifetime.

There's nothing in that moment except beauty and freedom and potential. And when an entire community shares that moment—when our accepted vision of reality is peeled back and we get a real glimpse of Paradise on Earth—the potential for sociocultural transformation is, by any definition of the word, revolutionary.

And if that moment can last—if it can survive not just the morning after, but the test of time, if it can linger positively in your memory as you slog through the day-to-day continuum of work and debt—then, perhaps, you will see the desire for change cohere into something substantial, and even formidable. And maybe even something that can win.

The danger of a politician harnessing the energy of the euphoric moment—the collective utopian vision—is, of course, demagoguery, and all the blood-letting that historically comes with it.

Totalitarianism and populist fascism aside, the warty second cousin of the demagogue is the charismatic leader. Even given a charismatic leader's good intentions, the problem with such a person is that when they go away, so does the movement.

In San Francisco, what has come to be termed the "progressive" movement—a grab-bag of Greens, disenchanted Democrats, and miscellaneous leftist politicos—seems, so far, to have lived and died on the ideals, charm, and lover-man good looks of Matt Gonzalez, who lost the election—albeit by a hairsbreadth—and who has now announced he's not running for the Board of Supervisors seat he holds.

So what happens now? Is it all on hold until Matt comes back? Or until the next big political hope comes swinging in on a vine?

We cannot go on like this. We need leaders, but the San Francisco of our dreams cannot live and die on their rise, their fall, or their political moods.

Utopia means "nowhere," and by necessity that means that our utopian San Francisco cannot be a goal, but a process. We will never get there, but in the process of trying we can make our city a much better place than it ever has been.

The problem is, many of the city's reform movements in the nineties were notable not only for the grandeur of their vision, but also their frequent failure to move past that initial burst of euphoric, community-building energy.

In 1999, Tom Ammiano gathered around him a giddy swirl of artists, musicians, queers, and plain-old-leftists. He made a hard run at Willie Brown's office, and he failed, badly. And except for the success of district elections, not very much of Brown's patronage-driven agenda was derailed at all.

Popular outrage at the dot.com boom's unprecedented "cultural clearcutting"—as ethnic communities, funky art spaces, and nightclubs alike were uprooted or shuttered by waves of expensive condominium projects colonizing low-rent neighborhoods—amounted to little more than a tempest in a teapot, in the end. Housing is still inhumanely expensive, and Oakland is benefiting greatly from our displaced creative communities. The vanished clubs and venues are gone, forever. The best that we can show for all our efforts is a new entertainment commission—instead of the SFPD—to govern how entertainment venues are permitted in San Francisco.

And the very fact that culture has to be permitted doesn't indicate much progress at all. If the question of art and culture is, as Situationist grandpappy Guy Debord said, "a question of producing ourselves, not things that enslave us," then San Francisco really is in deep shit. Our creative underground is going strong, but is still badly bruised by the dot.com boom. I don't say this as a good-old-days fogey—this is a matter of hard economics. Burning Man now costs a mint to attend, making its message of liberation through participatory creative expression quite inaccessible to broad and important swaths of the population. Extravagant, out-on-the-streets, reality-hacking creativity is tragically rare these days. Brian Goggins's grinningly skewed "Defenestration" installation—with rubbery, Looney Toons furniture leaping out of the windows of a decaying building on 6th Street and Howard—is steadily decaying, and worse still, seems to have been a one of a kind project, leaving our downtown destitute of anything except self-important corporate architecture. Projects like the 24-Hour Community Spacewalk—which in 1997 and 1998 covered huge segments of the Mission and South of Market with hundreds of multimedia installations, performance events, and participatory art parties—are now utterly absent from our lives. Instead, we have dreary commercial street fairs selling Budweiser for $5. This, from the town that coined the phrase "guerrilla theater" more than thirty years ago!

Consider, also, the transportation reform movement, a think-globally-act-locally phenomenon in San Francisco that is arguably one of the key emergence points. Despite the breathtaking success of Critical Mass as a mass movement that staked out psychological space on urban asphalt for bicyclists, despite the remarkable organizational focus and discipline of the San Francisco Bicycle Coalition, we have not significantly derailed the petro-centric culture of global climate change, oil wars, and pedestrian-unfriendly urban design.

This is big. Lots of people die all around the world because of our oil-dependent society. San Francisco could be leading the world in evolving past this culture of pollution and death, but the high hopes of our collective effort are tragically outweighed by the small scale of our success. We have a few more bike lanes in town, and more bicyclists on the road. Yes. But public transit remains grievously underused and unattractive as a commute option. Rush hour sucks, and is going to suck even more, given time and population growth. There is no car-free city center, following the lauded European model. The *San Francisco Chronicle* reported in May 2004 that the proposed Mexican and Jewish museums are both going bust on a $43 million parking garage near Yerba Buena Gardens. Car-free Saturdays in Golden Gate Park failed at the ballot box, and now Warren Hellman is ramming through an appalling 800-car underground parking garage in the middle of the park's previously idyllic Music Concourse. In 1998 the voters called for the removal of the freeway overpass thrust roughly between Valencia, Van Ness, Western Addition, and Upper Market, and somehow no one noticed that there was a new overpass built into the deal—this one double-wide.

These are terrible failures that enable behaviors that reinforce spiraling pollution, social alienation, unsustainable industries, and wage-slave debt financing. Countless millions of dollars are being poured into automobile-friendly projects that rip the guts out of communities and nurture the suicidal imperative to prop up Middle East dictatorships that sell us petroleum for cheap.

Outrage at the system and its consequences brought tens of thousands of people to the streets of San Francisco when George W. Bush invaded Iraq. Where is that energy now? What happened to the anger, the focus, the willingness to change?

What happened is that when those marchers finally wound up at Civic Center, all they found were a bunch of leftover left-wingers unloading decades-old rhetoric about yesterday's ongoing injustice. And then they went home. And nothing changed. And it was the same old story.

The 2003 mayoral election started out as a tiresome affair featuring the traditional array of flailing leftist Democrats versus a well-funded, heavily favored, Willie Brown–annointed limousine liberal. It was mind-deadeningly ordinary. Into this gaping political void stepped Matt Gonzalez, and he set the city on its ear. The man deserves great credit for bringing plainspoken, straightforward charm to the role of the idealistic, charismatic leader. He wasn't shrill or bludgeoningly ideological. He was willing to bring fresh ideas to the table, but didn't promise the moon. His fiscal pragmatism—including skepticism of bond financing—was intriguing.

Gonzalez gave this city's latent political energy a focus. The chronically disorganized leftists, reformists, and urban utopians were not only motivated, but coordinated. The folks who rallied hardest behind him—who put on the benefit concerts and staffed the phone banks and went door to door—were the seekers who live here for the spirit, the art, the music, the legacy of social innovation. They were, and are, part of a disparate urban Utopian movement—as many rockers as ravers, as many poets as painters, as many hippies as punks, as many proletarians as college kids, as many ecologists and computer programmers.

Coin all the stereotypes of the Left or the underground you like. These diverse groups coalesce around individual expressions of the common experience of euphoric community. And that experience is universally utopian in nature, despite the divergent nature of each subculture's mode of expression and rituals of participation.

And despite the common experience of euphoric community, the divergence between subcultures had the same inadvertant political effect as any program of "divide and conquer." Blame identity politics, blame fashion or genre snobbery, blame target-marketed consumerism or isolated creative or political subcultures, but until Gonzalez came along, these urban utopians were simply incapable of coordinated action toward mutual goals, and too individually marginalized to ever be able to match the political focus of San Francisco's trough-feeding Democratic machine, even considering the American reality of a willfully disenfranchised, cheerlessly apathetic electorate.

The Gonzalez campaign successfully tapped into the euphoric moment, and its extraordinary community-building potential. It almost shattered the cliché of the apathetic electorate, and it almost smashed Democratic Party machine politics into a million pieces. What an upset a win would have been! The news would have been easily as big Gavin Newsom's savvy playing of the gay marriage card, and far more terrifying to the national Democratic Party leadership than Ralph Nader ever could be.

What happens next, then? Do we sit and wonder what might have been? Do we idly wait for Gonzalez's next run for office? Do we hang all our hopes for humanitarian, inclusive, non-capital-focused political reform on the peg of one single politician?

If we do, then the urban utopians will remain a marginalized force, relegated to the coffee shops, and to occasional, sentimental reflections in essays about the Bay Area's colorful cultural history.

In fact, the Bay Area's greatest cultural achievements have pioneered the reclamation of the channels of democratic discourse. From the first Human Be-In to Critical Mass, from the ecstatic rock show to eclectic underground art spaces, from guerrilla theater to the uncensored, intellectually fertile Internet, San Francisco is an ongoing emergence point for new methods of claiming—or creating—public space for civic engagement.

Gonzalez has shown us that it's possible to unite the diverse utopian communities in this fair city. Now we must take it to the next level. It's crucial for progressive reformists to establish new methods of organizing and coordinating. Communities must learn how to identify goals, and agree on methods of achieving them.

Communication, discipline, focus, strategy, and tactics are essential. A disaffected veteran of one notable (and nameless) San Francisco arts collective and facility complained bitterly to me about "cluster" meetings—the co-op committees that set policy there—that lasted for hours, primarily because each participant found it necessary to explore their feelings about the issue of the day, rather than considering potentials and appropriate action.

Similarly, my own experiences at KUSF, a remarkable nonprofit community radio station that has played a crucial role in supporting noncorporate culture and ideas in San Francisco for almost thirty years, have been at once extraordinarily inspiring and enormously frustrating. As a volunteer DJ, producer, and director there since 1994, I have seen waves of staff come and go, and throughout it all the station has at best managed to eke out its own survival from one year to the next. Considering the astonishingly bitter infighting, wailing human tragedy, and monumental bureaucratic indifference that the station's volunteers endure, it's a miracle the place has survived this long—and a testament to both the redeeming significance of its cultural mission and the dedication of its individual staff members.

Therein lies the conundrum San Francisco's utopians must untangle. The strength of their individual visions is enduring. The beauty and promise of their moments of euphoric community is universal. The lack of coordination, the failure to communicate, the fragmentation, and the apathy are epidemic.

Gonzalez showed us that it's possible to tap into the euphoric community and the utopian impulse, and turn it into a potent political machine. Now San Francisco needs to establish new means and methods for grassroots political engagement. We are the *demos*, the foundation of democracy, and we must translate our vivid dreams of a more beautiful, humane city into a thriving reality. We don't need a charismatic leader to make this happen.

The first step has to be the establishment of new, inclusive spaces for civic engagement, encounters with mutually respected rules of participation that eschew vanity, pride, anger, and recrimination. I don't mean another post-Gonzalez "next steps" forum of irked progressives. I mean a thriving, inclusive, cross-cultural forum for identifying reformist priorities that can be enacted through ballot initiatives. Stuffy and tucked-in they may be, but Robert's Rules and rotating meeting facilitation may be a useful means of moving the conversation forward. As for a venue—the San Francisco Public Library offers many free meeting spaces around town.

The second step has to be an aggressive run at the on-the-take, money-focused co-option of our electoral system. To truly advance the cause of grassroots, ballot-driven direct democracy, we need to clear the airwaves and the mailboxes of the lies, distortion, and mudslinging of campaign advertising. Political ads should be banned, or rigorously limited by radical "truth in advertising" legislation—and damn the ACLU with their hypocritical support, in the name of free speech, of the "right" of the monied class to access the airwaves. Doing so clearly denies the right of free speech to those who do not have money.

Instead, why not a weekly issues forum and debates hosted by Bay Area broadcast media on a rotating basis? This would be an enormous improvement over deceitful TV campaign ads. Similarly, mailbox-clogging political junk mail could be replaced by a monthly issues bulletin to be mailed to every registered voter in this city, with candidate and issues advertising in the back—the only such advertising to be permitted in a given campaign—covering the costs of publication and delivery. Third Party and no-party participation in debates must be mandated.

The public needs to recognize its power, and stake it out. This can only come from active, vigorous, respectful discourse. It's not good enough to dream, it's not good enough to snatch at your glimpses of utopia and your moments of euphoria while you can. And you certainly cannot wait around for Matt Gonzalez to swing in on a vine and pull your ass out of the fire.

Instead, you should be waiting at the doors of City Hall, deciding judiciously whether to permit him entry.

Now that would be quite a city to live in, wouldn't it?

Interrupting the Monologue

Hugh D'Andrade

In November of 2003, I returned from vacation to a San Francisco in the middle of one of the periodic explosions of political extravagance for which it is justifiably famous. The mayoral race had failed to produce a clear winner, and a runoff election was scheduled for early December, matching the well-oiled, well-funded Democratic Party insider Gavin Newsom against the rumpled former public defender and Green Party underdog, Matt Gonzalez.

Having been out of town for a few weeks, I was a little surprised at the level of euphoria and excitement the campaign had stirred up. Everywhere I went, people were almost hysterically pro-Gonzalez, and even in circles that aren't normally very political, people were talking in an animated, excitable way about the election and what it meant. The political types I hang out with were in a virtual fever of organizing and campaigning. Everyone felt that a window of opportunity had opened momentarily, and the excitement was contagious.

In the Mission district, where I live and work, it was almost impossible to ignore the election—and as a radical with an anarchist background, ignore elections is what I usually do. But the level of popular support for Matt was truly impressive; the hundreds of official "Matt for Mayor" signs were one thing, but the many countless homemade signs, stickers, posters, even graffiti, were evidence that formerly marginalized voices were speaking out. People who are normally not involved in the usual grind of the electoral cycle had jumped in the ring. Matt's campaign touched a nerve, and in a city still reeling from years of dot.com-driven "development," it was truly a refreshing phenomenon.

Setting aside my usual ambivalence about electoral politics, I decided to get involved. I had time on my hands, being even more underemployed than usual. And I was curious to see if I could learn more about what was behind the Matt Gonzalez phenomenon—what, if anything, made this politician different. The Gonzalez campaign was "hiring" canvassers at the lofty sum of $62 a night, and so, in an act motivated at least as much by financial desperation as by political curiosity, I walked into the chaotic headquarters of Matt's campaign and offered my services. For the first time in my life, I would involve myself in an official campaign, working to elect an actual politician.

My political curiosity wasn't just about the Gonzalez campaign, but also about the rest of the city. It was obvious that the mayoral election had manifested the same divide that had been opened over the Iraq war, as ordinary life was disrupted by protests against the impending disaster. While those of us involved in the protests experienced an exhilaration that seemed to engulf the entire city, it was clear to anyone paying attention that our sensation of being a majority was an illusion. Most San Franciscans were not far from their fellow Americans in their support of the war. Getting outside the bohemian enclaves of the city during those months provided a bracing slap of political sobriety.

I could see that the Gonzalez campaign was going down a similar path. While certain circles were buzzing with nearly unanimous support, the rest of the city was clearly removed and somewhat baffled. The noise and the excitement of this political contest defined a high-stakes showdown between the liberal establishment and our newfound power—what we could call, for lack of a better term, "the alternative cultural progressive bloc."

I wanted to get involved, but I was tired of talking to hip culturatti like myself. How did things look to people in the Sunset? Hunters Point? South San Francisco? Or the neighborhood most bitterly reviled among progressive hipsters, the tragically unhip Marina district, home to our archnemesis, Gavin Newsom? My hope was that walking precincts for the Gonzalez campaign would give me some brief opportunity to get outside the usual circles and converse with people on the other side of my self-imposed exile. As one of those rare people who actually enjoys talking to strangers (especially about politics!) I was enthusiastic about the opportunity to walk up to someone's door and discuss the burning issues of the day.

Unfortunately, it was much more difficult than I imagined.

In January, as the Bush administration's imperial plans fell into place, tens of thousands of people marched together in massive displays of antiwar sentiment. Each rally grew in size and strength until February, when millions of people around the planet marched simultaneously in opposition to the looming disaster in Iraq, with apparently no effect on the Bush administration.

On March 20, the day the invasion of Iraq officially began, San Franciscans once again filled the streets, this time not content to offer symbolic resistance. On that day, and for several days after, over 20,000 people, organized into small, close-knit affinity groups, cooperated on a massive scale to shut down the financial heart of the city. The movement against the war had advanced from simple protest to an active assertion of social power.

For those of us involved, the lived experience was powerfully transforma-tive. Everywhere you looked was another small group of committed peo-ple, many young or simply new to political action, engaging in actions that in their creativity and imaginativeness far surpassed the ordinary, predictable dynamic of leftist marching and chanting. It was as if imagination itself had finally been so offended by the "inevitability" of war that it unleashed human ingenuity in all its splendor to stop business as usual. There were dozens of groups following a "menu" of choices to occupy and block inter-sections: bicyclists swirling through the city providing scouting and guid-ance to blockades; Aging Grannies Against War; Crafty Bitches Knitting Against War; and countless others.

One could have been forgiven for assuming San Francisco had achieved virtual unanimity in opposition. In the neighborhoods where I and most of my extended circles hang out there were no yellow ribbons of war support. The Mission, the Haight, the Downtown neighborhoods were awash in antiwar sentiment—simply walking out in public was to become an instant participant in some act of resistance staged by one of the hundreds of affin-ity groups. Everyone, it seemed, was against the war. Who were these peo-ple that actually thought Saddam was hiding weapons of mass destruction and planned September 11? Did anyone know them? Where were these mythical pro-war masses?

Our disruptions at the war's outset were to us an inspiring example of our own ability to cooperate in imaginative, nonviolent resistance. But they struck others as morally abhorrent. I had a few interesting e-mail conversa-tions with fellow San Franciscans offended—maybe "mortally outraged" is a better word—by our actions. One former marine saw our activities as deeply immoral, criminal acts. "What have you ever done for your country," he asked, "other than disruptive noise in the streets?"

The marine's question gave me pause. For one thing, as an internationalist, the idea of "doing something for my country" is somewhat foreign to me. And for another, my political activities almost entirely consist of what you could call "disruptive noise"—I'm involved in Critical Mass, played a role in bringing bicyclists into the streets during the war, and routinely plaster the city with political stickers and posters. I like disruptive noise. Like Howard Zinn, I think the problem is not civil disobedience, it's civil *obedi-ence*—the blind apathy of a public too lazy to challenge the crimes of the state. It was almost as if the marine and I were speaking different languages—or the same language in which words have different meanings.

The news media constantly bombard us with polling information that is difficult to believe, disturbing statistics about what our fellow Americans do and don't believe. 69% are convinced Saddam staged 9/11; 78% are positive that weapons of mass destruction will be found; 67% believe the United States is a Christian nation. No doubt a similar percentage also believes in Santa Claus or the Easter Bunny. While it is reasonable to question the accuracy of statistics and the methodology behind them, it is also unwise to ignore the broad truths the polling data express. Let's face it: radicals, progressives, and independents with some willingness to question authority, all together comprise a small fraction of the population, even in San Francisco. By taking part in these massive displays of unity, were we trying to convince ourselves and the world that we somehow amount to a majority, if only for a day? Were we, on some level, concealing from ourselves the uncomfortable fact that we are, most likely, a marginal minority?

For me, the war simply drove home once again the fact that I lived in a bubble. Not only did I live in one of the most left-wing cities in America, but I spent almost all my time in the most Left neighborhoods of that city. My relatively large circle of friends and acquaintances is almost entirely comprised of somewhat marginal, creative types—artists, students, writers, musicians, poets, activists, city planners, teachers. People who don't watch much television but who go to lots of independent films, people who read the papers but supplement their mainstream news sources with radical periodicals and well-informed perusal of the Web. Like most Americans, we shop compulsively, but we patronize the local hip shops and stores, almost never setting foot in a mall. And, crucially, we live in dense neighborhoods, where we have dozens of unexpected interactions with friends, neighbors and strangers every day—interactions that introduce us to new underground music, bits of news suppressed or underreported in the papers, local heroes on the Board of Supervisors running underdog campaigns for mayor.

Matt Gonzalez elicited a near-unanimous enthusiasm from our crowd because he was so obviously and conspicuously "one of us," a member of our extended "urban tribe" of creative, alternative types who gravitated to San Francisco to take part in its famous bohemian subcultures. We looked at him and immediately saw our own reflection: someone who lives with roommates, rides a bike to work, has dusty punk and jazz albums in his record collection, reads poetry, goes to gallery openings, and looks somewhat out of place in a business suit. One of the first things that Matt did on the Board of

Supervisors, which set him off from so many other politicians, was open his office to the art community, using it to stage shows of local artists.

With the city once again divided over serious political questions, the Gonzalez campaign was going to send me out into new territory, hopefully leaving my comfort zone to find out what made the city tick.

It was easy enough to sign up with the Gonzalez campaign. Their office, located in a prominent empty building at Mission and 14th, was a hive of buzzing activity. Walking in, I felt immediately at home, surrounded by laid-back hipsters with whom I could just as easily have swapped iTunes collections as share outrage over the latest policy statement from Willie Brown's heir-apparent. Here and there one or two of my political friends flitted about, looking incredibly harried and busy with important campaign work.

The first intimation that my experiment with canvassing was not going to be as interesting as I had hoped came during the initial training session. We introduced ourselves, talked a bit about Matt, and broke into teams to practice the prewritten "rap," a short script we were advised to memorize and use. One person would pretend to be the canvasser, and the other would be the person at the door. To my chagrin, I can still repeat it from memory:

"Hi, my name is Hugh and I'm with the Matt Gonzalez Campaign for Mayor. As you know, polls show we have a good chance to get Matt elected. The problem is that Gavin Newsom has raised over 3 million dollars . . . So we're going to door to door today, asking people who support Matt to chip in. Some of your neighbors have contributed $100 or $200. Is that something you would be able to do today?"

"Uhh . . . I don't have that kind of money."

"Oh, that's fine, I totally understand. Some other folks have been putting in $20 or $40. Is it possible you could do something like that?"

"Oh, no, I really don't have any money to give away."

"No problem. Thanks for your time! Can I give you a window sign to put up or some campaign literature?"

This wasn't exactly what I had in mind when I signed up. The focus on fundraising has always kept me away from electoral politics, and here I was, about to really rub my own nose in this dirty business. Did I really want to do this?

I decided to try it out. I could discard the silly speech and use my own communication skills, which would allow me to tailor my message and convey a more authentic voice for the campaign—more important values, as far as I was concerned.

But I was also disappointed by the fact that we weren't exactly getting into all those districts that had remained a mystery to me during the war. We started out in Bernal Heights, a slightly upscale neighbor to the trendy but low-budget Mission, home to plenty of strollers as well as cars with "Impeach Bush" bumper stickers. Not only is Bernal decidedly liberal, but it is also not the flattest neighborhood, which meant long hikes around windy San Francisco hills.

My trainer was a friendly, enthusiastic guy I'll call Gary. Judging from the way Gary could rattle off the rap about "some of your neighbors" pitching in $200 without sounding completely phony, I figured he was an old hand at this. I was amazed out how easy he made the whole process look. He could knock on a door and walk away with $50 or $100 in a way that I knew I never could.

That first night, after breaking off on my own, I didn't bring in any money, and I didn't have any interesting discussions, at least not with anyone on the other side of the fence. For the most part, I walked alone through quiet streets, marveling at how few people even leave their porch lights on (a green light for canvassers to harass you, obviously). It was a lonely experience, especially when I did actually find someone who would come to the door. For one thing, I found that my attempt at improvising a rap didn't work particularly well—I could feel people wanting to end the conversation as quickly as possible. It was difficult to feel that I was doing anything other than taking people away from their few moments of cherished quiet time with friends and family—or perhaps they were eager to get back to watching *Survivor*.

The best moments came when I would somehow stumble on a house that was enthusiastically pro-Matt. The people would come to the door, invite me in, talk excitedly about attending one of the millions of benefit parties for Matt. Straying wildly from the script I was given, I would ask about their opinion of Newsom's Care Not Cash policy. It was always gratifying to share a moment of quiet anger at corporate liberalism's attempt to scapegoat the poor.

One interesting household made up for all the bad vibes I'd been experiencing. Two kids answered the door, and enthusiastically asked if I had any Chinese-language Gonzalez for Mayor signs. "We're learning Cantonese in school!" they said. We talked for a while, and their friendly, bearded Dad told me they went to a school where they learned half the day in Cantonese, half in English. The kids were so smart and friendly and curious about their world that it made me feel somehow hopeful for the future. I think the Dad wrote out a check out for a big $20.

But for the most part my first night had been a bust. I hadn't broken even (meaning I hadn't raised enough to pay for my own $62 stipend), and I hadn't learned anything about how people who are different from me actually think.

As it turned out, my first night in Bernal was actually my best night canvassing for Gonzalez. The subsequent nights spent walking around other neighborhoods were even more alienating. I found myself longing for the comfort of Bernal's funky, informal suburbia.

One night we were in Laurel Heights, which is an upscale neighborhood somewhere on the edge of the diverse but quiet Richmond district. There aren't any hip bars or bookstores in Laurel Heights, and no trendy restaurants. Prior to this night, I had not even known this area was an actual "neighborhood." Certainly I'd never considered strolling here, talking to people. This was exactly the non-comfort zone I was looking for!

The first thing I noticed about Laurel Heights was how silly I felt walking at all in this neighborhood. This is a place designed to be driven through. The streets are wide, and the large houses have large, welcoming garages. There is almost no foot traffic at about 6 or 7 in the evening, and the only sound is the occasional whoosh of another SUV sweeping by.

I also noticed that, unlike so many other neighborhoods during this turbulent time, few residents cared to display their political allegiance with window signs or bumper stickers. It was as if, along with the quieting of urban noise that comes with suburban lawns and driveways, a quieting of political noise took place as well.

Predictably, there wasn't much space to forge a political connection with people, either. Like quiet Bernal, most houses kept their "Welcome, Canvassers" lights turned off. I had a difficult time finding anyone who would come to the door to talk to me, and when they did, they were very clear that they didn't have time to listen to my speech. And no, they didn't want a window sign.

At one point, outside one of the few apartment buildings in Laurel Heights, I came across a couple uncharacteristically using public space: they were awkwardly standing on the sidewalk having a smoke. I had to laugh at their appearance in this context—dressed in black, with wallet chains and nose rings, they could not have looked more out of place anywhere else in San Francisco. They bolstered my flagging spirits by expressing their enthusiasm for Matt's campaign and sharing their chagrin at having to live in such a dull neighborhood. They were very excited to have their own window signs, but alas, they weren't able to help me with my main mission of collecting money for the campaign.

Despite the lack of street life here (and thus the difficulty of starting a political conversation) I had my most interesting political conversation during my brief experiment—and oddly it had nothing to do with Matt Gonzalez! In a small side street where suddenly the houses were less posh, I found one house that was occupied by several students. Like the other young folks I met, they were very supportive, and actually cheered me up by commiserating with me on the awful grind of canvassing. "That job sucks, dude! Want some beer, man? Water? Anything? C'mon in!"

One of the housemates here was a young Israeli guy with one of those soothing, lilting accents that makes me wish I learned English as a second language. That day, the papers had carried news of more carnage in the occupied territories, and I asked him where he thought it would all end. He totally surprised me by saying, 1) that he supported Sharon, since he was doing what needed to be done despite the difficulty, and 2) that he thought eventually at some point, the Jews would be forced to leave and the country would cease to exist.

I was amazed. First, it was odd to find that someone who was Left enough to support an outsider like Gonzalez would have anything nice to say about Sharon. But more odd than that was his assertion that Jews might just up and leave. "Where would they go?" I asked. "How could a whole country just disappear like that?"

He shrugged. "Do you know how many people are in Israel? Only 6 million. That is less than live in some cities in the U.S."

I told him I thought the population of the entire Bay Area is about that.

"Exactly," he said. "It's a lot of people, but at the same time, it's not that many people. They could leave. They could all move to various countries, I don't know where."

After wandering around Laurel Heights for a while, getting absolutely no contact from anyone except the odd hip young person who somehow managed to slip into the neighborhood, I decided to call it quits. Right then, one of those oversized family SUVs drove past me, and from the cold of the street the driver looked downright cozy in her large, expensive bubble. As she entered her automatic garage and disappeared into her quiet, lonely house, I considered knocking. After all, this was one person I knew was home. What did an SUV driver think of the election? Of the housing crisis? Of the end of Willie Brown's long reign? But I knew this was one person who didn't want to talk to me. Her whole life—from the job she had probably left late to the massive, elevated vehicle to the house on a quiet street in a neighborhood no one has ever heard of—was designed to avoid bumping into people like me! This place was a refuge, a hidden garden away from the noises of the city and the annoying needs and demands of a society in turmoil.

I ran into one of my fellow canvassers, a heavyset smoker I'll call Joanne. It became apparent that she had stolen into my zone and checked all the houses—judging from her transparent denials, I figured that this must be some sort of breach of canvasser protocol. I certainly didn't mind, though I found it irritating to be lied to. But I was saddened to realize how much more this "job" meant to her than to me. I looked at her puffing away at her cigarette in this rich neighborhood and realized she was obviously a low-income person, as most of the young, hip Matt supporters I knew were. For a moment I wondered whether there wasn't an element of class struggle in the campaign after all!

I was cold, tired, and reduced to squabbling over "turf" with a career canvasser. This whole thing wasn't working out. I put in a couple more nights, collected another check, and called it quits.

Each time I finished canvassing and returned to the Mission with a carload of canvassers at about 10 at night, I couldn't help but notice how lively even the quiet parts of the Mission are on a weekday night. There are people in the streets, hanging out in bookstores, having a drink with friends. There is a cacophony of sounds and voices of many different types of people, all occupying the exact same space. Every possible surface is plastered with some form of communication, mostly small advertisements for shows, but a lot of do-it-yourself political agitations as well.

All this noise in my neighborhood contrasted with the hush and quiet, the orderliness, of the neighborhoods I had just left—neighborhoods where people don't generally bump into each other on the street or use signposts to agitate for issues. I wondered how much this fact impacted the kinds of politics you find in each area. The way social life is structured in neighborhoods like the Haight and the Mission makes it possible for ideas to circulate and social movements to develop, outside the controlling interest of the mainstream media. But how far could that go?

In trying to elect this guy mayor of a big city, we had succeeded in creating a huge amount of noise—not just window signs, but nightly parties and events—but only in a few select neighborhoods. It was as if we had been able to raise our voices to fever pitch, but we still couldn't raise our voices loud enough to be heard over the wall between our comfort zones and the rest of the city.

I had totally failed to do what I set out to do, which was find out what people outside my social scene thought about local politics. And, in the bigger picture, our whole movement, such as it is—whether it's trying to stop a war, elect Matt Gonzalez, defend the homeless, or get more low-income housing built—is failing as well. We are failing to do much more than talk amongst ourselves.

I've always found the old critical cliché "preaching to the converted" extremely annoying, partially because I do so much of it, and partially because I think the "converted" also need to be inspired from time to time so that they don't slip into apathy and amnesia. But the criticism stings because of the element of truth contained in it.

There is a paradoxical nature to our movements for social change. The very thing that makes them dynamic and exciting to be involved with—the fact that they are rooted in many subcultural niches—also makes them limited and exclusive. As I pointed out earlier, our affinity for Matt was not based so much on agreement with his politics as on a certain shared cultural sensibility. Few of us were even able to identify exactly what it was, beyond his perceived honesty, that made us supporters, or what he would do to improve San Francisco. But if you weren't in our club, you looked at Matt and thought, "so what?" Maybe you even preferred Newsom's greasy, slick hair to Matt's bed-head.

Phenomena like the Gonzalez campaign and the antiwar affinity groups have been relatively successful because they avoided the usual mistake of exclusively communicating through the dead zone of the media. Instead of trying to water down ideas to the point that they might be palatable to some mythical lowest common denominator, they built on existing social networks and spoke with the authenticity of face-to-face dialogue. These movements thrived in the social space opened by alternative lifestyles and the street life of dense urban bohemian neighborhoods. The movement for change, based in a cultural milieu, expresses itself and communicates with cultural signifiers—and is thus somewhat opaque to non-participants.

This type of politics, in which cultural values replace genuine political conversation, comes fraught with peril. I would hate to become known as the guy who compared Matt Gonzalez to Ronald Reagan, but it is a fact that Reagan's appeal was exactly this. His supporters largely opposed his policies (tax cuts for the rich, covert imperial war, and so on), but were swayed by his sentimental sociability, which spoke to many people's affection for "old-fashioned values." He had a cultural appeal that circumvented the conventional politics of the day and united people behind him in a powerful grassroots coalition.

We also can't forget that the movement for Gonzalez unfolded within the logic of a political campaign. Progressive political campaigns—like the one to elect Gonzalez, or to elect Medea Benjamin, or Ralph Nader, or Eugene Debs for that matter—desperately need to raise money (like the campaigns of their conservative rivals) and raise it fast. Everything is subordinated to this guiding principle. This puts a limit on what they can do, what questions they can ask, how far their program can go.

Beyond that essential problem, there is also confusion about what actually drives social change. Reformers often make the easy assumption that the state is the director of society, and that to change social life, all that is required is grabbing the controls of state power and driving society in the correct direction. As radicals have pointed out for generations now, this is akin to assuming that the world is flat. The real mechanisms of change are much more complex and mysterious than they at first appear. The state's power is constrained within a network of visible and invisible forces that run the gamut from corporate power to public opinion. Beyond that, real social power is based in human communities, not the state. Transforming life begins with this social power.

The story of bicycle activism in San Francisco over the last few years illustrates this point. Back in the early nineties, the San Francisco Bike Coalition was a tiny group with scant resources, lacking in any political clout. The city bureaucracy was strongly resistant to implementing reforms to protect bicyclists or encourage cycling.

That all began to change when bicyclists started meeting once a month to ride home together in Critical Mass. Organized informally, without overt political demands or central committees, Critical Mass created a public space where bicyclists could experience and feel their own social power, and experiment with changing their city one Friday at a time. It didn't happen overnight, but eventually bicycling became an issue no politician in San Francisco could afford to ignore. Today, more than a decade since the founding of Critical Mass, there are ongoing improvements—still sadly inadequate, but welcome nonetheless—being made to the city's bicycle infrastructure.

Some people imagine that San Francisco needs a charismatic leader who will bring honesty and vision to city planning. But it will take imaginative, visionary, and eminently simple practices like Critical Mass to turn things around, carried out by ordinary people. Does the endless procession of progressive electoral campaigns help or hinder the process of discovering and using social power? We as individuals and communities have the power to remake the world, but we mostly don't believe it, and rarely use it.

In the first weeks of the war, a Critical Mass splinter group called Bikes Not Bombs met every day to continue protesting. After the March 20 shutdown of the financial district, the media emphasized a backlash among ordinary people horrified by the inconvenience caused by protestors. While many affinity groups responded by avoiding disruptions, Bikes Not Bombs kept those tactics in circulation. As we knew from years of riding in Critical Mass, it only takes a small group of determined bicyclists to really jam up the downtown area. We didn't make too many friends among the shoppers and commuters, although there was a fair amount of support. We did distract war supporters—who thought they could merrily sip their latté on their way home to watch the latest upbeat war news on TV—with a loud, discordant note of angry dissent.

During those months, I often rode the 38 Geary out to the Richmond district to visit my sister and her new baby girl. Each time, I couldn't help noticing the palpable ebbing of my antiwar rage—as if, as the bus hurtled down Geary, away from Downtown and the Mission, the noise of the social struggle faded and dissolved. Out in the avenues, all was order and normalcy, and it was hard to remember why I had been so angry. It was all too easy—and such a relief!—to retreat into a world of private concerns. There was food to be bought, laundry to be done, money to be made . . .

If I had turned to my neighbor on the bus to discuss my feelings about the war, I might have had more success than I did as a canvasser for Matt Gonzalez. For the most part, my attempts at dialogue were thwarted at every turn. Canvassing is clearly a poor way to conduct political dialogue. My chances of making even a small dent were limited—as our political movements are also limited—by the fact that most Americans are not engaging in any dialogue at all. Cocooned in air-conditioned offices, navigating the city in giant SUVs, returning to homes sequestered from the noise and hassle of city life, and immersed in a mediated world of dazzling info-tainment, the wider public is busily receiving a prepackaged monologue. Celebrity newscasters, celebrity politicians, and celebrity businessmen speak, while the public listens, watches, absorbs.

Our movements for social change all begin with dialogue. Conversing amongst ourselves, conversing with the power structure, conversing with political opponents. We seek to instigate dialogue and extend the terms of the debate. We depend on unscripted social interaction and genuine, face-to-face political discourse, thriving on the turbulence and unpredictability of urban life. This turbulence and messy diversity contrasts with the calm, orderly, neutral tones of the corporate voice that constantly announces its own inevitability—the voice of "journalists" on cable news, but also the smooth voice that advertises the luxury of chocolate and wristwatches. The voice that states unequivocally that weapons of mass destruction will soon be found, and announces that the next mayor of San Francisco has already been decided, long before a single vote has been cast.

The recent antiwar movement and the Gonzalez campaign show us that diverse movements can link up in large, decentralized networks to raise issues and challenge the system. Recent campaigns, thankfully, have escaped the conventional leftist logic of building large "popular front" organizations or parties. Moreover, the Gonzalez campaign in particular shows that a large slice of the population is willing to break from a self- defeating loyalty to the liberal Democratic establishment.

These two promising movements have remained limited culturally and geographically. Dominant social patterns favor isolation in an environment where the voice of power speaks and acknowledges no other. It is clear that certain sectors of the population have had some success in breaking out of the traps set by the power structure. But to go beyond organizing hipsters, the movements of the future will have to puncture the sealed world of disembodied images, and find a way to interrupt the monologue—to insist on meaningful dialogue with a population that has forgotten how to think and speak for itself.

One Small Piece of Gold at a Time

Marlena Sonn

The dungeon had only been closed for a month or two when I heard that Matt Gonzalez was running for mayor.

I remember feeling a strong flash of irritation and disbelief, mixed with the pleasure of a passing acquaintance being in the running. I had met Matt a few times at Adobe Books' legendary art parties ten years ago, and followed his quirky and wonderful rise from a public defender to president of the Board of Supervisors. But I had cut my electoral teeth on Tom Ammiano's write-in campaign of '99, felt Angela Alioto was more "electable" against Willie Brown's heir Gavin Newsom, and didn't know who to vote for, now that Matt was in the ring. In other words, I was in the same boat as every other progressive in the city.

But I loved the figure that Matt Gonzalez cut; he was, above all, one of us, a freak of nature. A poetry reading, punk rock listening, lover of the arts, and antagonist to politics as usual; who would think such a creature could be mayor of San Francisco? He was leading the revolution not only against the Willie Brown machine, but also against a ossified progressive movement that believed that elected office was a wait-in-line position.

Meanwhile, I had spent the last eight years building up my practice as a dominatrix. My career path was unexpected, but one that a ladies' education at Barnard College prepared me for startlingly well. It was fun, creative, and most important, politically correct. It had always been my dream as a Marxist and political activist to make the captains of industry beg for forgiveness. And here I was doing it on a daily basis! I was engrossed in the continual exploration of power, in love with the luxurious trappings of the theatre of SM. My North Beach dungeon was a cross between a sound stage and a salon, where conversations about art, human nature, and politics were held after rituals exposed the vulnerable hidden nature of my slaves.

Yet somehow I always felt guilty. The unfairness of the world had always been, and continues to be, intolerable. To witness the poverty of my friends, to know it intimately as an artist who wanted time more than money, left a hollow feeling after flying home from a weekend at the Ritz-Carlton, pretending to be rich. I had seen how the other half lived, and although I had entrée through the side door, I could not embrace the life of being a kept woman. Who was

I to leave behind the ghetto, when others couldn't? Yet who was I, middle-class hellion, to be downwardly mobile, which is the ultimate exercise in privilege? Touching these ethical themes were painful in my twenties, so I drank and partied away these questions, figuring I'd sort it out later.

Being a dominatrix left me a lot of time to pursue other hobbies, such as being in a sixteen-woman synchronized sixties gogo dance troupe, and indulging in being a news junkie. My activism languished after college, where I, like many people, spontaneously marched off campus at the start of the first Iraq war, participated in clinic defense against Operation Rescue, and was arrested for a number of worthy causes. But it was the exodus of friends and the eviction scandals of the late nineties that re-engaged the bombthrower in me. When my dance troupe, the Devilettes, lost our dance studio, I helped stage a performance marathon and rally that drew 1500 people and ended in a small group occupying the building for eighteen days. The renters of this town were pissed off, and we threw the bums out that fall, electing the most progressive Board of Supervisors anyone could remember.

That was the summer of 2000. Then the next year I watched my hometown burn for months, and on Christmas Eve of 2001 I cut up 500 pounds of potatoes and squash for the emergency workers in lower Manhattan, serving the men I used to throw rocks at. The men I used to call "pigs" I now called "sir." The games I played in the dungeon with Intel wannabes weren't fun now that they were really happening in plain sight at Guantánamo. A life of running wild and playing bedroom games turned gray in 2002. I decided to retire.

Switching careers left me a bit lost, and broke. I had thrown a fabulous benefit for the St. James Infirmary, the nation's only free health clinic for sex workers, and established a fund-raising department for the little organization that was threatened to be squashed by massive city and federal budget cuts. For a while I worked part time as I phased out my last visits with my most loyal slaves, and marveled that a single hour of my time as a dominatrix was worth more than a week's pay at a clinic literally saving lives. My hours were endless for a cause that I believed in, and latex fairy tales never last forever. I needed a job, and I needed it quick.

So the "Yes on L" (living wage) campaign came along, a chance to make a difference and make the rent. By then the mayoral race was a bloodbath, with Tom loyalists and Angela pragmatists cursing and scoffing at the third progressive running. I sat it out, working instead on the initiative to raise the minimum wage, an earnest little bit of fingerflipping to The Man toward which everyone felt agreeable. And it gave me a taste of a game I started to like; I wanted to get into the action for the runoff.

So I decided to throw thirty parties for any progressive that got into the race against Gavin.

I had assumed that Matt would make it, after visiting the campaign headquarters of all three progressives. It was obvious to anyone who could look past what the media or the progressive establishment said; there was an excitement, an air of expectation, at Matt's headquarters that Angela or Tom just couldn't match. I made a cheap little flyer that cribbed some text from the Green Party Web site and added the tag line "Join us as we embark on 30 parties in 30 days!" On the election night, I had them ready as the numbers rolled in: 20% for Matt, good enough for second place. I was at the "Yes on L" party, and dropped one into Supervisor Chris Daly's hand. He looked at me, and said, "This is so crazy it just might work."

To say that I was determined is an understatement. I came in hungry, stubborn, and refusing to deviate at all from my dream, which was to manifest the most parties any political campaign had ever seen. In my mind, every night would be a celebration that we even made it this far, a loud and major "fuck you" to the kingmakers and politics as usual. I wanted to take the natural shape of the events and puff it up, make it bigger, crazier. I wanted to package Matt's inherent rock-star shine and turn the campaign into a Major League Tour. And I wanted something to call my own, a title, a little bit of land on which I could build a way out of sex work, a plug to fill the eight-year hole in my résumé that listed me as an attitude adjustment specialist. I was actually quite lucky to jump onto a train quickly gaining speed; my own survival and future depended on hanging on tight.

The first party was scheduled for Adobe Books, and the place where the Rock 'n' Roll Runoff baseball jersey was born. I had compiled a list of the events that had come together by that Saturday. It was on the back of the second flyer, which was just as cheap as the first, and ready to be photocopied. By Saturday, four days after the general election, there were twenty-six parties scheduled. The rap sheet listed the neighborhood, time, date, and title of the event, and as it circulated in the crowd it caught on: people laughed, shook their head, and then said, " I want to throw a party too!" And then Tom Scott from Queers for Matt said, "This list should be on the back of a jersey, just like an old Iron Maiden t-shirt."

By Monday the t-shirt was in the works, and the Events team was in place; two friends were recruited to volunteer full-time, and I was fighting for an office. In the mass explosion that was headquarters, it was a battle to get a phone and DSL line, and a major coup to score a wall-sized whiteboard. Every day the campaign expanded exponentially. Every day more and more volunteers flooded in, took over a corner, and said "We're not leaving. We know how to help Matt!" With more bodies than rooms, desks, or chairs, and priorities shifting in the campaign, half of my time was spent making sure the Events team wasn't usurped by some other, more determined volunteers with young legs ready to storm City Hall.

Every day was a glorious battle. The Events department went from being party planners to a giant bulletin board, as calls flooded in from people who were determined to throw a party for Matt. My own parties withered and blew away as I spent most of my time just trying to catch up with all the phone calls and getting people what they needed: campaign materials, posters, volunteers, speakers, and most important, Matt. Everyone wanted Matt at their party. One woman who was fixated on having him began crying when I said that he was previously engaged. People begged and yelled, and they wouldn't stop calling. One crackpot offered $100,000 to stage an event where Matt would get his hair cut; the ladies of the campaign were outraged and felt that his messy tresses were perfect just the way they were.

The interruptions were constant. I would arrive at the office at 10 A.M., and enjoy a few hours of regroup and planning. By noon the place would be a tornado of activity and by 2 P.M., I wouldn't be surprised if I had answered at least 250 questions. Everything from, "What's the next hot party?" to "Where's Matt going to be?" to "Where's the bathroom?" New volunteers were looking for guidance and wandered through anyone's office looking for it, often feeling very urgent about being paid attention to *right away*. On days we were all in the office together, three or four separate conversations would be held in simultaneously in an office the size of a large coffin, t-shirts were flying out the door, and piles of money were stacked in bags at my feet, waiting to be counted and submitted to the treasurer.

And the money flowed in, a tidal wave of one-dollar bills. There had been this grim determination at the start of the runoff to make it on a shoestring, in the face of millions of dollars being spent by the opposition. There was a hopeful $250,000 mentioned as a "goal," but one that seemed about as far off as the little leprechaun that would accompany it at the end of the rainbow. But I knew we could make it, and more.

The thing that I wanted to give the campaign more than anything in the world was access to money. Not that I had it myself. But I had seen the other side, and knew that there was plenty to go around, if only we could claim it as our own. This was the thing that I would work on, the dirty work that no one else would touch. Because we needed it so badly, and it was my chance to shine and to serve. It was a fierce longing that kept me up at night, representing the missing link between our movement and City Hall. All the injustice and the poverty that I had witnessed, the wrenching exodus of friends and evictions of artists during the dot.com boom, somehow all this could be absolved with the victory of our campaign. All we needed was the money.

But the greatest resistance to this dream came from within our own ranks, so used to condemning the pursuit of money as a shallow, evil thing, and afraid to ask for anything. I had been surrounded my entire life by artists and activists who suffered from an awful deprivation, and yet our eyes were closed to the abundance around us. So used to a poverty mentality, the concept of asking for more was completely alien. Why could we not imagine having more, all of us? All the tainted meanings had stripped money of its neutral role as a marker of time, an expediter and enabler for our own imaginations.

While I felt hollow asking for myself, I loved dreaming big for this campaign that somehow felt like a winner, and shamelessly demanded top dollar from everyone I knew. The bar was set at $1,500 per party, with some pulling in $20,000, a few upward of that. Most donations came in very small increments. The t-shirts alone raised in the ballpark of $60,000, $20 at a time. It was the volume of events, the enthusiasm of dozens of grassroots fund-raisers, and a few high-powered individuals that helped level the playing field, which was still uneven, but becoming more manageable. By December the campaign had raised over $800,000, $550,000 of that during the runoff. Instead of combating a 20 to 1 advantage, we slimmed it down, fighting instead against the ticking clock, and the banked absentee votes that San Franciscans cast before even getting to know Matt.

All the while there were parties going on. At some point halfway through the runoff, the events team said "*no more parties.*" We were up to 118, and there were upward of seven events a night. Swanky affairs at Shanghai 1930, art auctions, and Mansions for Matt brunches in Pacific Heights. Grimy noise rock shows in warehouses, coffee klatches, bookstore readings, and Burning Man voter registration drives hosted by the founder himself, Larry Harvey. Jonathan Richman played songs for the kids at Moms for Matt, right before Gary Indiana, Mr. San Francisco Leather, hosted Leathermen for Matt at the Eagle. Although I failed in my bid to have City Lights unfurl new Matt banners on the side of their building, it was quite a kick to get a phone call from Lawrence Ferlinghetti letting me know that he was personally walking house signs all over North Beach to hang in cafés.

Of course I loved the parties, although they meant more work once I got there. The hardest part was assuring anxious hosts that Matt would indeed be arriving; even if I had a firm ETA from Liz Ross, Matt's scheduler, there was suspicion that it was too good to be true. There was always an edge to a party before he got there, a flinty hardness until he arrived. When he stepped through the door, the crowd would errupt in relieved applause. Once he was there, the event's tone would just flip; the warmth and excitement would overwhelm the room, as the crowd would get noisy and raucus with his presence.

There were so many beautiful moments, but my favorite was "Votestration II," the rally on the steps of City Hall. To encourage early voting the weekend before election day, one event planner booked out UN Plaza, erected a stage, and lined up bands. Matt was due there at 2 P.M. When I arrived at 1, there were fifteen people. My stomach pitched upside down as Matt, his father, Danny Glover, Public Defender Jeff Adachi and Chris Daly were all due on the spot in an hour.

Bad went to worse when I looked across the street: Willie Brown had set up his own PA system, and Gavin Newsom had decided to march from the Western Addition to City Hall with black activists from the Bayview. Microphones were set up and powered through the gilded gates Willie had so lovingly refurbished and treated as his own. A cordon of speakers was already set up across the street, screaming into the microphone at top volume. The battle of the PA systems had begun.

A call to Alli Starr, the campaign's miracle worker, set off the SOS. Busloads of volunteers came down from headquarters, with more coming from the district offices. Text messages were sent out to cell phones all over San Francisco, and the events organizers were working their phones above the din of two PAs facing each other and turned up to 11. People started trickling in, and I called every café and bar within twenty blocks to send their patrons to City Hall for an hour. When the barristas and barmaids heard that it was a rally for Matt, the response was uniform; a loud cattle call would ring out from the folks who just got a raise with Matt's minimum-wage legislation.

By the time Matt arrived, there were 400 supporters cheering and welcoming him to the stage. We had mobilized 400 people within an hour.

Brown looked down at us from his balcony, the final aria for the diva of City Hall. It was sour. The screams and whoops of his cronies blistered our ears as Matt raised his voice and started yelling back to be heard above the din. Frustrated by the immense noise Willie was aiming at us, the Events team positioned our bright yellow double-decker bus on the street between City Hall and UN Plaza. Within a few minutes, by bouncing and amplifying the sound back to Willie with a blockade of metal and glass, his supporters gave up and retired inside for their catered lunch. Gavin never showed up. We won that round, and snickered when the Battle of the PAs made the front page the next day.

We would never have guessed at that moment, when we were right at the gates, that we actually weren't coming home.

The frenzy of the runoff campaign was everything you've heard about and remember. It was amazing fun and excellent politics. We felt alive and meaningful. For many it was the moment that turned activists into electoral insiders; cynical after years of fruitless battles, it restored our hopes in a system that we had long condemned as decayed beyond redemption. The anarchists voted for the first time in years, because they finally had someone and something to vote for. We argued about which was more effective, direct action or electoral reform, but we all agreed to coordinate both flanks of the progressive movement. Inside or outside, by working together we could break up the corruption that was sucking San Francisco dry.

So much of this had everything to do with the candidate, and then nothing at all. Matt, unlike most politicians, had something outside of politics that defined him. A leader who was passionate about things besides legislation and dealmaking, he was real and whole. His air of command and intelligence was his inherent nature, and yet he was also a person with likes and dislikes. The android was losing, 52–48, throughout the evening. The early absentee vote banked by the Newsom campaign ultimately saved the coronation, but lost on election day. It was a sign that San Francisco preferred humanity over sound bites.

But somehow, despite Matt being Matt the Person, Matt the Candidate became a cipher for all the individual dreams people had for San Francisco. He captured people's imaginations; but by being barely there he also allowed those imaginations to turn into something much bigger than the man or the campaign. The perfect embodiment of what people saw as their own potential, the identification gave rise to a movement ready to come in from the fringes. We were dismissed as "the perfect storm," as if the confluence of events were a fluke. The disorganization of the campaign became legendary within forty-eight hours of the runoff, and we were heavily criticized for it. Yet it was this beautiful confusion that let people feel like they could own it, let their imaginations run wild and create something out of nothing. This is the spirit of democracy. Our job was not to assist in a coronation; it was to turn San Francisco into a giant soapbox where people could shout out loud whatever was on their minds.

The momentum brought everyone out of their specialized lives into this bigger thing that nobody could have anticipated. Not only was headquarters a messy vortex of talent, it often felt like a cross between a high school reunion and *This Is Your Life*. I worked on events with my old college buddies, and ran into numerous activists who helped organize actions from years past. There was the submissive whom I met during a kinky speed-dating event; he came in religiously to wash the endless dishes that the campaign volunteers produced. Old boyfriends came to smoke cigars in the back rooms, and to exchange a little inside gossip with the campaign's strategists. Bands that used to play with the Devilettes offered to put on shows, donate PAs, and register new voters. The parade never ended. One out of five people that voted for Matt also knew someone who worked on the campaign. We were, and are, a community.

I think every political junkie has a moment that hardens the curiosity of dabbling in campaigns into a routine, a way of life. The challenge to activists committed to working within the system is to re-create the perfect storm again and again, with each engagement drawing in the young legs that are destined to support, then usurp, political establishment, including our own.

Matt's campaign was my perfect storm. In those moments after the returns, I was not sad because we lost. I was sad that it was over. But the end simply brought me to a new beginning of working another campaign, a national outfit that wanted to have a little bit of our San Francisco sparkle. One more campaign, one more bit of commitment that I can make a change from within the system, no matter how unlikely it may seem. The crazy fluke had given me a chance to realize the disparate best in me, and to forge a new life encompassing both the Domme and the activist.

The theater of pain seems far away now, with its scripted archetypal shiny boots of leather. For me, it was always a lesser mystery that echoed the political battlefield. To learn to exert one's force of will, to train and nurture others, to understand money, power, and the world that hoards these things, these were the lessons I learned in the dungeon. Every lesson and skill I acquired in the theater of SM is now a tool to serve a dream of what could be: a progressive governing majority, not just in San Francisco.

Six months after the campaign, in the inevitable contraction after such vast expansion, we pause. With the vortex broken up, and the progressives heading for yet another knife fight in phone booth in November's district elections, the goal now becomes to keep the Left from destroying itself. No monolithic machine, no real sense of pointed organization; these things may in fact be impossible in true participatory democracy.

But we can, in the course of picking one's battles, remember to always leave something behind to give strength to our future. The strength lies in preserving our gains and widening the circle. The gains are made with people. Some uninitiated kid who has never worked in politics before, embraced and given the experience she needs to go out and fight her own battles. Continual conversations with people less involved, to invite them in with their own thoughts and dreams. A growing progressive base that maybe agrees to disagree on local issues, but closes ranks and communicates to the rest of America that Center and Right does not represent us all.

This is what we hope for and build today on the foundation of last year's campaign, the Board of Supervisors sweep of 2000, and Tom Ammiano's runoff of 1999. We can have a progressive governing majority; we are moving toward it with a sense of lightness and momentum that I never could have imagined before the runoff of 2003. Although it was, in fact, the best month of my life, I hope for better. Matt's campaign has raised the bar for all of us.

From the Streets to Elections

Alli Starr

We didn't have the money, the luxury of time or the force of the old-guard Democrats on our side. What we had was people—thousands of people who came from every corner of the city to help elect Matt Gonzalez mayor of San Francisco. Gonzalez's grassroots campaign forced a runoff election between the outspoken Green Party candidate and Gavin Newsom, a trumped-up, old-money Democrat. For many participants, this campaign was their first involvement in any social justice movement. Others, jaded by prior experience in electoral politics, were given new inspiration. People came from all walks of life to build a citywide movement, strengthened by a common vision of a San Francisco led by us, not by the wealthy minority.

Throughout the race, Gonzalez's personal integrity and dedication to finding in-depth solutions to the city's problems stood in stark contrast to Newsom's slick style and opportunistic candidacy. Even a casual glance at the two candidates' political histories shows that Gonzalez's record is one of courageous leadership and service to working-class people. Elite restaurateur Newsom, on the other hand, is known for following the herd, only supporting the underdog when it looked good in the court of public opinion.

Despite the odds, we believed we had a real chance to make government in San Francisco more accountable. Up against an ultimately insurmountable money machine, we almost did.

The Runoff Begins

In October 2003, I got a call from a friend who happened to be at the Gonzalez headquarters right after the runoff election was announced. They needed experienced organizers immediately; a staff position had opened up. I needed a job so I joined the campaign as Volunteer Coordinator. Although I have been an arts activist and social justice organizer for fifteen years, this was my first time working directly on an electoral campaign. Several of us who had cut our teeth on direct-action organizing and guerrilla media found our skills in demand. And there was something unique about this campaign; we were cross-fertilizing diverse movements and developing hybrid strategies that might move us all forward.

During the absolute chaos and fervor of the thirty days before the runoff, we compiled a database of over 5,000 people who flooded campaign headquarters to help. What began as a hierarchical structure became a horizontal wave of mass activity; democratic participation, rare in electoral campaigns, fueled our effort. Many people gave every waking hour to help out. Some gave up vacation days or simply took a leave from their jobs. Many more were underemployed computer professionals, teachers, artists, and others who devoted their days to phone banking, setting up voter registration tables, doing visibility actions, raising funds, stapling signs, hosting events, tabling at concerts, entering data, copying maps, transporting voters, making buttons and much more. Of course these activities make up every election campaign, regardless of how it's organized. This one was different because there was no administration micromanaging the work, and a great deal of the work occurred outside the official campaign altogether. Volunteers embraced tasks they'd never tried before and shared skills with new volunteers without prompting. San Franciscans all over the city stepped up to coordinate projects that could never have been managed from the campaign headquarters—from psychedelic posters instigated by Chuck and Ron from Firehouse, to Cyrus and his amazing flame-covered yellow fire truck cruising the city. No top-down model could have supported the empowered participation we experienced.

In my role working with both staff and volunteers, I tried to challenge some predictable, outmoded cultures of organizing. Both Republican and Democratic parties reinforce institutionalized racism within the electoral process. In corporate culture—and often in the nonprofit world—oppressive power dynamics make people feel like machine parts instead of human beings. I've seen how race, gender, and class privilege play out, especially in stressful situations where organizers don't value relationship-building. As a white woman, I believed it was important to support other women and people of color who stepped up to challenge negative gender and race dynamics during the campaign.

Those who get hit the hardest by far-right policies are also the most marginalized and exploited in our society. Poor people of color are sent to the front lines to fight wealthy white men's wars against other poor people of color; and the most disenfranchised are on the front lines of battles at home against enforced poverty and police abuse. Most electoral campaigns tend to ignore, lie to, and exploit working-class people and communities of color. While the Gonzalez campaign did not ignore these communities, it was unable to mobilize sufficient support from them in such a short time. As Richard Marquez, a Green Party member, community organizer, and field coordinator of the Gonzalez campaign, says, "We were playing catch-up to address the aspirations of the neighborhoods of color largely on the east side of the city. We did not have enough resources to build a coalition presence in those neighborhoods. We almost pulled off a miracle. We were attempting to do the impossible: to build a progressive coalition in less than ninety days."

Although the demographics broadened to some degree as the campaign went on, Gonzalez's base was comprised largely of white progressives and alternative culture types. "In the beginning," Marquez explains, "it took time to trust each other. The culture of the campaign was not hip-hop and/or immigrant-based—it was a very white, post-punk, English-only culture." Marquez notes that district elections strategically segment the city so that supervisors can focus on their own districts. As supervisor, Gonzalez had raised the progressive bar with "living-wage" legislation, corporate taxation, and a commitment to artists, but the culture of his campaign often didn't resonate with communities of color, says Marquez. "If we had started six months earlier we could have recruited the unheralded heroes and heroines, the younger leaders of color in Asian/Pacific Islander, African American and Latino communities. Where we were able to reach those leaders we were able to close the gap."

Many of us who are members of the Green Party feel that the Greens are still in their infancy when it comes to issues of multiracial solidarity. Marquez agrees that the Green Party, while trying to fight the good fight, has barely begun to democratize participation in communities of color. "As the campaign went on, Matt became more multicultural in his presentation of his own Mexican-American ancestry when addressing communities of color," says Marquez.

We weren't always successful, but we tried to honor everyone who walked in the door. Reception staffers were encouraged to respectfully welcome each person into the building. As basic as it might seem, when people feel seen and appreciated, they keep coming back. What could have become a sea of competition became a strangely connected family whose members were still trying to remember one other's names as we worked together.

With three phones ringing, six people worked furiously within feet of each other in a 10x10 office space, and five new volunteers were waiting to plug in at any given moment, I learned to quickly assess each person's experience and interests. After determining what role might be best suited for someone, I delegated clear tasks and leadership duties that empowered people to take action and feel respected for their contribution.

Election Day was like a strange dream. Most of us hadn't slept a full night in weeks. I knew in the pit of my stomach that it was unlikely we'd win; Newsom's people were pulling out all the stops. The Democrats brought former vice president Al Gore and then former president Bill Clinton to San Francisco to awaken the Democratic machine. They also bought votes in poorer communities like Hunters Point, and they created a web of heinous lies about Matt and his family that were printed in the *San Francisco Chronicle*.

People later described the city as swarming with "wet bumblebees" as Gonzalez supporters walked every neighborhood in yellow rain ponchos. Neighborhood campaign centers roared with intensity as all of our various "get out the vote" efforts coalesced in a final mad push. But when the votes were counted, Newsom had won, but by a margin far narrower than was expected. Thousands of people crowded into the headquarters at Mission and Duboce Streets for Gonzalez's concession speech and the party that followed. I was barely able to stand, but my spirits were revived by volunteer after volunteer who came up to me, glowing with excitement for what we had done together. They said they had never been so inspired in their lives. For many, this was just the beginning.

The Aftermath

After the election, there was much discussion about how to further build on the momentum created by the campaign. Some supporters wanted to build a new organization, but Matt was concerned that the group's values might become too watered-down or too "middle-of-the-road Democrat." Understandably, he didn't want to end up fighting a group with his name on it. I wasn't a big proponent of centralizing energy in a new organization. Bantering with Matt, I said that working on an electoral campaign was one of the least "radical" things some of us had done. He responded by contrasting the value of appointing a "progressive" to the school board to "throwing rocks" at the 1999 WTO protests in Seattle. I didn't say anything more, but if he had been in Seattle, he would have seen that the 50,000 teachers, steelworkers, artists, and others were not throwing rocks, but actually shutting down the meeting of the most powerful trade-policy maker on the globe.

That moment illuminated the chasm between the different ideologies that tried to align themselves during the campaign. Our perspectives come from where we are standing. While Matt courageously worked as a trial lawyer for the San Francisco Public Defender's office and as a San Francisco Supervisor, I've been defusing police violence with dance performances in the streets, building alternative educational models, and building youth and women-led arts activism organizations. I am interested in the diversity of our experiences and the intersection where our collective wisdom meets and mixes, strengthening our various movements for social and environmental justice.

Grassroots activists put energy into community organizing, assisting local struggles, or organizing cultural events and protests. Although I'm a registered Green and I vote in every election, I feel that marking the ballot is the least of my activism. As a woman, I never forget the thousands of women who worked tirelessly for over 150 years for my right to vote, but I remain skeptical about participating in a system designed to keep the wealthy in power. My mother always said, "If voting worked, they'd make it illegal!"

The Gonzalez campaign attracted people not naturally drawn to electoral politics. We were compelled by the vision and honesty that Matt brought to the table. We were motivated by the opportunity to rid our city of the sold-out, pseudo-liberal machine that has held San Francisco in its grip. And we were inspired by a grassroots movement that grew beyond the confines of a typical electoral campaign and even beyond one man's candidacy.

Chris Crass illuminates some of these complexities in his recent article, "Beyond Voting: Anarchist Organizing, Electoral Politics and Developing Strategy for Liberation."

> *"How do we as radical organizers, left activists and anarchists relate to elections and electoral politics in general? Are the elections an opportunity for strategic intervention or a waste of time? . . . For me, anarchism is fundamentally based in a belief in the capacity of people to share power with each other . . . We are largely successful practicing this in groups and communities of dozens. Our tactics, strategies and theories need to deal with societies of millions . . . Voting and elections will not achieve revolutionary change. But this is not the point as no isolated tactic or campaign will . . . I do not believe that we should unconditionally do electoral work. I believe that we need to be strategic about when and how to be involved. I do electoral work not in spite of my anarchist politics, but because I'm an anarchist committed to building broad movements for social, economic, racial and environmental justice."*

How can we maintain our radicalism while working within the system? At the same time, what can we do to break out of radical activist ghettos to build mass movements with the power to make systemic change? Finally, how can we demonstrate that what is deemed "radical" is incredibly basic: everyone deserves human rights, health care, education, housing, art, a clean environment, and direct democracy.

The Gonzalez campaign spawned dozens of projects and organizing groups. Many of us still call each other weekly to get strategic advice, share updates, and invite one another to social justice events. Some ongoing clusters of activity include the D-5 Hive, working on issues of concern to residents of San Francisco's district five; The Progressive Voter Project, which works in under-served communities to increase voter registration, encourage permanent absentee voter status, and enlarge voter turnout; www.sfprogressive.com, an exciting new progressive Web site; and NextSteps, a post-campaign activist listserv and organizing meeting group. San Francisco Neighborhood Assemblies Network Initiative promotes neighborhood dialogue, responsiblity, and community building.

A group of Gonzalez supporters/policy wonks loosely calling themselves the "San Francisco Policy Institute" still gets together. Other people jumped into working on the www.indyvoter.org site, Dennis Kucinich's presidential campaign and the League of Pissed Off Voters/Hip-Hop Voters. Several who worked with the campaign have secured first-time appointments to city commissions and committees. Since Gonzalez decided to leave his post on the San Francisco Board of Supervisors, over thirty progressive hopefuls—many of whom worked on his mayoral campaign—are now running for district five supervisor in November 2004.

The relationships I developed during this campaign are priceless. People who were utter strangers to me in October have become allies and colleagues. Powerful connections were made between people who will stand up for each other in these trying times. That, to me, is the true meaning of movement building. A week or so after the election, I threw a small party for close comrades. With very short notice, over forty people showed up. The excitement to continue what the campaign had advanced overwhelmed our disappointment.

While the Gonzalez campaign will be remembered forever as a citywide explosion of political hope and excitement, there is much work to be done if we are to be effective. Our organizations need to address race, gender, and privilege; subtle and not-so-subtle power dynamics continue to sabotage our best efforts. We can work toward better styles of communication and leadership that reflect a more feminist, anti-racist, pro-queer, and non-authoritarian consciousness that builds respect, consensus, and group empowerment.

In these days of George W, corporate media takeovers, Arnold, racist oil wars, U.S. empire-building, global warming, deepening poverty, unemployment, rampant electoral corruption, and violence against women, people of color and the poor, we have our work cut out for us. I believe we can learn from our mistakes and strengthen social justice movements. As long as we honor each other as human beings and don't give up, we really can turn things around. Our strength will never be in weapons, money, or propaganda. Our greatest resource, our most cherished force for liberation, is the power of our people.

Into the Fray

Alejandro Murguía

Democracy comes in many forms—democracies, in fact, are as varied as lizards in a pet shop. But the basic dictionary definition of democracy is a government in which supreme power is exercised by the people via elections—hence government by the people, supposedly (and why not?) for their benefit. In other words, all of us, the common people, should constitute the source of political power, determine what laws are established, and distribute our wealth for the good of society.

From its origins, our own system of democracy has maintained a rather oblique sense of participation via the people. In the United States—so arrogant about its democratic traditions—the founding fathers were suspicious about any kind of direct democracy. And during the first half of the twentieth century, the two mainstream political parties basically denied, suppressed, or intimidated the voting rights of women and ethnic groups. Hardly an example of democracy in action, *qué no*?

Today, for a variety of reasons, only about 40% of eligible voters actually step into the booth. The low voter turnout indicates that democracy in this country is stagnant and does not invite participation. You don't have to be a prophet to see that neither of the two establishment parties is anxious for a more active electorate. An apathetic electorate allows both parties to serve corporate interests and big campaign donors. History shows that the two main parties haven't exactly been champions of participatory democracy.

Even in San Francisco, the most liberal city in the U.S., the majority of voters tend to be wealthy and upper-middle class whites, and share similar interests and world-view as the Democrat-Republican machine. But the interests of a working class Latino family in the Mission district are not the same as the interests of a wealthy family in Pacific Heights, a district that voted overwhelmingly for Democrat Gavin Newsom.

The question is not will the Democrats stand up for Latinos but rather can this city have a functioning democracy if a portion of its population is marginalized from the political process?

One way to empower the Latino community would be to invite the Democrats' top elected officials, Representative Nancy Pelosi, and Senators Barbara Boxer and Diane Feinstein to a forum in the Mission District (something that's never done) so there can be open debate regarding issues like the Palestinian-Israeli conflict, health care, housing, immigration, or funding for education or the arts. Such a forum would allow the Democrats to see the faces of a constituency they have ignored, and it would also make them accountable to those they claim to represent. It would also give a human face to those affected by their actions—schools falling apart, displaced families, lack of jobs, or even training in new technology. But don't hold your breath on a community forum any time soon, because, in reality, the above named politicos speak only for the fat cats who line their campaign coffers. To paraphrase Bob Dylan "Money doesn't talk, it swears."

The people in La Missión, Excelsior and Bayview-Hunters Point, forgotten, ignored, and silenced for so long, also pay taxes—only they don't get much back: their housing and schools are dilapidated and murderous violence is rampant. So for these marginalized neighborhoods, more estranged than ever from political power, their only hope in a democracy is grassroots candidates that will oppose the Democrat-Republican stranglehold on the city, which has been marked by corruption, deception and favoritism.

I've always judged the strength of a democracy not by how much money candidates raise for their campaigns, nor by which of the two almost identical parties poll the most votes, but by how amply involved are the people in elections. In October and November 2003, during the Matt Gonzalez campaign for mayor of San Francisco, the spontaneous participation of a varied cross-section of people was like a fresh breeze blowing through a South of Market alley. For the first time in decades, people who'd been left out of the electoral process or who'd been ignored by machine politics suddenly became involved in a campaign that pitted a long-shot underdog against the most formidable party machine ever assembled in San Francisco.

Especially heartening was the participation of artists and writers, reminiscent of other popular movements in this hemisphere. In 1970 the Chilean Unidad Popular movement of Salvador Allende, was strongly supported by poet Pablo Neruda and other Chilean artists and writers. Jamaican prime minister Michael Manley was actively supported by reggae great Bob Marley. In 1979, the early Sandinista movement in Nicaragua mobilized poets and writers such as Ernesto Cardenal, Sergio Ramirez, and Gioconda Belli.

Part of the mystique, glory, and appeal of San Francisco is its artistic-bohemian aura and milieu. The participation of so many marginalized groups, especially neighborhood artists and writers in November 2003, was a powerful challenge to the Democratic machine, which under Willie Brown had left many people despairing, including myself, of ever again having a reason to vote. The Democratic Party candidate for mayor, Gavin Newsom, donated money to the George W. Bush/Republican Party campaign for president! I mean—how much closer can their interests be aligned?

The spontaneous energy created by volunteers in the Gonzalez campaign even evoked memories of the Civil Rights movement of the 1950s and 1960s. Marginalized people of color forced open the doors of the political process, not because a party organized them but because they felt the urge to change a system that had very deliberately left them out (although the same system never hesitates to tax or draft these citizens for its wars).

What appeared as a fresh breeze for the previously marginalized electorate was interpreted by the Democratic Party machine as a storm warning aimed at its interests. The party machine used all its power to turn back this popular movement by doing what the Republicans do. Boxer, Feinstein and Pelosi, as well as other Democrats, sent out desperate campaign literature to warn that electing a Green candidate would ruin the city. In a dirty trick to discredit them, Gonzalez campaigners were told by Newsom people to protest Al Gore's public appearance in town. Voter registration rolls included dead people; illegal (not to mention unethical) pressure was placed on employees by city department heads to vote Democrat; and the Elections Department gave the wrong date on which absentee ballots would be mailed out, so that absentee voters began casting votes before Gonzalez campaign mailers with information about his platform could be sent out. The Democrats won the election, not on election day—that count went to Gonzalez by ten thousand votes—but because of absentee ballots. The Democrats didn't crush the popular sentiment, but running scared in San Francisco, they employed all the tricks of the party machine to win the mayoralty for Newsom.

The people who came out for Matt Gonzalez did so precisely because they are fed up not with democracy but with a two-horse race. Considering that the Gonzalez campaign was a late starter and relied on volunteers (whereas the Democrat mayoral candidate had been running for two years), had the full backing of the political machine that has controlled San Francisco for decades (even bringing in former President Bill Clinton), and spent more per vote than any other previous candidate for mayor—considering all this, it is staggering that the Democrats had such a thin margin, showing just how vulnerable they are. It also shows the untapped strength of the marginalized electorate.

That the Democrats have lost touch with what is called "the street" is obvious in other areas as well. During the massive demonstrations in San Francisco against the impending war in Iraq, none of the top three Democratic Party politicos (Pelosi, Boxer, and Feinstein) even acknowledged that over 60,000 people were marching in the streets of San Francisco. Correct me if I'm wrong, but I didn't see Mayor Brown (a Democrat, no less, who criticized the public outrage against the war), nor his hand-picked candidate for mayor, either attend or acknowledge the people's opposition to the Iraq war.

So how will the people have their voice and concerns heard? For many, including myself, playing the Democratic-Republican game is just falling into the wishful thinking trap. The other alternative is to open up the game, encourage more participation not less, but independent of the two parties.

I was very encouraged by how marginalized folks jumped into the fray, using their own inventiveness and spontaneity to challenge the entrenched powers-that-be. Never before in my thirty years of living in the city have artists, writers, working people, and local denizens come out in such force. I saw people riding on bikes plastered with "Matt for Mayor" posters. Districts like the Mission and the Haight turned out in force to vote for someone who would represent them. Windows in many neighborhoods sported Matt Gonzalez posters for months *after* the election. It's true that Matt Gonzalez didn't win, but the November election was not about an individual anyway. It was about the common people making an effort to take back their government. The election was a moral victory in the sense of people standing up to the arrogant, party machine that thought it could buy the election the way it has always bought elections—with false promises, fear-mongering, and big money from corporate interests. It was a political victory for the common people in the sense that we had an opportunity to flex our political-electoral muscles. The real test, though, will be in future elections.

How do we stay outside the bogus two-party system, but still participate in the game? It is best to start small—there's really no other choice. Local neighborhood activists—especially in those areas traditionally ignored by the machine, like La Missión, the Outer Mission, the Haight, and Bayview-Hunters Point should run as independents against the Democrats. And they should form alliances with all those the Democrat-Republican machines have ignored: artists, writers, and working-people, as well as with the Green Party and other small political parties. Seek advice or endorsements from progressive politicians like Art Agnos, one of the few Democrats to back Gonzalez. Challenge the status quo in every election, from the board of education right on up to the seat in the House of Representatives, currently held (ho hum) by a Democrat.

Perhaps with candidates that are more conscientious, we can have a more humane approach to some important issues. A favorite pet peeve of both Democrats and Republicans is undocumented immigration. But the flood of undocumented workers is caused by U.S. policy toward Latin America, a policy that follows an interventionist, "let's overthrow the government and set up a dictatorship" model. But the politicos want it both ways—destabilize a country, then bash those who flee the chaos. Invariably the refugees come from countries we have attacked, invaded, or embargoed—Nicaragua, El Salvador, Guatemala, Cuba. They also come from those places we have trampled over economically—the northern border of Mexico is an example, which we have ruined with maquiladoras. It's the classic imperialist-colonist blowback. In fact, Haiti and Nicaragua, the two poorest countries in the hemisphere, provide lots of undocumented immigrants. They also have the distinction of being the two countries most intervened in and meddled with by the U.S. in the last hundred years. Coming here, even undocumented, is the only way many people can survive the conditions the U.S. has imposed on their countries.

We need, at a national and local level, a noninterventionist attitude toward the rest of the continent. That doesn't mean a let's-hide-our-head-in-the-sand attitude à la Gavin Newsom ("I don't care what happens in Colombia"). The San Francisco tourist industry survives on the back of immigrants, documented or not. Practically every manual job in a hotel, restaurant, or tourist joint is held by an immigrant or person of color. Immigrants do it all in this city, from washing cars to teaching law, practicing surgery to making *pan dulce*. A politician that attacks immigrants is what in Spanish we call *un farzante*, a braggart and a fraud.

Latin American countries have long recognized the economic power of their immigrants and are now acknowledging their political power too. Mexico, for example, is considering legislation to permit Mexicans in the U.S. to vote in Mexican elections. Nicaragua is considering the same. Why not empower the immigrant community of La Missión to participate in local elections?

We need neighborhood political action groups that will develop priorities and leadership. Neighborhood activism in La Missión goes as far back as I can remember to the days of the Mission Coalition Organization in the mid-1960s, and the arts groups that founded Galeria de la Raza and the Mission Cultural Center for Latino Arts. A new generation of grassroots activism could write the next chapter of the Mission District, already rich with a cultural-economic-political history.

The challenge of course is to move La Missión from the margins of power to the center. So with the street *conjuntos*: why couldn't we have a musicians' plaza set up at the currently abandoned and boarded-up Taco Bell eyesore on the corner of Valencia and Mission Streets? This could provide a gathering place for these workers, similar to Plaza Garibaldi in Mexico City, famous for its mariachis; it could also serve as a hiring hall, providing a source of revenue for both workers and the City (and raise the level of professionalism among the musicians). Incorporate the street sellers on Mission Street with the concept of *tianguis*, mobile street markets, for the flower sellers and the *paleteros* and all the rest of the *ambulantes*.

The creative energy of La Missión could be channeled into a *Centro de Artesanias*, where local artisans would have a place to create and sell their wares. The long abandoned National Guard armory site at 14th and Mission could house such a center, each floor a particular craft—say furniture and other house-and-garden items, handcrafted of wood, iron, steel, fabric—whatever the artist's instinct desires. The center could provide the more expensive tools, such as lathes or acetylene torches, and the artisans could lease the space to work and/or sell their wares. Master craftsmen and women could mentor and be given a place in the center. There could even be a cooperative for small wine production and handcrafted beers. The center provides the tanks and fermentation equipment, the rest would be up to the locals. For example, a guy on Treat Street goes to the cooperative, brings his own hops or buys them on site, rents the equipment, brews ten gallons and stores it right there, in stainless steel containers. On Sundays, for the football game, he'd pick up a gallon of his own handcrafted brewsky from the cooperative then kick back with his family and friends to enjoy. Could life be any better than that?

And La Missión, known for it rich literary and bohemian character, could host an intercontinental gathering of poets. The Mission Cultural Center for Latino Arts, along with local bookstores and literary arts centers could invite participants from all over the continent, including Cuba, Haiti, and Nicaragua, to read, dialogue, and experience our city in a week long Poetry Festival of the Americas. This festival would enrich both the coffers and ambience of the Mission, the city, and the hemisphere. How come we haven't made this happen before?

And what about the world famous murals that first drew attention to La Missión in the early seventies? For the most part they are now neglected and in some cases have been destroyed by corporations that didn't get it. These murals are integral to La Missión. A case in point—the Lily Ann mural by Chuy Campusano—a three-story masterpiece of abstract Chicano arté—now a whitewashed symbol of the greed and disrespect the dot.commers left us. In spite of the dot.com boom and the so-called media gulch that has overrun the northeast part of the barrio—there have been zero jobs for this community. And where were the politicians while this economic war was waged on us? The Latino community and the working-class community survived out of our own sheer will—against the desires of those who want to see us run out or made invisible. But we are here and we are not leaving.

I believe the disenfranchised Latino electorate of San Francisco has the *cojones* to create a prototype of a political party—similar to La Raza Unida Party of the 1970s and 1980s. If the Democrats fear the Greens or Ralph Nader, wait until Latinos organize. Then we'll have a real horse race. Because in the last analysis, only someone from the neighborhood will stand up for the neighborhood. The error is in believing that only the rich will vote their interests.

If we as outsiders make a strong enough challenge, then sooner or later the pendulum of power must swing in our direction. We are, after all, the major-ity. It is our government whether we like it or not. In the classic definition of democracy the power rests in our hands. We will spend our own money on whatever we want and need: quality schools, safe neighborhoods, health care, restoration of our murals (and funding for new ones), more arts and less war, exactly what the Democrat-Republicans do not provide. (Which raises a question, perhaps for another day: If the wealthiest country in the world doesn't provide its citizen with the basic human necessities, how is it gov-ernment of, by and for the people?) Just think of the possibilities of a real government by the people—if just one B-1 bomber was scrapped from the budget, we'd have $200 million for something tangible, like a new hospital, or new schools, or new job training centers, or affordable housing. And any-one who says one less bomber makes us somehow vulnerable is a snake-oil salesman with his hand in the till.

The key lesson of the November campaign is that common people can make a difference. We can't wait for the party machines to organize us. We have to do it ourselves, with our own energy and our own resources and our own platforms with our own candidates who have our interests in mind. We have absolutely nothing to lose since we don't have a voice any-way—but we just might have our own future to gain.

In the Heat of the Campaign

Michael Rauner

Michelle Monogan distributes campaign literature on Market Street in the Castro.

A campaign table at a Gonzalez for Mayor rally in the Civic Center.

Matt Gonzalez with Campaign Manager
Enrique Pearce at Gallery 111 Minna during
the election night party on November 4th as
Gonzalez entered the runoff election.

Dave Snyder and Jim Dorenkott preparing for a SFBC bicycling event for the campaign.

Matt Gonzalez with Carlos Petroni at the Immigrant Rights Day on Mission Street.

Vote Yesterday

Michelle Tea

I was talking to Heidi today at El Rio. We were out on the back patio leaning against the giant Carmen Miranda, wedged in between a dozen youngish, queerish people clutching their skinny cocktail glasses and cigarettes. *I saw Matt Gonzalez yesterday*, she told me. *He was walking down the street and it seemed like he was talking to himself. I hope he's okay.* Heidi's face was squished with concern. I'm Sure He Just Had One of Those Cell Phone Earpieces Going, I assured her. They Make Everyone Seem Crazy. Heidi nodded and we both sat quietly in the unquiet throng of revelers. What was the occasion? It was a giant outdoor party in honor, like most San Francisco events, of us: that we are queer or otherwise inexcusably weird, misfit toys cast out of our homes and hometowns and gathered together here by events random and deliberate to be among each other, to make art and set up homes, to find and fuck and befriend each other, to howl, occasionally, in unison, at how bad things are, how terribly and deeply unright the world is, the whole world, even our own city. Especially our own city, which had seduced us to it with promises of a freaky fairyland and did a bait-and-switch on our ass upon our arrival: freaky fairyland, yes, but you will pay to live here, pay way too much in rent, get paid way too little in your crap-ass jobs slinging coffee or dancing naked or some godforsaken do-gooder social service gig that pays you pennies to take care of people with schizophrenia and addictions and no place to live. You will be surrounded by like-minded people, sweet relief, but you will be governed by a series of dimwitted, mean-spirited assholes.

When I got to town Mayor Frank Jordan was sicking the cops, his people, onto kids ladling out soup to hungry folk at Civic Center. A girl I was crashing with got arrested for chucking a stale bagel at a cop's head. Food Not Bombs indeed. It seemed like a real Ding Dong the Witch Is Dead moment when we got Willie Brown elected. Surely a man who dressed so good, had such a flair for style, was African-American, was not an old fuddy white guy who used to be cop of all things, surely Willie Brown would save us. We thought that big party he threw to celebrate his inauguration was a party for *us*, that we'd all won when he won, that he was welcoming us back into the city. As it turned out, he just liked to blow money. A gold-encrusted City Hall? What better symbol of a government by and for the upper classes? Soon the city was falling apart and in case you weren't sure exactly how the mayor felt about your poverty, your upwardly mobile rents, and your dwindling quality of working-class life, he went and told Ivy from the 'zine *Turd Filled Donut* that if you couldn't afford to live here maybe you should move. Ivy printed the interview, the *Guardian* excerpted the incredible quote, and it was official: Willie Brown is all the asshole you suspect him to be, and more.

I was on tour for Tom Ammiano's write-in campaign against Willie Brown in 1999. I came home to Queer Nation–style stickers proclaiming "I'm A Tom Boy!" stuck all over the city, and heard stories about my most unlikely friends. Strung-out, cynical queers, who wear their alienation like band t-shirts, were campaigning door-to-door for the supervisor. I was in Las Vegas when he lost, saw it projected on a mute television above the bar at the Peppermill Lounge—Ammiano graceful and a little sad, Brown grinning in a shower of confetti or something—it was clear what had happened. I cried a little cry into the thick fluff of my Piña Colada and went on with life.

This time around, fall 2003, I was prepared to get out on the streets and campaign for Tom Ammiano, but the only thing I wound up doing was reading some stories at a benefit show. Man, I love Tom Ammiano. I love how gay he is. I love his hairdo, that little silver pompadour. Once I was at a Board of Supervisors meeting, testifying about the amount of toxic lead paint in crumbling Tenderloin apartments. Folks were throwing around the words *table* and *chair* and Mr. Ammiano, perhaps a bit tired with the dull back-and-forth of it, quipped, *Table and chair, chair and table*, in this very understated but over-it queeny humor and I instantly loved him for livening up the moment, even if hardly anybody else caught it. Once I saw him in the produce aisle at The Good Life up on Cortland and he told me he liked my boots. I was too shy to tell him that I liked his pompadour, but I felt shiny all day from his compliment. God, *Imagine If He Was Our Mayor!* I would exclaim dreamily to my friends. The gayest mayor ever, a mayor who appreciated platform leopard-print boots. Of course, this sort of shallow read of a politician's position on things via his interest in fashion has severely backfired before—Willie Brown in his goddamn *suits*, the frigging *fedoras* everyone liked to moan over—but it was just one more thing that was good about Tom Ammiano, whom I adored, whom I wanted as my gay dad and if not that, my mayor.

Who's this Matt Gonzalez? I squinted a hostile, cowboy squint in the direction of the poster tacked to the wall at La Bohème. A really cute poster, silkscreened in good colors, a quirky green, some orange, on chunky paper. Our Ideas Are Better, the wonked, inky letters bragged across the page. And there was Matt Gonzalez, disheveled, unassuming, sort of cute. Oh right, he's the head of the Board of Supervisors. Wow, I didn't realize he was, you know, cool or whatever. I got pissed at myself for falling into the simple aesthetics of the campaign poster. God, am I so easily manipulated by propaganda or what! So it looks like one of my friends made it, so the dude looks like someone I'd go thrifting with, so what? Why was he encroaching upon Tom Ammiano's turf? It was clearly time for Tom to rule San Francisco, and now some hipster campaign was bucking up out of the muck to steal his votes.

I got an e-mail from my best friend asking me to read at a Matt Gonzalez benefit at the Makeout Room. Um, I'm Already Doing Benefits for Tom Ammiano, I typed in this tone that implied, And Why Aren't You?! My boyfriend did a benefit for Tom that week and reported, sadly, that there weren't exactly a ton of people there. Maybe it wasn't well publicized? Maybe there were just a lot of other Tom benefits going on that same night? Maybe Tom is just too fucking gay? That's what I surmised from a friend who was campaigning in the Castro, where votes for Tom should have been *Duh*, laid out on the counters of all the local businesses like the giant bins of free condoms. But, incredibly, a lot of gay people weren't voting for Tom because . . . he's too gay! Gay people didn't like his, um, voice. His wicked gay, fierce, and lispy voice. The wonderful queer intonations I had yearned to hear delivering impassioned and triumphant speeches. This same voice struck fear in the hearts of the self-loathing queens who had beat the lisp out of their speech, who had cultivated a bland machismo and dudish lifestyle that washed over their anxiety of things queer—nelly faggots, swaggering dagger females, and everyone else who upset the progress of assimilation like a bull in the Pottery Barn.

Okay, so I went to the little church around the corner and in the roomy basement I cast my vote and as tends to happen, my vote lost. I decided to abandon my simmering resentment of Matt Gonzalez, who had stolen Tom's votes. I was, after all, someone who had been viciously screamed at in late night barrooms by drunken imbeciles who insisted my support of Ralph Nader is why we are all now suffering the rule of George W. I understand the infuriating and futile arguments and did not want to lob them at my Gonzalez-voting comrades. Especially because now it was only Gonzalez who could save us from the greasy, evil specter of Gavin Newsom.

Gavin Newsom. A name born to be shunted out from the mouth in a tone I'd recently heard described as "WASP-y lockjaw." You know the accent. Think James Spader in any movie he did during the 1980s. Gavin with the famously bad hairdo, rising like an Exxon oil-slick tsunami above his bony brow. *Now, Michelle, that's not nice,* my own *mother* scolded me during her first-ever visit to San Francisco, smack in the middle of the campaign. We were cruising through the Castro on a tour of the city. This Is Where All The Gay People Are, I generalized grandly. Then I looked up and saw a larger-than-life billboard of Gavin Newsom, rising up off the roof of some gay business. Eww, That's Him! I shrieked and pointed, so my mother could understand exactly who it was I'd been railing against, maniacally, all week. God, Look At His Hair, Look At That! *Now, Michelle, that's not nice,* she chastised. She had, after all, lived through my teenage years, a time when I was having everything from insults to chunks of brick hurled at me because of my own fucked-up hairdo. She must have thought that such a traumatic experience should have given me sympathy for others with laughable hair, but no. Instead, it taught me a powerful tool to humiliate your enemy— make fun of their hair. And I wasn't alone with this knowledge—nobody could deal with Gavin's hair. As the race progressed, even the *Chronicle*, which had gathered a cast of supposed fashion experts to critique the candidates, talked some shit about Gavin's 'do. They poo-pooed Matt's look too—his cowlicky coif, baggy suits, and Doc Martens, but you'd expect them to do that. Glancing at the ridiculous article while waiting in line for my morning coffee, I felt glad that even the conservatively groomed in the city took issue with Gavin's bulging hair-helmet.

I started doing Gonzalez benefits slowly, just one at first, a comedy one above a bikrim yoga studio in the Mission. I frantically begged my way onto the bill, eager to reverse my early snub of the candidate. The thought of Mayor Newsom, famous hater of the poor and the homeless, denizen of the Marina, terrified me. What did I know about the Marina? I went to couples' counseling there, once. I bought makeup at the BeneFit store, once. And I'd seen people from the Marina on drunken slumming binges in the Mission, requesting directions to SkyLark on a breath of burped Slanted Door cuisine. Did I want one of those yahoos running my town? Even my boyfriend's aunt, a stunningly conservative woman who once uttered the words, "I hate the homeless! I spit on the homeless!"—even she didn't want Gavin for mayor, concerned that his housing policies would put her rent-controlled apartment in jeopardy. I felt deeply buoyed by Aunt Doris' disdain for Gavin Newsom. If she saw through his slick and moneyed facade, then others of her ilk would, too, and that's who Gonzalez needed to convince. Not the Mission artists swooning over his cute posters, but the cranky Aunt Doris's of the city.

Twelve-step programs brought me closer to Matt Gonzalez. Outside an Al-Anon meeting I bumped into a guy I hadn't seen forever, one of a gang of folks speedily scheduling fund-raising benefits. I'll Do Anything, I volunteered. Not Just Read, I'll Do The Door, Whatever You Need, Call Me. I scribbled my number into his notebook with a pencil. Later I was waiting to be let into an AA meeting and bam, there was Matt Gonzalez, strolling down the street, on his way to a meet-and-greet at a bar down the road. I'd been talking and thinking about this man so much I'd forgotten he was actually a real person. He'd become a sort of concept, like peace or love or justice. Gonzalez. He stood for good stuff for the city—living wage, free Muni. A Green Party member, not a weasely Democrat or absurd Republican. A third-party candidate—the genderqueer of the political system. There he was, in his rumply suit, a tall man, a big guy, super cute. I got all giddy and excited, seeing him there. Like when I met Billy Idol as a teenager, or the poet Eileen Myles as an adult. I became deliriously nervous and obnoxiously full of stares. One of my fellow alcoholics managed to trot over and shake the candidate's hand, offer some praise and the promise of a vote. I was in awe of my friend's composure in the face of such fame and greatness, but he has a lot more time sober than I do.

I got my first Matt Gonzalez placard from a table outside the Bernal Heights Neighborhood Center. Both candidates had faced off earlier, and had left behind tables full of paraphernalia and some volunteers. I took a bright yellow cardboard sign and walked it home. Across the street a little kid, maybe eight years old, held her own cumbersome sign, and screamed, *Gavin Newsom stinks! Gavin Newsom stinks!* She was yelling it at the Newsom workers climbing into the SUV parked in front of her. The little girl hollered and shook her giant sign. I sighed with deep happiness. Older conservative women, bratty little children, everyone united in their loathing of Gavin Newsom. Carrying my sign home, there was no way to not feel like I was in a parade of sorts, a march of one. My sign waved and flapped, I submitted to its unwieldy proclamation, I pranced it up the hills to my house. And something was changed. I was no longer simply trying to defeat Gavin Newsom, engaged in the familiar stance of Against. No, this fresh new purpose I felt was not a weary posture of defensiveness. I was actually *for* something—I was in favor of Matt Gonzalez, thought him deeply deserving of mayoral office, felt invested in his campaign, wanted badly for him to win, thought hopefully that it might actually happen, and perhaps had a crush on him as well.

At a benefit in the Mission I sold t-shirts. They were so cute. Some were simple white Ts with Matt's trustworthy face silkscreened in pixelated green, others were balls-out rocker shirts, with three-quarter-length sleeves and a cool logo on the front, "tour dates"—benefit shows—listed on the back. I coveted them, planned to splurge on one eventually. I pressured my sister from Los Angeles to help out the campaign during her visit, something she was happy to do, having spent the recent season of war feeling frustrated in apolitical L.A. Our campaign supervisor was a wiry and energetic man named Tom. Tom had the sort of boundless vitality possessed by Jack LaLanne; I wondered if he was fasting and was maybe super-high on low blood sugar. Tom helped us fold and organize the shirts, heaping praise onto Kathleen for her shirt-folding abilities. *I love to fold*, she modestly admitted. We were joined by my old friend Chris, whom I hadn't seen in a long time, Gonzalez pins dangling from his jacket. Some others folks loitered around the table where we sold stuff all night. Eventually Matt himself walked in and everyone got a little ga-ga. I was embarrassed to see that the special feelings I'd been feeling for our candidate weren't so special. It looked like maybe everyone had a bit of a crush on Matt. The girl who'd organized the benefit, looped on booze and pills and bursting out of a creatively-scissored evening gown, swooned into his arms. My sister stared. I watched the crush form in her eyes. *He's so cute*, she said. And then, right as she said it, Matt, feet away, turned and caught her eye, held it a minute, and turned back to his people. Oh My God! I gasped. *He really looked at me*, Kathleen seemed lightheaded from the bolt of charisma. We Have Crushes On Matt, I explained to Tom, who was standing nearby. *Well, if anyone has a chance with him it'd be you girls*, he flattered. Me and Kathleen sank into a fantasy that involved Kathleen finally moving to San Francisco, dating Matt Gonzalez, and becoming the first lady of San Francisco.

Matt clambered onto the stage and delivered a speech in which he called Gavin Newsom a "fucking liar." It's always thrilling to hear someone unexpectedly use the word *fuck*, and it's extra great when it's a politician you're having an unlikely crush on. Everyone went wild when he said that. And it was true, Gavin was a fucking liar. A phony "Green Party" protest of Al Gore's San Francisco visit had been sent out on the Internet, encouraging protesters to "wear green" and perhaps "dress like trees." It had been traced back to Newsom's campaign. Then there was Willie Brown's bombastic accusations of Gonzalez's racism, hurled on Newsom's behalf. Later, Matt came over to the table to autograph some stunningly beautiful silk-screened campaign posters. He took a second to thank me and Kathleen, and shake our star-struck hands. Then he turned to the guy waiting at his side, my boyfriend's cousin, visiting from Colorado and wanting an autograph on the t-shirt he just bought. *Man, I never heard a politician ever call someone a fucking liar!* he gushed. He was starstruck, too. We packed up the table, and I waited for my boyfriend. Rocco had just performed and he was stuck in a clutch of people I'd never seen before buying his $5 CDs. Already the Gonzalez campaign had cross-pollinated the San Francisco arts scene, pulling people out to shows they wouldn't normally go to. Walking home that night, heading up Mission, the city felt wider, the night larger. Our Gonzalez pins clattered on our jackets.

Tom kept calling my voice mail to get me to come fold and sell shirts at the nightly benefits. I got other calls too; I read tarot cards at a candlelit table during a fund-raiser thrown by local filmmakers. I MC'd a giant rock show at the Great American Music Hall, noteworthy for how flagrantly I botched the performers' names and introductions. I wasn't too familiar with any of the bands and they all sort of looked alike in their white-dude, ski-hatted rocker way. I mispronounced Mark Eitzel's name repeatedly, and then actually mistook him for the singer from Cake, whose name I never learned, and called him, on the mike, "Mr. Cake." As in, *Hey folks, it's Mr. Cake, weren't they great?!* Thank God I'd tricked-out my Gonzalez T-shirt, studded it with rhinestones and customized it with scissors and safety pins. I hoped that my dazzling shirt would distract the audience from my shoddy MCing. Jonathan Richman, whom I've adored since discovering The Modern Lovers when I too lived in Boston, spoke eloquently between songs about what a beautiful person Matt Gonzalez is. It was super touching. After his set, the two men, Richman and Gonzalez, did ceremonious shots of liquor in the corner. God, on top of all else, Matt Gonzalez is *friends* with Jonathan Richman? Would it even be legal to have such a cool mayor?

I dashed back and forth between Rocco, sitting now with his new friends, Lara and Melinda, a couple of girls who bought his CDs the other night, and the blinding stage. Lara had a sticker on her purse that read "Why does my girlfriend think Matt Gonzalez is so fucking hot?" Everyone really did have a crush on him. I tried to shake my own, uncomfortable with being part of a mass attraction, but it stayed lodged in me. He had those real sensitive doe-eyes and that great voice, soft but with some sort of hard twang right underneath. Not even his speech that night—a terribly long-winded thing about the Whig Party that lost me after the first twenty minutes—not even that lapse into arcane egomania, shut my crush down. *God, what was that speech?* Rocco marveled later on, and I'd shake my head like a proud mom and concede that yes, it was boring and yes, it went on for too long, but how cute that he's so passionate about the Whigs! Rocco looked at me like I was insane, but I could tell that he had the stirrings of his own Gonzalez campaign crush—on Lara—so we let each other be. The hectic campaign atmosphere, full of hope and passion and played out nightly in the city's bars and clubs, was conducive, I believed, to romance. I wondered how many actual single people were falling in love with their fellow volunteers or at least getting laid.

At the very end of the show, so late, midnight now, the crowd down to those who bought raffle tickets and were waiting to see if they'd won any of the creative prizes—a ride to the airport, piano lessons from pianist Marc Cappelle, a beer with Matt. I was pulling the winning ticket for relationship advice from Mark Eitzel, making goofy cracks about it hopefully going to someone in a lousy relationship, and watched as the curly-haired female winner walked reluctantly up to the stage. You Look Like You Need A Lot Of Help! I quipped cheerfully, and the lady froze and stared at me as if I had just called her, I don't know, a fucked up crazy-ass bitch. *That's not nice*, she snapped at me, and Mark Eitzel, to my right, consoled her, *You're right, it's not.* I had only just called him Mr. Cake, I guess I couldn't expect any solidarity from him. I explained into the mike that, hey, don't we *all* need a little help? I know I do!

At Trader Joe's I apprehended a Gonzalez volunteer and got a handful of little newsletters to distribute through my neighborhood. When I got home I saw that someone had already scattered them across everyone's doorstep—modest newsprint things, wholly different than the glossy card stock Newsom mailers that came nonconsensually through my mail slot each afternoon. One featured a glossy portrait of an upset-looking Latina schoolchild, matched up with some text about how Gonzalez was failing the children; another was a full-color photo of a bunch of people with slapstick expressions trying to squeeze into a phone booth, representing Gonzalez's supposed wish to force families to sleep eighteen to a tenement apartment. On the one hand, the flyers were blatantly manipulative, their claims obviously suspicious; on the other, people were jackasses who believe what they're told. Newsom's flyers shone with the slickness of television, that familiar box of truth. I kicked them out of my hallway and into the street.

Another day I wound through the Mission, the state streets up around 24th—Florida, Alabama. *Voted already!* a little man shooed me away from his gate. *Gonzalez!* A lot of people had already cast their vote, and in this neighborhood it seemed unanimous—Gonzalez. The yellow signs were propped in many windows, and the house that occasionally sported a Newsom sign seemed laughable, reactionary, like that crazy Republican notary in Noe Valley who uses his storefront to rail against "loony liberals." I could hardly take the Newsom signs in the Mission seriously, felt sad for the angry people that would hang such signs, worried about their houses getting defaced. *Hey nice pink shoes*, a man sitting in his truck drinking a tall boy in a brown paper bag yelled out the window to me. My shoes were tiny fuscia thrifted things with a low and worn-down heel, not the most comfortable shoes to canvas in but hey, I was representing Gonzalez and wanted to look my best. I walked over to the truck, campaign paraphernalia in my hand. You Guys Going To Vote For Gonzalez? I chirped. There were three of them wedged in the cab, all drinking afternoon beers, at least one of them already tanked. Never, ever would I actually engage with a boozing dude who starts a conversation with me by using the word *nice*, but this was a new era of being in San Francisco, a new feeling of community that rolled out of me like some new emotion, an extravagant benevolence that allowed me to feel compassion for the foolishness of Newsom supporters and to interface with drunk dudes harassing my shoes on the street. *Yeah, he's Green. I like Green Party, I voted Green for him already*, one of the men slurred. *What's he all about*, challenged the original shoe-commenter. *What's he gonna do for me?* Ah . . . I fumbled. My mind blanked out in the face of the vastness of Gonzalez's plans. I mean, I got the big picture, right, but the details, the little bits, my mind sort of short-circuited. *I'm disabled*, the guy continued. *What's he gonna do for disabled people?* He's Going To Help All Working People, All Poor People, All People Who Need A Hand In The City, I spoke earnestly. I'd read some material detailing Matt's position on homelessness and was touched by his immediate assertion that homeless people are people in our community, a part of our city, included. So simple, but who the fuck's said that, ever? I tried to communicate the scraps of information I'd gleaned over the past week. The dudes seemed satisfied. Well, I Got A Lot Of Houses To Hit, I explained, waving my plastic bags, heavy and bulging with propaganda, at them. *Bye-bye pink shoooooooes,* the guy chortled.

Another time I went to North Beach. The way it worked was, you walked into the crazy hive that was Gonzalez headquarters, and you looked at all the different volunteer stations, figuring out what you wanted to do. Me and Rocco liked hitting the streets, it seemed most important. Then you said "hi" to all your friends who were there, then you said "Wow, Oh My God!'" to all the people you hadn't seen in eight years with whom you were suddenly reuniting. Like Daniel, last seen in New Orleans while on tour, who had dragged me to "his bar" a fag bar in the French Quarter, where he did me the dangerous favor of comping me athletically alcoholic cocktails all night. Now he was setting up a community space down on Sixth Street, writing a vegan cookbook and helping direct the Gonzalez campaign. After these tiny moments of social activity you gave smiles to all the people you sort of know but not really, or the ones that you know but you're not sure if they know you so you just give a shy smile, and then the ones you've never met but you've been riding the bus with, passing in the streets, seeing at shows, for years. Then you get your assignment.

Rocco was off searching for Lara, who had been selling t-shirts there the day before. She wasn't around. Rocco seemed dejected as we stood on Mission, waiting to begin the elaborate bus trip that would deliver us to North Beach. What's Up? I asked. He was sulking. *I have spring fever*, he said. It was November, the fall. Not that San Francisco has seasons anyway. *I feel restless.* "Spring fever" and "restless" are Rocco's code words for "I have a crush on someone." You Have A Crush, I said. On Lara.

The day before election day me and Rocco stood at the volunteer table at headquarters, looking for a neighborhood. I pondered waking up the next morning at 5 A.M. and standing down on César Chavez with a sign. Could I do it? How committed was I, really? *We need people in the Marina*, the woman heading the booth, a poet I knew from the queer open mike K'vetsch, said in a slightly pleading tone. Everyone looked at each other. Nobody wanted to campaign for Gonzalez in the Marina. I thought, I'd have to get really dressed up and summon all my rage and attitude for that. I didn't feel capable. I felt blissed out on community and possibility. I selected the Bell Market on 24th Street, in Noe Valley. *Hey, anyone need a ride? Anywhere, anywhere at all? I'll take ya.* This is coming from an older biker-looking dude with long gray hair and a matching gray handlebar mustache/beard combo. His t-shirt bore a silkscreen of Gavin Newsom as the Cat in the Hat with some sort of pithy joke underneath. Hey, Yeah, We're Going To 24th Street, I jumped on the offer. Probably it goes without saying that, without the soothing mantle of common cause the campaign had draped around our collective shoulders, I would not in a million years get in a car with this dude. With any dude, to be fair. This dude's name was Jackson, and he led us to his beat-up long white Cadillac, the interior deep red, smokey and equally battered. We cruised up to Noe Valley, Jackson comfortably telling us all about his life as a schoolbus driver. I had been envisioning Jackson as either a Hell's Angel or a professional wrestler, but now I understood him to be an aging Otto the schoobus driver from *The Simpsons*.

He pulled up to the curb before the Bell Market parking lot, and behold— it is Gavin Newsom. It is him, in the flesh, in the hair. He stands with his wife, Kimberly Newsom, who I was once sort of hot for, watching her cool in the background in footage from the dog-mauling trial, but when I learned she was married to Gavin I lost respect for her. And to be honest, she seemed slightly less hot in person, but again, this could have been due to her proximity to her husband. She wore stiletto boots of plum-colored suede. I thought about how she used to be a lingerie model. I can't remember where I first learned this, it seemed to be common knowledge at this point. What I also didn't know is if that meant she was, you know, a model who had gotten a lot of lingerie contracts, or if she's been a *lingerie model,* a sex worker, one who works the nebulous Lingerie Model outfits, which seems to be a strange gray area encompassing stripping, peep-show work, and occasionally prostitution. Or all of them or none of them—who knows? It's a mystery to me. But I had worked in the sex industry myself, as a straight-up prostitute, and I liked the idea of having a former sex worker first lady, but not if she had to bring her husband along.

Jackson bounded out of his car, leaving it idling at the curb. He wanted to show Newsom his t-shirt, which insulted him. *Hey, check this out,* he crowed, pulling the fabric taught so the candidate could clearly read it. Newsom sort of smiled and shrugged. His handlers waited, tensed for something larger to erupt, but nothing did. Jackson went back to his car and hauled himself away. Which left me and Rocco and Gavin Newsom and Kimberly. This was incredible. Of all the places we could have selected, we picked this magical one. Truly, I wished the station had gone to someone younger, someone angrier and more confrontational—a Gay Shame kid, or a member of the Biotic Baking Brigade. The moment was sort of being wasted. Rocco and I took our post at the other end of the parking lot and wondered if they would make us leave. They didn't. I slung the Gonzalez signs around my neck, sandwich board–style, the way we were supposed to. I looked really stupid. So stupid, in fact, that I feared I might be costing Gonzalez votes, here in fashionable Noe Valley. Rocco just refused to wear his. Mine blew about my body in the wind as I lunged at passersby and tried to deliver some campaign literature to them. Few wanted any. Many of these people had already voted and didn't go out of their way to say, . . . *and for Gonzalez!* They simply said, *Voted already.* Many new mothers pushing stroller-full-of-baby glared silently at me or snapped No! like I was trying to sell them crack. This didn't feel very promising. This was worse than North Beach, where I had expected such hostility but had been met with civil curiosity. Here in Noe Valley, where I imagined socially conscious yoga moms would be all over Matt, they were instead sort of rude, like maybe they really really *needed* a yoga class, or were suffering from postpartum depression.

Gavin, who had pranced into Bell Market, was now leaving again, pausing to take pictures with imbecile employees. I felt defeated. An old man walked by and started yelling at me about the unions, how the unions didn't want Gonzalez and Gonzalez was antiunion. I started yelling back at him. We had a stupid fight there on 24th Street, brief but embarrassing. He trotted off with his grandson, a little kid who looked back fearfully at me like I was the evil person who yelled at his Grampy, which I was. I stood there bereft in my sandwich board. Now Rocco was tense with me, for making a scene in a sandwich board. We had a fight too. Fuck This, I proclaimed, and dragged my campaign materials up to Castro to wait for a bus home. I was done for the night.

The next morning, on election day, I got up and voted at the church around the corner. *You gotta take that off,* the old man manning the polls said kindly, motioning to my Queers for Gonzalez pin. I had a lot of Gonzalez pins. I had little ones people were wearing as earrings, I had your basic Gonzalez yellow pins, I had Queers for Gonzalez, Poets for Gonzalez, I had a simple, full-color picture of his face, the one I called my *Tiger Beat* Gonzalez pin. Then I had a shitload of specifically Green Party Gonzalez pins I'd been conned into accepting by a very charismatic Green Party dude at one of the benefits I MC'd. I had tried to get rid of them but really, everyone already had like twelve Gonzalez pins. I left them on top of a trash can at the bus stop at Mission and Eight Street.

After I voted I walked to therapy. It was up on 24th Street in Noe Valley, scant blocks away from the scene of my humiliation yesterday. I walked there, taking an unusual route that weaved through residential streets I'd never walked down. A man on a bicycle pulled out of his garage, a Gonzalez sign rigged to his basket with bungee cords. I passed a couple of blonde girls talking on cell phones outside a skin-care salon. *Well, if Gavin doesn't win I don't know what will happen,* one whined, real worry in her voice. Maybe we would win, today. The city would win, my part of the city, the part that has not yet won in the eleven years I've been here. The broke part, the messy part, the queer or weird part, the old and disheveled part, the part that needs the help, that really, really needs the win. That deserves it. In therapy I actually talk about the election. I'm So Invested, I tell my therapist. I Don't Know What I'll Do If Gonzalez Doesn't Win. I'm Going To Get Really Depressed. It's Going To Be Really Hard On Me. Because I'd let myself believe it was possible, that change here in San Francisco could happen. I'd been swept away on hope and good cheer. Now I considered the possibility that we would maybe lose. I considered the possibility that my therapist voted for Newsom. I don't know if I could get past that. Thankfully I never find out.

Here's something startling: in the paper the other day Newsom was quoted saying something about battling Schwarzenegger, about standing up to him and his rotten plan for California. It was startling because I had forgotten that Newsom was a Democrat. I'd lumped him in with Schwarzenegger and Bush the same way whoever printed up those "Compassionate Conservatives" posters did—full-color jobs depicting the faces of the president, the governor, and Newsom. They were so convincingly real I once snarled at someone who tried to hand one to me. I thought they were serious. Realizing that Newsom was anti-Schwarzenegger made me wonder. Have the Democrats really become Republicans with marginally better social attitudes and less religion? Are they really that indistinguishable, or am I ruined (no, refined) from a decade in San Francisco, so that a candidate who would seem embraceable anywhere else in the country is hideously, conservatively unacceptable here?

By the time I get home from therapy, still quite early in the afternoon, the polls and whatnot are calling it a done deal: Newsom's ahead. Newsom's gonna win. For Gonzalez to win, pundits muse, X, Y, and Z would need to happen and the chances of that are slim and so, with hours and hours before the polls close, the race is deemed essentially won and I am left tending to the results with the dumb faith of someone who hopes their beloved will come out of the damn coma. They're still breathing, right? Couldn't something . . . happen? A miracle? A surge of Gonzalez votes from some uncounted corner of the city?

I had said that if Gonzalez lost I couldn't go to the election night party at the headquarters. I'd feel too emotional and would walk around dripping tears and feeling insane in public, which I dislike. But as the sun set and the results became official and Newsom proclaimed our mayor, I realized there was no way I couldn't see the thing through to the end. I had to be among my community of fellow losers, to resume our defensive posture of hating the world, to exchange the hope we'd carried all month for regulation cynicism. I put on my iridescent pink sequin skirt and hooker boots and took the 14 Mission. Along the way the bus stopped and other sad people on route to Gonzalez HQ climbed aboard. Kat and Cookie, two punk girls with dyed black hair, who play in bands and do burlesque and write, shuffled on board with beer, came to the back to sit with me and Rocco. Is It True? I asked, a last, futile hope surfacing. I mean, I hadn't heard a poll report in like an hour. What if something had happened? Cookie nodded somberly.

So many people were at headquarters. They were at capacity. Throngs of supporters were stuffed down the side alley, people on bikes, clutching beers, craning their heads to catch a glimpse of the speeches being made from a gated patio. Lucky for me Tom the t-shirt guy was at the door, and scooted us inside to the overcrowded warehouse. Back behind the initial volunteer room was a labyrinth of rooms. On the patio Matt Gonzalez had just finished speaking and was being ushered out on a wave of applause, trailed by news cameras. Another room had some sort of jam band kicking to life, a room full of tables and chairs where people were milling about in varying states of dejection. A room full of food, mounds of decadent vegan food. Everyone was there. There's Rocco's old boss, there's my old psychic, there's my ex-girlfriend, my old bandmate. Lots of friends. I didn't know what to do with myself, beyond scarfing some snacks. The front room got opened up into a big dance party. I stood around awkwardly while everyone else drank bottles of beers and got sweaty on the dance floor. Rocco danced with Lara. I hate to dance. I'm not proud of it, it's just the way it is. I gave a wave goodbye and split.

At the end of the night Lara, who had spoken to Matt Gonzalez, the object of her campaign crush, a couple times throughout the month, mostly seeking some sort of absolution for the fact that she worked for the Transamerica Corporation, finally gave the man her number as he was leaving his party. And then he invited her along to wherever it was he was going. Last Rocco saw of her he was helping her into a cab. Rocco was delirious with it—what happened? Where did they go? He was dying to call her and get the gossipy details, but—was that weird? I sighed, drowsy with the onset of my predicted postcampaign depression. Fricking Lara. She gets my boyfriend's spring-fever attentions and then she gets to go off with Matt Gonzalez. What's her magic charm? And, what's going to happen next? There's talk of keeping this community, the one that formed around the campaign, intact, to mobilize around other causes, but that won't happen. I notice a flyer posted up on a telephone pole on Mission advertising a benefit to help Matt recoup some financial losses.

I get a phone call from a boy I worked on a benefit with inviting me to a dinner at his house but when I return the call he realizes he had called the wrong Michelle. Oops. And so life drifts back to its normal place. That afternoon I go for lunch at the St. Francis Soda Fountain, me and Rocco and our friend Rick, whose husband, ill for many years, recently died, and I hadn't seen him since. I feel tender and awkward toward Rick, whose persona is that of a brassy old comedienne from the forties, draping his heartache in laughs. Together we all eat eggs and potatoes. At one point the door opens and a girl runs in with a t-shirt she hands to our waitress. It's a yellow cotton shirt, and silkscreened on the back is a big red heart, broken, a lightening-bolt crack down its center. Underneath it reads, *Vote Yesterday*.

It felt so lousy taking my Gonzalez signs out of my window, such a terrible concession. It was like Newsom and his pack of voters, my therapist among them, was standing over my shoulder cackling gleefully like a pack of harpies. The small, skinny flyer I'd taped in the window of our front door stayed up forever, I just couldn't bear to remove it. *Um, are you ever going to take that down?* Rocco asked one afternoon as we sat beneath it on our front stoop. Oh Yeah, Yeah, I said, embarrassed. I Just Keep Forgetting. Which was half-true. I peeled the tape from the glass and threw the small bit of paper in the trash. All around the city I see Gonzalez signs in people's windows, still, and wonder if we all need some sort of support group in order to move on, to be there for each other as we remove the signs, and everything they represent, from our windows.

Engagement and Enragement

Michael "Med-o" Whitson

*The Goddess of Political Lying flies with a huge Looking-glass in her hands
to dazzle the Crowd, and make them see, according as she turns it, their Ruin
in their Interest, and their Interest in their Ruin.*

—Jonathan Swift

I was walking down the street and saw a woman in the distance pacing
back and forth on the sidewalk. She seemed very agitated. I drew nearer and heard her screaming to no one in particular, "I married a fucking faggot!" I was put off by both the comment and her unpredictable rage.
"That's right, my husband is a fucking faggot! You don't want to hear me,
do you? I'm *fat* and *ugly* and y*ou* don't want to hear me!" I actually didn't
think she was either fat or ugly, just a slightly overweight, kinda trailer-
trash, thirty-something, white woman. Except for her venomous use of language, she didn't appear much different from many of my family's friends
that I knew growing up in a small logging town in rural Washington. But
it was clear she was crazed, acting out in public, simultaneously out of place
and quite at home on the streets of San Francisco.

What made this scene particularly surreal was that it was happening directly
in front of my neighborhood polling station during the special gubernatorial
recall election of October 2003. I was temporarily dazed by her wild behavior and stopped about thirty feet away from her and the entrance to the polls.

Why was I voting, anyway? Mostly to vote against the collective entity called
"Arnold Schwarzenegger." It seemed so wrong, the Republican power grab
to oust Gray Davis and replace him with Arnold. This seemed an incorrect use
of the recall mechanism. But why? It was easy to despise Gray Davis on political grounds. He loved killing people; he loved prisons and the prison guard
union; he had recently arranged a sleazy, behind-the-scenes, sweetheart deal
with energy corporations to "solve" California's energy "crisis." Finally, I trust-
ed his milquetoast, perma-smile about as much as a psychic surgeon's sleight-
of-hand substitution of chicken livers for the supposed toxic organs extracted
from a cancer patient. Like most of his predecessors, Davis certainly deserved
to be recalled . . . but wait . . . no . . . not in this way . . . not by Arnold!

My philosophical quandary and political stupor were suddenly shattered by
renewed raging from the impromptu election greeter in front of the polling

place. Again she screamed, "I married a faggot." (Then louder) *"I fucked Arnold!"* (Even louder) *"I gave Arnold herpes!! I gave Arnold genital warts!!!!"* She was now in a full, bellowing rage.

This last outburst made it clear. I should stop standing around pondering dilemmas and just go in and vote, damn it! It was both hilarious and tragic to witness the larger insanity of society being transmitted through the emotional antennae of someone over the edge of madness. This realization forced me to respond to a more immediate dilemma. Should I piss my pants laughing or, with equal misgivings, empathize with an inspired nutcase quite off her rocker? Feeling confused by either response, I decided to vote instead. So I marched in and voted "no" on the recall even though it seemed a meaningless gesture. Frankly (and with embarrassment) I have to admit that being inside the polling station felt a lot less compelling than being outside on the street. The entire time I was voting, I was looking forward to more of the unique free speech outside. Sadly, by the time I emerged, the woman was being forcefully shoved into a police car. As they drove her away, I could see her reddened face pressed against the window. She was screaming so loudly I could hear her passionate protestations piercing through the rolled-up windows, *"It was me; I groped Arnold! God damn it, I groped Arnold!"*

Less than a month later, I was back at the same polling place for San Francisco's mayoral election. Although a lot less surreal, this time another unsettling incident occurred. Two young women in their early twenties ahead of me inside the voting room gave their names to the first of three election workers sitting at the table containing the voter roll and ballots. Neither could be found on the voter roll. When questioned, each assured the election workers that they had indeed registered to vote (for the first time ever) about a week ahead of the deadline for voter registration. Although I didn't confirm this, it seemed obvious by their youth, appearance, and the fact they were residents of the Haight-Ashbury neighborhood that they were almost certainly there to vote for Matt Gonzalez of the Green Party for mayor. It also seemed very likely that this was the only reason they had registered to vote. So it came as a great shock when they were told they were not on the voter roll. One of them said with considerable concern to the election workers, "I really want to vote. What should I do?" There was not an immediate consensus among the workers about the proper procedure to follow. One hesitantly suggested, "Maybe the best thing to do is to fill out a provisional ballot?" The young woman replied even more earnestly, "Are you sure . . . are you sure my vote will count then?" No one in the room replied with easy authority or confidence to her query.

It then dawned on me that the two women were probably in the wrong polling place and that their names would be on the voter roll at the polls across the street. In the previous election I went to the same polling place I had gone to in every election for the last fourteen years only to find out I had been reassigned. I informed them of what had happened to me and suggested they go across the street where their names should be on the voter roll. This explanation evoked a big sigh of relief from the election workers as well as the two women, resolutely determined to vote in their first election. They walked out with a renewed buoyancy and determination in their steps.

These two seemingly unrelated anecdotes reflect a split deep within my political psyche. The mad barker in front of the polls perversely expresses a politics of enragement. The first-time voters conversely exemplify a politics of engagement. Together they illuminate opposite poles in the contradiction called "participatory representative democracy." The internal contradiction generated by a system fundamentally based on representation while also promoting full participation breeds a crazy political schizophrenia. The ensuing conflicts between representative and participatory impulses lead to gnarly psycho-political dilemmas.

A primary conflict arises between electoral politics and citizen direct action. Electoral politics, because it is rooted in a structure of representation, acts as a brake on grassroots social power. Unmediated participation through direct action threatens to become irrational, dangerous, uncontrollable. This is precisely why the aristocratic architects of American democracy created representative institutions. These institutions act first to suppress and then to mediate direct interventions of passion, rage, riots, strikes, and protests. Such unmediated political participation is contagious unless systems of social control act to curb it. Totalitarian rule is the crudest form of such control. Representative democracy is a more sophisticated and deceptive structure to manage impulses of social outrage. On the surface, it offers an alternative that appears more sane, rational, and egalitarian—the rule of law and equality over the rule of mob and might. The lived reality, of course, is much different.

I feel much more alive as a citizen, much more of a participant by cocreating collective political power at open, public protests. At the core of such acts of resistance and civil disobedience is a personal enragement about social injustice. This is where I most identify with the mad barker in front of the polls going off on Arnold. My biggest concern about acting from political rage is that I will end up like her—hauled off by the police spouting the occasional insight lost amid an avalanche of inspired ravings my fellow citizens regard as utter nonsense. Fear of police violence and imprisonment in response to public protest plays a crucial role in strengthening the popularity of electoral politics. Authorities stigmatize grassroots direct action as crazy and counterproductive. Voting is safer. Voting is fairer. Voting is civilized.

There is widespread confusion among Americans about enjoying the equal right but not the equal ability to participate in elections. This confusion helps sustain the legitimacy of American representative democracy. All citizens eighteen and over (with the exception of convicted felons in some states) have the right to vote, to run for office, to sponsor referenda, to freely circulate their political opinions, and so forth. These are all important democratic rights that theoretically should produce both the opportunity and conditions for political equality. But something very different has happened. The goal of political equality has been subverted by the overarching influences of money and corporate media in determining election outcomes. Coupled with regressive cultural tendencies toward celebrity worship, spectacle, and submission to authority (especially paternal authority keen to manufacture and manipulate public fear), the practice of democracy has taken a serious wrong turn. Any credible notion of broad political equality can't even pass the laugh test today. Yet the ideology of political equality remains strong.

The principle of one person/one vote as the bedrock of democracy is a profoundly egalitarian one. But American democracy didn't start on that premise. It has taken all 200+ years to expand the right to vote to all citizens equally. After legalized slavery was ended during the Civil War and the suffrage movement gained the right for women to vote in 1920, America seemed poised to enjoy universal democratic equality. But as the Florida debacle of 2000 showed, even the Voting Rights Act of 1965 has not yet guaranteed the equal right to vote to thousands of African Americans. Nevertheless, it is widely accepted that the trajectory of American democracy is toward universal suffrage.

The popular acceptance of voting as the culminating moment of democratic participation has always felt false to me. So much so, during the 1992 national election, I helped promote a "National Day of Mourning" that asked citizens to take an additional step beyond the duty to vote. The event encouraged citizens, whether they voted or not, to gather outside of polling places to wail, shake, wring their hands, and so on, as a public ceremony of political impotence. It was a visceral counterpoint to voting as a satisfying expression of political participation, pointedly asking, "Is this the best we can do?" "Isn't it pathetic that this is what we accept as good citizenship?"

Because the winners of elections do exert real political power, I engage in elections and voting. Here, my deeper dread is that after all the electoral hoopla is stripped away, I'm really in the same predicament as the first-time voters mentioned earlier. Trapped inside a Kafkaesque nightmare, I can only wander from one polling place to another searching for my name on the voter rolls, hoping that my vote will be counted. Even if it is counted, I will be haunted by its likely irrelevance. Will it make any difference at all? How am I supposed to derive meaning from this act?

Apparently, I am not alone in these concerns. Over the last three decades Americans have increasingly stopped voting. There are no longer national elections in which even 50% of potential voters go to the polls. What would have been an unacceptable crisis prior to Watergate goes unnoticed today. An unacknowledged crisis of legitimacy, however, neither sees a problem nor demands change. There is no broad, articulated recognition that American democracy is based on a big lie; that despite its stated values electoral politics does not create, much less allow, a level playing field; that the way economics and class power relations shape election outcomes makes a mockery of democracy; that for most working-class, poor, and marginalized citizens neither voting nor meeting with their elected representatives has any realistic impact on improving their lives. Instead, experts blame the decline in voting on alienated voters, apathetic citizens, and lazy, self-absorbed people happy to enjoy the privileges of democracy—American style—without the responsibilities. While such a view may be warranted in some instances, it is a fundamental error to blame individual failings as the source for an ongoing disenchantment with voting.

Such naïve perceptions are less accepted as you travel south from U.S. borders. A 2004 report on Latin America by the United Nations Development Program reveals widespread distrust of representative democracy. Over 18,000 citizens from eighteen nations stretching from Mexico to Argentina generated harsh critiques of their relatively new experience with democracy. All the nations had emerged from unrepresentative one-party states or repressive military rule over the last twenty-five years. Yet 55% of the citizen respondents across all class lines said they would give up democratic government if it would result in greater economic equality and benefits. Despite gains in civil liberties after the demise of dictatorship, most Latin American democracies have not resulted in equal protection before the law, much less a better economic life for average citizens. Instead, intense social friction has resulted when the "right" of political equality rubs up against the lack of movement toward economic equality. The UN report's director, Argentina's former foreign minister

Dante Caputo, summarized it this way: Latin Americans wonder "why a system that is virtually a synonym for equality exists side by side with the highest level of inequality in the world." When was the last time you heard an American offer such a sharp critique of representative democracy? American criticism rarely attacks the institutions of representative democracy. Instead it proposes ameliorative reforms: get big money out of politics; institute campaign finance reform; or create a viable third party. Public discourse gets sidetracked from a deeper vision of equality and democracy.

The fundamental issues that I care about are categorically excluded from any sane engagement with electoral politics—for example, abolishing the buying and selling of human time; dismantling the war economy; private profit; the false scarcity that prevents basic food, housing, and health care for all; a culture of civility that values the arts (especially the art of conflict, inevitable in a complex, multitendency society). These and other core issues are completely off limits within the narrow discourse that candidates, pollsters, and "voters" consider realistic and worthwhile. My experiences of social power are maximized outside of elections where I have developed a practice of grassroots direct action and confrontational politics.

When I vote, it is predominantly a defensive act to prevent a worse candidate or popular initiative from gaining political power. I believe that politicians, parties, and their policies do not *lead* toward progressive change but rather *follow* when forced by successful confrontational movements to do so. The system that politicians inhabit is so inherently corrupt and reformist that positive change only occurs when confrontational movements raise social costs so high that it becomes smarter (and cheaper!) to change policies than to keep fighting the opposition.

An important exception to these assumptions occurs where citizens engage with local government. Although rare, here it is possible for citizens to work in concert with a responsive elected official and collectively express grassroots political power. When San Francisco readopted district elections for the Board of Supervisors in 1999, the normal, dominating influence of money and advertising in determining winning candidates was disrupted. As opposed to citywide supervisors, district elections created a smaller, more directly responsive system where candidates could campaign face to face with their constituents. This creates the potential for much greater accountability. The critical mass of money, media, and spectacle that routinely determines electoral outcomes and renders grassroots participation irrelevant exerts much less influence in these decentralized district elections. But at the larger municipal, state, and federal levels such antidemocratic forces are usually unstoppable.

Democracy and the Economy

Economic forces widely perceived by ordinary citizens as being *non*political undercut the principles of egalitarian democracy. Much in the same way that "the separation of church and state" has functioned as a compelling ideology within American democracy, the (false) "separation of economics and democracy" has served to bolster the illusion of political equality. Economic influences supposedly external to democracy (such as enormous fund-raising operations and advertising expenditures) have become an absolute requirement for running a successful election campaign. Presidential elections now start two years before the actual election in what is known as "The Money Primary," where candidates jockey to raise the most money for the approaching campaigns. The blatant antidemocratic impact of these class-weighted economic practices mostly goes uncontested by the citizenry. It is class blindness and a strong, shared belief in the egalitarian ethos of one person/one vote that allows the body politic to tolerate the corrupting power of such anti-democratic, economic forces upon *free* elections.

The underlying force driving this subversion of democracy arises from the inherent inequalities produced by capitalism. As the twentieth-century American cultural historian C. Wright Mills succinctly put it: "Politically equality is not possible as long as there is economic inequality." Unless you can deliver a lot of money or votes, your ability to democratically "participate" is quite constricted. In this way, an individual's ability to express political power is governed by forces that are in no way democratic. We are not all on an even playing field, despite the rhetoric, when class relations and economic power are excluded in the calculus of democracy. But the civil right to participate on an equal basis is guaranteed. Herein lies the confusing contradiction that allows American democracy to be widely accepted by its own citizens as the fairest and best of all possible systems in spite of its blatant bias toward the wealthy and their interests. The largest blocs of capital manage the "electoral economy" to support the candidates and causes that reflect their interests. Class position largely determines which candidates have the connections and can marshal the resources necessary to mount a successful campaign. Apart from a small but slowly growing movement to repeal "corporate personhood," there is no popular debate to radically restructure democracy that incorporates both political and economic changes.

Maybe it is time to look backward in order to move forward. Revolutionary America was galvanized by the slogan "No Taxation without Representation!" What might the current update be? "No Representation without

Participation" expresses a lively contradiction itself. It places primacy on empowered participation while recognizing that in a large, complex society it is neither possible nor desirable for each citizen to be intimately involved in the making of every single microdecision. Not everyone wants to be involved in deciding whether a stop sign should be placed at the intersection in front of my house. We all, however, should be able to participate in the bigger decisions that significantly affect our lives (for example, decide how our shared collective wealth is allocated; what percentage of taxes should go to schools versus prisons, and so on.) A practical tension occurs between the tremendous number of relatively unimportant microdecisions and the much fewer but very important macrodecisions that need to be made. This tension generates the basic argument for representative democracy, that we need a division of labor even in our self-government.

Imagine a democracy that included more than voting on specific referenda or candidates to represent us. As it is, American democracy gives us no voice; no way to participate equally in the larger decisions of our economic lives. Supposedly, the invisible hand of the marketplace cultivates free choice among the jobs, products, and services available to all. This is pure fiction of course, as large blocs of capital systematically design and manipulate the markets and jobs that we get to choose from. Our class status, as well, largely determines the jobs we can get and what we can buy.

Nowhere within the current American ideology of democracy and free choice is there a process to collectively debate and make choices about the economy and the work we do in it. Public decisionmaking regarding the overall design of economic production and ensuing work processes is completely absent from our conception of democratic practice. Imagine expanding the notion of democratic practice to ask and answer these two basic questions:

1) What work is worth doing from a social standpoint rather than from a strictly profit motive?

2) What is the best way to prioritize and do the work (the economic activity that produces and reproduces our social and material world) that is popularly valued?

Imagine a world in which such decisions were seen as inalienable, democratic rights. Imagine that our role as producers and citizens was to design and direct our economy—as opposed to the abstraction called "the Economy." The current core inequalities in representative democracy cannot be remedied through reforms (like campaign finance laws) applied only to the electoral system. The most important step toward creating authentic political equality requires making radical changes far beyond the electoral arena. It is only by first eliminating the inequities of the larger economic system that the conditions for genuine political equality can emerge. Currently, such thinking is completely absent from public discourse regarding democracy. That absence underscores an even greater problem inherent to representative democracy.

"Real" versus "Felt" Social Power

"Real" grassroots social power occurs when people collectively resist repressive institutions and policies and the force of this resistance creates positive changes in the objective conditions of life. The civil rights and anti–Vietnam war movements are well-known recent examples of this in the U.S. Real power is wielded when the reproduction of existing power is successfully challenged. Essential elements of this reproduction are: 1) accumulation of capital; 2) control of social institutions; 3) definition of social norms; 4) claiming of public space; 5) directing the collective imagination and climate of ideas.

"Felt" social power is a less measurable, more problematic phenomenon. It is the belief and perceived experience that purposeful citizen action will result in positive change. It can "feel" powerful to militantly march in the streets with thousands of others. It can also "feel" powerful to vote for an insurgent candidacy that might win. Such felt power starts with desire; specifically the desire to resist the injustices of the status quo and create a better world. This is a necessary but insufficient precursor to the development of real social power. Although important, simply acting on the collective desire for progressive change will not by itself improve objective conditions. This desire and action must be wedded with political contestation in which citizens leverage their collective power to force change upon an entrenched system actively opposing it.

Direct grassroots confrontation often can move from felt to real social power since it is not mediated by a system of representation. Electoral politics not only blocks such movement; it functions to encourage a false sense of felt power. Such false projection often percolates up from a cultural reservoir of unmet yearnings for social transformation. Whether it is Howard Dean, Dennis Kucinich, Ralph Nader, or Matt Gonzalez, there is always some candidate who symbolizes the great, unmet hope for truth and justice among progressives. It is both sad and cruel how such yearnings are hoisted upon candidates that either can't be elected or won't be able to deliver even if they are. Relinquishing our individual power to leaders and elected officials in the hope that they will fairly "represent" our interests leads to recurrent disappointment.

Unresponsive representation was on stark display in early 2003. Despite massive, spirited demonstrations in the U.S. and around the world opposing the proposed U.S. invasion of Iraq, the Bush administration summarily dismissed these protests. Many U.S. and Bay Area antiwar activists encouraged by the large, broad-based turnout against a military invasion then had to face the political impotence of these actions. The intensity of global and domestic protests aimed at preventing a war before it even happened was unprecedented both in its grassroots strength and its failure to change public policy.

The twenty-first century so far has been particularly unkind to U.S. citizens working for progressive change. The Bush administration's skillful manipulation of 9/11 and public fear has provided fertile ground for the worst fascistic tendencies by both government and the citizenry. A deadening call and response of Terrorism/Security has been invoked with a vengeance. The resulting cultural climate has been a disaster for lovers of freedom. It has left many of us depressed, confused, and looking for something hopeful.

Grassroots direct action is by no means immune to a false sense of felt power. When you are a participant in a spirited, mass protest it is easy (perhaps even natural) to inflate the felt power of that moment. This is especially so when we are hungry for hope. Being a veteran of large direct-action resistance for nearly three decades, I have experienced this over and over. For participants in the antiwar movement(s), especially since 1991, virtually unchecked warmongering by the U.S. military must at least raise some doubts about the usefulness of our actions. At its worst, false inflations of grassroots power go completely unexamined. Direct action can become self-referential, self-important, moralistic, and cultlike. Then the logic of activism for the sake of activism can result in robotic-like protests that may appear militant but have little social meaning outside of an earnest subculture of participants. This is particularly troubling, when in conversations with activists at direct action protests (or the meetings to plan or evaluate such actions) there is no interest or *time* for political theory or history. More often, there is a strong subcultural bias against such "intellectual" diversions. Like the Nike commercial, for increasing numbers of direct-action protestors, "just do it" has become an operating credo that eclipses the inclusion of theory or history as part of the action in activism. (This should come as no surprise from a culture that popularly elected a body builder/action hero as the governor of the nation's most populous state.) Just-do-it activists are *too busy* to let critical discourse get in the way of the urgent need for immediate activist response. This is a breeding ground for inflated, felt social power. Resistance, however well intentioned, that is primarily rooted in immediacy and (re)action is often politically shortsighted. The resulting blurry vision obscures the value that critical historical perspective or a broad-based cultural frame of reference can contribute toward developing successful strategies and tactics.

It is difficult to evaluate the full impact of "felt" grassroots power. Even when objective conditions don't improve as a result of a protest or movement, there can still be an increase in public awareness. Sometimes that awareness contributes to future progressive change. Other times, there is no positive change in popular consciousness or a competing reactionary ideology enjoys more potency instead. The integrated system of capitalism and representative democracy is incredibly resilient and adaptive. When it can't effectively suppress grassroots power, it tries to integrate and control it. Fortunately, empowered citizens sometimes collectively create a very different outcome.

The Dynamic Movement from Felt to Real Social Power

The experience of authentic grassroots social power is thrilling for most people. How and when it becomes "real" social power is a complex, dialectical process that can't be reduced to a simple formula. I remember thinking in November 1999 as I was leaving San Francisco to go to the anti-WTO (World Trade Organization) protests in Seattle how this would probably be yet another one of those large protests with no discernable impact. I was never so happy to be so wrong! After years of radical somnambulism in America, a powerful culture of resistance finally asserted itself again. Prior to this uprising, you would have been considered a raving lunatic for professing that effective protest would emerge in the U.S. amid an unprecedented pro-capitalist, economic boom. Yet it erupted that week in Seattle and galvanized a savvy international, grassroots attack upon the WTO both from outside and within the organization. Up until then, the WTO had been a pernicious global capitalist institution on the offensive and taking no prisoners. Nearly six years later it has not recovered and is still defensively floundering; its latest failure was in Cancún in September 2003.

A crucial component of creating real social power is reclaiming public space. Whether at the workplace, on a bus, or in the street, the making and taking of public space is vital. San Francisco's decade-long Critical Mass bicycle actions illustrate a unique way of claiming public space. It is a monthly, open gathering of 1,000 to 5,000 bicyclists who ride together through the streets of downtown San Francisco. This mass of bicyclists reverses the usual power relations on the street, overturning the norm where they are at the mercy of dominant, dangerous automobile traffic. Instead, automobiles have to wait for bicyclists riding en masse as they create safer and more pleasant conditions not possible in normal traffic. It is an act of resistance as well as a highly visible demonstration of a less polluting, more enjoyable transportation alternative. The palpable experience of felt social power is profound, at least on those streets in those moments. How this alters objective conditions is difficult to gauge. Critical Mass defines itself as a cultural gathering rather than a political action. It has no specific demands. It has no leaders. Yet its mere presence has created a momentum and legitimacy for politicians to try to offer some kind of tangible policy or benefit to this potential constituency. It uniquely expresses social power for participants and observers. Seizing public space in a society that has largely eliminated it in favor of commodity exchange and the banal daily movement from home to work to shopping is in itself a vital assertion of social power.

Perhaps Critical Mass's greatest expression of real grassroots power has been its spontaneous appearance across the world. It spread to hundreds of cities on five continents. In San Francisco, authorities have been unable to prevent or even control the event despite attempts to do so. It has been unstoppable even when then-mayor Willie Brown in July 1997 orchestrated a concerted media campaign against Critical Mass and instructed the S.F. Police Department to shut it down. The authorities simply couldn't devise a strategy to control a leaderless, decentralized, highly mobile mass that improvised on the fly without a pre-planned route and that could spontaneously break into splinter groups and just as spontaneously regroup later. The publicity against it and the massive police presence to control it completely backfired. The grassroots response was a larger, more militant turnout than ever before.

There are many more traditional ways collective direct action can catalyze positive changes in objective conditions. The most profound occur when mass movements successfully contest and change both social attitudes and public policies. The women's suffrage movement and the later civil rights and feminist movements are prime examples of altering oppressive attitudes and repressive laws to expand basic human rights. U.S. history is full of strikes and protests contesting workplace exploitation. The humane reduction of the standard workday and week to eight hours a day and 40 hours a week was a result of ongoing strikes and public protests throughout the late nineteenth and early twentieth centuries.

This is an example of felt social power that took decades to become real.

Workers *felt* they had the right to work less and enjoy life more; activists *felt* this was a popular view; and an oppositional movement *felt* that through concerted strikes and protests working people could force business to accept their demands. These felt desires only became real as people persistently protested and were successful at forcing public acceptance. The crucial leverage here was literally *striking* at the point of production. When workers strike business is disrupted and loses money. Even when they aren't on strike, disgruntled workers can be less productive and more disruptive until their demands are met. At a certain point business realized it was smarter and cheaper to give in than to keep fighting. Still, it took decades of protracted struggle to finally get the 8-hour day, 40-hour week broadly accepted. The value of radical persistence and patience seems forgotten today in our culture of sound bites and immediate results. It is important to remember that it took over eighty years from the initial protests of the ANC until the formal ending of apartheid in South Africa.

Radical persistence and patience shape our approach to social change. Although off her rocker, the opening anecdote of the mad barker in front of the polls captured the sense of rage than can spark us to publicly confront injustice. There is immediacy in rage that demands change now, not tomorrow, and certainly not eighty years later. That urgency is critical to cracking open "normal life," to inspiring and mobilizing a larger collective response. Yet history illustrates that creating enduring radical change is usually more glacial than like lightning. The necessity to inspire by being on fire, to keep persisting with urgency while still remaining patient, is an inescapable contradiction for those committed to progressive change.

Voting and elections, however, provide a false practice for radical patience. The anecdote of the first-time voters speaks to the skillful co-optation of both radical patience and desire. American representative democracy gives society's rulers a powerful means to maintain their control: a system calibrated to tolerate spaces of felt power without ever relinquishing real power. It is up to us at the grassroots to see through these deceptions. It is up to us at the grassroots to collectively act upon and claim our real social power.

On the Lower Frequencies
Life in Abandoned San Francisco

Erick Lyle

The Bayview Bank faces Mission Street at 22nd with an enormous windowless wall, effectively a blank, white canvas. But if you look at the wall, you can see, slightly faded but still clearly visible, a series of red, green, and white splotches where paint struck the wall years ago.

I pass the bank almost every day and rarely think about the splotches of paint, but sometimes I'll stop and look at them and the years reel past in my mind. How did it happen that we went from nonstop fighting eviction and gentrification to fighting against the new president's visions of perpetual worldwide war, without even a slight break?

So much has happened since. But I remember happily that night, years ago, when three friends and I climbed to the roof of the former Leed's shoe store across the street from the bank with buckets of paint and a couple bags of party balloons we bought on Mission Street.

In an event typical of the era, the dot.com company BigStep evicted all the Latino community nonprofits to occupy the entire Bayview Bank building. So, we went to Leed's with a three-man slingshot, the balloons, and the paint.

We had chosen red, green, and white for the colors of the Mexican flag, and cheerfully fired sloppy wet balls of paint across the street for hours, laughing as they exploded, Jackson Pollock–like across the bank's wall.

I heard it made TV news and I read about it later. It was a fun thing to do. Not long after, BigStep went under and the dot.com economy disappeared. The nonprofits started coming back to the building, too. But no one ever bothered to clean the graffiti off the building and today it stands as a reminder of the day-to-day battles of the late nineties in the Mission, an unplanned monument to the struggle of that time.

I stop to look at the paint splotches and it all comes back to me—picketing landlord offices, the March of the Evicted, going out all night to wheat paste posters for marches. I remember watching the things you loved about your neighborhood disappear and watching a new, seemingly invincible race, the dot.commers, march through the ruins like a conquering army, laughing on their way to the bar. In late 2000, when the gentrification battles of the Mission had reached their highest intensity before everything rolled back, many of the groups that had been fighting back in the Mission decided to come together under the banner of the Mission Anti-Displacement Coalition (MAC). For a while, it truly seemed like anything would go. Old Latino organizers were working side by side with white tagger kids. There was a feeling of excitement that it was all new, that you couldn't tell where it would end up.

At one point artist—later 949 Market squat organizer—Heart 101 approached MAC and offered to do wheat-pasting for them. They told him to go out and tell people to do wheat-pasting, graffiti, whatever! It was time, they said, to see a unified neighborhood identity in street art and it didn't matter whether it was legal or not.

We ended up making huge posters reading "No Nos Vamos" (We won't go) in bold, black text on white paper and wheat-pasting them all over the neighborhood. The blocks of text looked impressive as I rode past the next day, the whole neighborhood subconscious now visible in the streets, united against gentrification.

But, as usually happens, the energy of widely different grassroots groups working together was soon diverted into election campaigns, this time to pass legislation that would curb live/work loft development and to elect several progressive candidates to the Board of Supervisors. I look back now and have mixed feelings. On the one hand, electing a new Board of Supervisors in late 2000 was a much-needed victory for antigentrification forces and a rebuke to Willie Brown.

On the other hand, a chance to build a new Mission organization across racial lines was lost. When the election was over, the energy dissipated, and the larger groups stopped meeting. Later in the year, when gentrification started to drive the poor out of the 6th Street area, it was almost impossible to get anyone outside the area or in the media to listen or care. After the election, the eviction issue was over. After all, we had *won*. What was left to do?

II.

"What we're for and not what we're against" was the rallying cry of the punks, artists, and activists that came together in spring 2001 to take over a long, abandoned Market Street pool hall. We turned an enormous, dusty, forgotten building into a community space that in its four-month-long existence was part art gallery, part rock club, and café with a free breakfast program.

The birth of the 949 Market space came at a rare time in the city's recent history, a brief break between battles. After the dot.com crash and before the permanent war, twenty-five or thirty veterans of the Mission's battles against gentrification got sick of their community always being under attack and always organizing to resist whatever crisis was next. We decided instead to not fight against something, but to build the world that we wanted.

In the vast, empty space we found when we opened the squat, it was possible to imagine anything happening, right there, hidden in plain sight just a block from tourists shopping and riding the cable cars. We thought, "What if you just had all the space you needed to do whatever you wanted? What would you do? What would it *look* like?"

First we cleaned and planned. Committees formed to clean up the dust and debris that accumulated in the former Palace Billiards since it had closed in 1988, and to talk together about what kind of events we wanted to have happen in the space. We decided to have one huge show with art, music, speakers, and free food. Different artists came to the space to plan huge murals together, all loosely based around the theme "What we're for and not what we're against." For a whole month, we cleaned and painted and explored the building's premises and the abandoned St. Francis Theater next door, trying to build a perfect show space out of the rubble. All the stuff we needed from the popcorn buckets in which we would later serve the vegan dinner, to the theater's old sound system speaker (which we used for the show's PA) we found right there.

Working on the space at 949 Market had that same exciting, unpredictable energy that the early MAC times had. My favorite memories are of what it felt like to walk into the squat as we planned the opening night show and see people spread out across the room, carefully painting murals or nailing movie seats into the ground where the films would be shown, or trying to figure out how to rig up water for the toilets.

On March 30, 2001, we finally had our "Grand Opening Night" for the space. An estimated 600 people showed up on a Friday night on Market Street to see four bands, speakers, and some films and to eat a free, vegan dinner. But the real show-stopper was the art itself. When you walked up the stairs off of Market you'd enter this enormous room, covered from floor to ceiling for hundreds of feet with big, colorful murals, flowing into each other.

We counted on the event's sheer size to keep cops away. After all, how could 600 people be attending a free concert *right on Market Street* with all this

Murals from 949 Market Street.

artwork in it *without permission?* When we turned out to be right and the event went off without a hitch, we started planning for more events.

Next, we started a weekly breakfast café in the squat, because we felt that people really needed a calm, beautiful place where they could come together and eat free food. A different group of people than those who had been in charge of the first show came forward to run the café. Food pickups were organized. Restaurant equipment was, uh, appropriated. The group did outreach to homeless folks in the neighborhood and invited them specifically to come and eat and chill out at the space (while also making sure to inform them that it wasn't quite legal).

There were several more shows and several weeks of free food before the space was evicted, uneventfully, when it was discovered by workers hired by the building's owners, one morning in June. It was heartbreaking to lose the murals, the results of months of hard work, and, for me, a place to live. But after being on the losing end of several electoral campaigns over the years, I realized what was different about 949 Market. When we lost an election, it felt like we had lost everything. When the squat got busted, it still felt like we had won *something.* Instead of finding a candidate to elect and hoping that they would represent our interests in office, this could be a first step in organizing in our own interests and creating a community strong enough that the candidates would have to come to us.

III.

What has been most remarkable about the last few years in San Francisco was the great speed in which events happened and whole eras came and went. In late 2000, I was attending tenants' rights marches seemingly every day. In the midst of this came the publishing of Rebecca Solnit's *Hollow City*, an actual hardcover book with the urgency of a flyer, full of photos of the marches I'd just attended. It even had pictures of flyers that I had wheatpasted around town and a mention of the Bayview Bank paint bombing.

I read in the book that the Clarion Alley Mural Project warehouse might be sold and the artists who lived in it might be evicted. In just a couple months, the warehouse was sold; the artists took a settlement and were leaving the City. My band played at the last party there. By the time another month went by, the economy was slowing down and the expected demolition of the warehouse hadn't taken place. The building was sitting there empty.

The warehouse at 47 Clarion had almost forty years of underground history, starting with the wild parties the drag troupe The Cockettes held there back in the sixties up to the mural scene of the nineties. The eviction of the historic space had been a well-publicized symbol of how bad things had become in the Mission. Maybe if I couldn't write another chapter in 47 Clarion's history, I could at least add an afterword. Late one night, a friend and I popped the lock off the front door and I moved in to my new squat.

It ended up being a great, free place to live with running water and grand skylights set in the ceiling (no electricity, though). I decorated my kitchen writing space with rough sketches of Aaron Noble's murals that he'd left behind. I lived there for four months with a key to my own lock on the front door, going in and out like I owned the place. No one noticed. Too much changed too often for neighbors to keep track anymore in the Mission.

One day, I went to the soup kitchen at Martin de Porres. Around the corner from Marty's, I noticed a gathering of twenty-something, white hipster kids. They stood, smoking and talking, in a configuration that resembled a younger version of the group of homeless men milling around outside the soup kitchen down the block. But they were standing in front of a dot.com company that was housed in an old, redbrick building. When one guy, probably about five years younger than me, stubbed out his smoke and opened the front door, I impulsively nodded "hello" and followed him inside.

A guard at the front desk didn't look up. As I passed the lobby, some employees headed out didn't give me a second look either. I strode confidently around the work area, poking my head into conference rooms and greeting people in the halls. I found the main work area, a vast, high-ceilinged room filled with young, white kids stationed in front of computers. One kid looked at me as I approached, nodded, and went back to typing. I realized I could probably sit down at a computer and pretend I worked there for days and no one would ever know I didn't belong there. Apparently no one knew just who worked there.

I later read an article in *The Baffler* about doing exactly that, showing up at a dot.com in New York City and pretending to work, but that sounded boring to me. I went for the beer! I soon found the fabled beer-stocked fridges and cabinets overflowing with food in an employee kitchen. I made a sandwich, enjoyed some Odwalla juices, and got some coffee for the road, noting that there were not one, but two good beers on tap. After that I went back a few times, avoiding Martin de Porres's gas-producing split-pea soup in favor of dot.com sandwiches and trail mix and the occasional fancy beer raised in toast to my new coworkers. But being somewhere that could be anywhere with people that could be anybody was just too damn creepy, and I quit going. At least Martin de Porres was like a family.

Underground scenes had to adapt quickly to the city's shifting landscape. As we struggled to survive the rapid change and impermanence, our events and protests started to embody it. Without the anchor of genuine community space, illegal street takeovers and shows in squats became common.

In 1998, gentrifying code enforcement officers shut down all the punk rock venues in the Mission, so bands like Miami and Shotwell started putting on hit-and-run punk shows in Mission Street doorways and BART plazas. A hundred punks and neighborhood passersby would gather in a doorway to watch a couple of bands switching off, playing two or three songs each, in case the cops came. But the cops never came and we always got away with it. We used a generator for electricity until someone realized we could plug into electrical outlets that were in MUNI bus shelters.

The boarded-up Mission storefronts were also ever-changing canvases for graffiti, a neighborhood history written in scraps of wheat-pasted flyers and stencils, layered over and under the nightly spray of free art (that would soon appear *inside* the hipster galleries opening around the neighborhood). The neighborhood transition was being documented and erased daily on the plywood slats surrounding the deep pits in the earth where buildings had been torn down to make way for condos. By 2001, a new graffiti police task force out of Mission Station was cracking down, meticulously photographing graffiti to build grand jury cases against graffiti writers. Some artists responded by quitting "graffiti" and instead trying a whole new approach—painting enormous, illegal murals in broad daylight. Aaron Noble came back to town to work with Andrew Schultz on a huge piece on a crumbling wall in China Basin that they worked on for weeks, right out in the open. Graff writer Heart 101 and I also used paint rollers and extensions to paint a block-long, 20-foot high, text piece reading NO MORE PRISONS on 3rd Street, right where people stuck in traffic from the Giants' games would have to look at it everyday. It took us four or five hours to paint and countless cops rolled by while we were working, but what cop has the imagination to think that a project so huge, undertaken in public, could be illegal?

The buildings we painted on were torn down soon to make way for the Mission Bay biotech campus in China Basin. My squat on Clarion Alley was finally torn down, too, and I left town for a few months. When I got back in early 2002, it was a new era all over again. I came home to a ghost town. Suddenly, there were potential squats everywhere. Vacancy rates South of

Market were as high as 40%. Newly completed loft spaces faded in the Mission sun, unsold, as the clock struck twelve for the dot.com economy and the briefly hip former ghetto turned back into a pumpkin before our eyes. I found a cute one-story abandoned warehouse in an alley South of Market and used a cordless drill to get the door open. I was pleased to find that it had working electricity and was fairly clean, but I would have to figure out how to get the water turned on to make it my new squat. The day I started moving in, I was carrying in an old futon I'd found on big trash night, when I met my new neighbor. He lived in the abandoned house across the street!

The next day, I checked out a café in my new neighborhood, taking a long, leisurely morning with the paper. The other patrons all seemed to have been stranded there in some arrested state of hipness, beached when some long-forgotten wave of Cool from a previous gentrifying boom period had broken. There were middle-aged women, still with dyed pink hair and leopard-print creepers; sad-looking balding men with goatees. At the counter, I overheard a young guy, about my age, chuckle to the tattooed and pierced girl at the register, "Well, it looks like I lost all my money!"

"Let me guess," she sneered. "Stock market?"

"Yeah!" he said. "It's all true! I was a day trader! Remember how I used to sit in here all day? I was a day trader!"

But she'd already moved down the counter to the next customer. I got a refill and considered the sweet urban irony of me and the former day trader, now scrounging for refills in the same café, while me and my friends set out with crowbars to open up the now empty places where his kind had worked.

Like many, I'd expected a dot.com collapse to give poor people and underground artists more breathing room. But as the summer unfolded, it seemed like somehow we'd gone to the Great Depression II overnight. There were no jobs and homeless people filled the doorways of now empty office space. Our country, we were told, was now engaged in a perpetual war that would last beyond our lifetimes. With more people needing help than ever, rich kid Supervisor and mayoral candidate Gavin Newsom began efforts to slash welfare checks for the city's poorest residents.

Jobs fled the city. Reeling from the discovery of its role in the growing Enron scandal, accounting firm Arthur Anderson alone laid off thousands in San Francisco. Somehow I found a job, though. I'm the guy who sorted Arthur Anderson's trash. I got hired at SCRAP, a nonprofit that accepts used items that would otherwise be thrown into the landfill, and then offers them for sale, cheap, as art supplies. When I started working there, Arthur Anderson donated countless boxes of whatever was left in their offices when they closed their doors. I spent nearly my whole three months at SCRAP sorting piles of Arthur Anderson's Post-It Note pads, old transparent tape dispensers and staplers, envelopes, and pens that didn't work. I still have an electrical power strip that says "Arthur Anderson" on it that I took from work one day to use at a generator show at the 16th and Mission BART that I'd set up.

Arthur Anderson's closing left hundreds of people in the Bay Area out of work, but their office closure *created* at least one job: mine.

Despite the collapse of the dot.com economy that had driven Mayor Willie Brown's neighborhood planning policies, the new "progressive" supervisors (that MAC's energy had helped elect) never seized the opportunity to forcefully articulate a vision for the city's future and implement a Left agenda. Supervisor Tom Ammiano, the presumptive progressive mayoral candidate in 2004, and the rest of the much-heralded new board of 2000, stood by and watched as Supervisor Gavin Newsom and his powerful backers from the Democratic Party machine made getting rid of homeless people the number one issue for the 2004 mayor's race a full two years before the election.

Newsom, the young, rich, owner of a Marina district wine bar and friend to the Getty family, was apparently the galvanizing force that a San Francisco Left, largely dormant since September 11, 2001, needed to stir itself. But there was a sense of a bitter déjà vu. Newsom was Dot.com Man all over again—the straight, white, rich guy who was coming to suck the soul from *our* city. But what was *our* city all about anyway? What did we want? We'd lost the moment and all we could do was react.

My old SOMA squat became a base to plan alterations of the billboards featuring Newsom's hateful antihomeless ads. We spent the summer riding around on our bikes all night, gluing our paper over Newsom's billboards. I was proud that, despite everything, we'd found a way to carve out some space for ourselves. When our alterations were taken down after a few days, though, I'd just feel desperate using street art to fight a multimillionaire. After all, even the billboards were owned by Clear Channel!

As election day in November 2002 neared, so too did war with Iraq. I grimly sorted through Arthur Anderson's old trash at work while listening to news on *NPR* of hundreds of thousands protesting across the world against the potential U.S. invasion of Iraq. Many of us who'd been involved in 949 Market had now morphed into a group calling itself "Punks Against War."

We were dissatisfied and frustrated with the traditional weekend antiwar marches that took place far from any actual neighborhoods at a time when downtown was largely empty. Though the size of the marches that were taking place against Bush's proposed war was inspiring, we wondered if there wasn't a way to have smaller antiwar events in our neighborhood that people going about their daily lives might be able to see and join. The idea that came out of this was the Anti-War Parade on Mission Street. There was a large ANSWER march planned for a Sunday afternoon, downtown, so we decided to have a parade in our neighborhood the day before to invite people from the Mission in Spanish to go and support the larger march. We wanted to have a parade instead of a march—a festive event that would appeal to the Latino families who would be walking on Mission Street on a Saturday. We passed out hundreds of free burritos at the 24th and Mission BART plaza and then paraded down Mission, about fifty of us in various costumes following behind a trailer with a band playing on it. Parents stopped to hold their kids up on their shoulders so they could get a better look, while we tossed candy to the kids and fanned out along the sidewalks, passing out antiwar literature in Spanish. Many people thanked us for having bilingual information and, of course, many people already were against the war. Surprisingly, the cars stuck behind us were honking and waving, too, and giving us the thumbs up, or yelling, "No war!" as they passed us.

That day sticks out in my mind as a time when the usual walls keeping different races apart in the Mission seemed to fall away and you could feel everyone together against this stupid war. It stands out, too, as the kind of action with music and festivity and, most important, generosity to the larger community, that really brings people together.

The next day 100,000 or so folks marched against the war downtown. But only a couple weeks later, Prop N (Gavin Newsom's legislation that scapegoated homeless persons) won in the election by a landslide and it felt like, once again, we'd worked all year for nothing.

IV.

Much has been made of the tremendous energy generated by last year's Gonzalez for Mayor campaign. The buzz and excitement of people getting into politics for the first time, the tireless volunteers, and how close progressives came, is already the stuff of legend. "Next time we can really WIN!" celebrated the campaigners for Gonzalez, while warning that we had to capture the campaign's energy and build a movement now.

But what if we already have a movement that *did* "win"? In all the buzz around the Gonzalez campaign, the truly historic shutdown of the city of San Francisco on March 20, 2003, when the U.S. invaded Iraq seems to have been forgotten.

In early 2003, as it became clear that a U.S. invasion of Iraq was inevitable, the call went out to protesters to shut down the city and bring "business as usual" to a standstill, when the war started. Flyers around town advertised open meetings where affinity groups could take responsibility for shutting down key intersections in whatever creative manner they chose. I went to check out a meeting at New College and was amazed to see the map filling up with claimed intersections to be shut down as a crowd of people calmly discussed bringing a major US city to a standstill. The confidence, the feeling of freedom in the very planning, reminded me of the days leading up to the opening of 949 Market. It seemed like almost anything would be possible in conjunction with the shutdown, from traditional lockdowns in the heart of the financial district to street parties, food servings, and group bike rides filling the streets all across the city.

This was the first time in ages I'd heard people talking about what they were going to *do* together to demonstrate the power of their community. Here was the buzz and excitement of first-time political participation and the tireless volunteers, but the idea of the shutdown was based not on the slimy compromise and pragmatism of electoral politics, but on our actual beliefs.

The possibility of a shutdown city inspired a vision of what might be possible, what we could get away with. Punks Against War decided once again to occupy a squat in a highly visible location downtown.

The theme for our action was "It's not the war; it's the way we live." The war was just the logical outcome of current U.S. policy—what happens when you spend all your money on weapons instead of schools, housing, or health care. The war was a smokescreen to divert attention from massive budget cuts, the corporate looting of America, and our shrinking civil liberties under the Patriot Act. For our action, we chose the former site of Denis Peron's pot club on Market near 10th, a four-story abandoned building. You could enter it fairly easily by climbing up the fire escape to the top floor and kicking in a window. The plan was to prepare the squat before the start of the war and then open it to the public the night of the big protest, presumably after the city had been brought to a standstill all day.

Opening the squat would not be a symbolic act where we called the media

TRADITIONAL SIT-DOWN DINNER
Government and Corporate

Financial/Corporate

A) City Corpse/UK Consulate—Sansome & Market
B) Carlyle Group/TransAmerica Pyramid—
   600 Montgomery
C) Pacific Stock Exchange (2nd floor)—220 Bush (near Kearny)
D) Bechtel, 50 Beale Street

Media

E) CBS Westinghoue Electric—221 Main St. Near Howard

Federal

G) Federal Building—Golden Gate & Polk
H) Federal Reserve—101 Market
J) Military Recruitment Center—670 Davis

DRIVE-THRU SERVICE AUTO BRIGADE

"This approach might provide some of us older people, in particular, with a more viable method for prolonged participation." From the person who started this idea, which was used by the movement that toppled Slobadan Milosevic. Drive through downtown very, very slowly. Or team up with one or two other drivers and take two or three lanes on one street. Support bicyclists and help the street blockade actions. Or simply stop your car and refuse to move for as long as you are comfortable doing so. Run out of gas. Or just leave it. Transform the City. Stop the War.

NO TIME TO DINE? TRY OUR TAKE OUT!

BIKES NOT BOMBS
Bicycling: A QUIET STATEMENT AGAINST OIL WARS.

Join the mobile Bikes not Bombs. Bring your bike (or rollerblades, or skateboard or any human-powered wheels) with signs, flags, and decorations to Main and Market at 7am (or whenever you can make it) and support all the stationary action, fill the streets with bicycles, get the word out.... Your affinity group can be its own moving anti-war bike ride.

A MOVEABL
Intersections

Primi Piatti (1st Co

1) Lombard & Van Ne
2) Polk & Broadway
3) Polk & Bush
4) Market & Franklin
5) Division & Van Nes
6) 6th & Brannan
7) 5th & Mission (SF (
8) 3rd & Folsom
9) Harrison & 2nd
10) Harrison & Fremc
11) Embarcadero & M
12) Broadway @ Colu

Secondi Piatti (2nd

13¹ & 13²) Stockton Tu
14) Powell & Bush
15) Market & 6th
16) 16th & Valencia/M
17) Howard & Fremo
18) Embarcadero & W
19) Embarcadero & B
20) Parking Lot of You
   a. Civic Center (M
   b. Sutter/Stockto
   c. 5th/Mission (e

and waited to be arrested for civil disobedience We intended to take the building and use it to demonstrate ways people could create the world we want to live in. We would provide free food, first aid, and have a safe, free space for people to meet and discuss the day's events and plan for the next day. Then, on the second day, we would have a big, free meal and a show.

We were counting on the city being so out of police control that our squat

ST
·eries

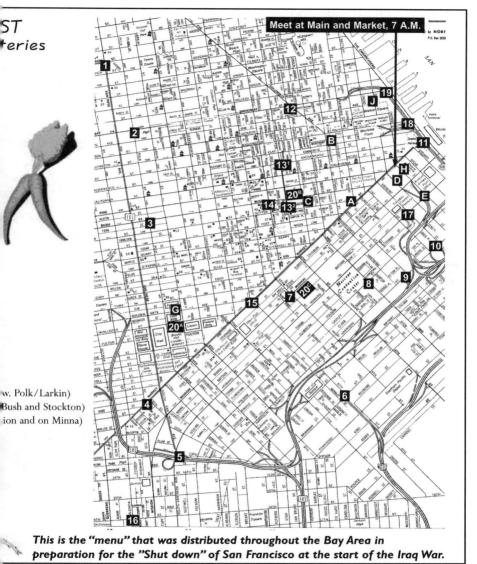

w. Polk/Larkin)
Bush and Stockton)
ion and on Minna)

This is the "menu" that was distributed throughout the Bay Area in preparation for the "Shut down" of San Francisco at the start of the Iraq War.

would fly under the radar for a couple of days, long enough for many people to know about it. Then we'd announce that we were going to serve free food every night in the squat and hold the building until the end of the war. If we could get large crowds to come, the space would develop a life of its own. People would propose ideas for the space and make their own plans there. If enough people were coming to eat, after a few days, there might be enough people who took it seriously enough to try and defend the squat from arrest. Or it could just get busted right away. Who knew? But even if it only lasted a day, I'd feel pretty good about taking back some space and feeding a couple hundred folks in it. We had nothing to lose.

We put our own locks on the front door and slowly moved supplies in while the U.S. moved troops slowly into the Persian Gulf. We spent weeks planning everything: who would bring the food, who would talk to police, how to maintain safety and security. By the time March 20 came we were ready.

But who knew how well the shutdown of San Francisco would actually *work*? The day's protests were so big and far-reaching across the city that it was impossible to get a sense of it while it was happening. I rode my bike around with hundreds of strangers all day, slowing traffic and marveling at how quiet everything was. I didn't get my first sense of the enormity of the shutdown until people showed up at the squat from all corners of the city that night, talking excitedly about what they'd seen all day. The sense of victory was indescribable as we opened the front door and unfurled our banner that read "It's not the war, it's the way we live" from the top-floor window. The fact that groups could announce their intention to shut down the city, plan openly for months to do it, and still actually have the numbers and creativity to pull it off is a far more inspiring show of movement strength to me than anything that could ever happen in a mayor's race. Market Street was under protester control all day, and Police Chief Fagan declared the city to be in the grips of "absolute anarchy," which you have to admit is way cooler than saying the city was in the absolute grip of the Green Party. That night went well. Several hundred people came to the squat to hang out, eat and drink beer, and celebrate the day's events in a free space. But the day after the shutdown didn't go as well for the protesters. Heavy-handed and often illegal police tactics, designed to avoid a repeat of the shutdown, kept most of the second day's protest from even starting.

When I reported to the squat that night to open it up, things looked bad. The cops had surrounded three separate marches and were slowly doing mass arrests, all within one block of the squat. I wasn't sure if they knew about the squat, but we were surrounded either way. We went inside and began preparing for the meal and show anyway, and opened the doors as planned at 8 o'clock. About a hundred people were eating when the cops showed up.

I am proud that our carefully planned evacuation drill worked. While I'd been delaying the cops' entrance, the back door had been opened into the alley. As the cops marched in, they seemed to think that they were backing the crowd into the corner. But the closer they got, the smaller the crowd got, until we had all filed calmly out the back door, avoiding a single arrest!

As the summer settled into a daily grind of war headlines, it became hard to remember just what that power of thousands of people working together and winning on March 20 had felt like. A dull, aching post-street war funk seemed to set in across the city, a fog that didn't lift for many until the Gonzalez campaign was under way.

V.

When I think of all the unpaid effort that went into 949 Market and the SF Shutdown, I see a vision of how much energy is really out there and that people are willing to make sweeping change in this city. Today, the city's dispirited, post-dot.com streets resemble a battleground where a war has just recently stopped. Homeless bodies pile in doorways in front of empty buildings and an out-of-control police force tries to pacify the remaining ungentrified neighborhoods. This is a divided city in need of a progressive New Deal, and more.

But, in the Gonzalez campaign, another opportunity was lost to assert a comprehensive progressive vision of what we want to see happen in the city and how we can make it happen. The mayor's race was about person-alities, not politics.

Much of the role of the mayor in San Francisco is symbolic, about how the mayor's personality both reflects and shapes the aspirations of our times. It was an accident of history that brought the imperious and thoroughly crooked Willie Brown back home to San Francisco just in time to preside over the thoroughly crooked dot.com times. But who else could have so embodied the era and shaped the city in his image, ruling from a golden-domed City Hall?

Gonzalez, too, is of the times, and the fact that he almost won says a lot about how much this city has changed in the four years since Tom Ammiano ran his upstart, write-in campaign. In 1999, Ammiano tried to rally all the tenants, people of color, working poor, and activists that remained after the dot.com boom. In 2003, Gonzalez, instead, rallied many of the young, white hipsters who remained after the dot.com bust. The Gonzalez campaign, with its art parties and Internet energy, was a gentrified progressivism, what a progressive vision looks like when it abandons traditional progressive organizing bases.

Eight years of Willie Brown had driven many people of color and work-ing poor from the city. Instead of addressing the concerns of weakened progressive neighborhood institutions, Gonzalez chose to emphasize those of his qualities ("He played bass in a rock band!") that would appeal to the displacers. The young people drawn to the campaign saw themselves in Gonzalez, a young lefty who held art shows in his City Hall office and actually knew who The Clash were; a candidate for a young, white, starving artist scene that wasn't *rich* but only a simulacra of the poor. When Gonzalez supporters speak of making a livable city, one senses they aren't talking about stopping police brutality in neighborhoods of color; they're imagining bike lanes. They're talking about banning genetically modified foods, not putting actual food on the table.

Had the Gonzalez campaign taken more vocal radical positions, he most likely would have won the close election, by exciting voters in the neighborhoods that had the most to gain from a progressive agenda. For reasons I could never understand, Gonzalez failed to campaign heavily in Hunters Point. A strong stand on police brutality and environmental justice may have brought out the vote, but, presented with a choice between two different brands of young, "good looking" white guys, voters in the Bayview and Visitacion Valley stayed home in droves, showing the lowest voter turnout in the city. The only other neighborhoods in the city with voter turnout under 50% were also among the city's poorest—Ingleside, Excelsior, the Tenderloin, and South of Market.

While Gonzalez raced around the city to "Mutts for Matt" campaign stops, Newsom had a high-visibility Bayview campaign office and was present in the neighborhood all the time. Communities of color, wary of being forgotten or taken for granted by progressives, ultimately went for the safe bet and the Democratic Party machine. At least the Democrats always hand out free turkeys on Thanksgiving.

Mission Street today is, like South of Market, appearing trapped in some arrested state of "hip." The poorly built lofts fall apart and resemble the cheaply made public housing that used to be in the neighborhood. The Beauty Bar is still there, but the blue gang graffiti won't stay hidden under the yellow paint they cover it with. An uneasy truce has developed between the Latino families who walk past daytime fruit stands and the nightly hipster bar crawl.

I rarely remember to notice the paint splotches on the Bayview Bank, but they did catch my eye on that rainy night last December when Gonzalez lost to Newsom. I thought of 1999. Ammiano's insurgent campaign had been fueled by anger at the long lines of young rich kids, who came to the Mission to cram into former Latino working-class bars, now turned into yuppie dives, like Doc's Clock. After Gonzalez gave his concession speech he headed down Mission Street to drink a consolation beer with his supporters. In 2003, the ex-candidate drank at Doc's Clock.

As venerable indie rocker Jonathan Richman played inside the bar, some friends and I drank whiskey outside in the cool rain. Even then, I'd already heard people wondering about how they could keep "the energy" alive. It seemed better to wonder how much of the energy would have been kept alive if Gonzalez had *won*? Would a Gonzalez victory have ushered in a sweeping transformation of everyday life in the city with the urgency and creativity of the year's antiwar events, or would we still be standing here in the rain, outside of Doc's Clock? Was this a movement or just a scene?

Staring at the paint splotches that night, I remembered rolling down Mission Street on a flatbed truck during the antiwar parade and playing punk shows in the Leed's doorway across the street. I remembered months spent dreaming of and getting away with a different way of life in 949 Market. I remembered Market Street shut down for a full day and the feeling of raw, unchallenged possibility in the joyful streets.

I still wish Gonzalez had won, but I only want to go to an art show in City Hall when City Hall is abandoned and taken over by squatters!

"130 Parties in 30 Days"

The Matt Gonzalez Mayoral Campaign & the Restructuring of the Culture Industry

David Rosen

Matt Gonzalez's mayoral campaign forged a spirited grassroots out-reach movement that drew upon the energies, money, and votes of those who have long been dismissed as a disaffected sector of the citizenry. Known by some in the campaign as "nightlife people," these were largely young people (in their twenties and thirties), mostly white, and strongly identified with alternative or independent arts, media, and culture—the "alt-cult" community. The Gonzalez campaign's outreach to this com-munity was expressed through numerous voter-registration and fund-raising gatherings that took place at house parties, bar fests, poetry slams, gallery auc-tions, and other get-togethers. This community was his core constituency.

Gonzalez's outreach to those sharing an alternative *cultural* sensibility suc-ceeded in drawing new and previously disaffected voters into the political process. This cultural appeal was marked by an apparently self-conscious decision by Gonzalez to forgo the more traditional ideological political appeal common to most electoral campaigns.

Cultural politics played a different, and in some ways more interesting, role in the Gonzalez campaign than in most electoral campaigns. All campaigns include cultural elements, for fund-raising purposes if nothing else. The Newsom campaign had its cultural components, identified with the city's "bourgeois" arts sector. But the Gonzalez campaign did more than merely appeal to a different, "alternative," cultural community. By de-emphasizing more traditional ideological or programmatic appeals, it attempted to imple-ment a different notion of political identity and political organizing. At its core, it identified with and cultivated an electoral constituency that was not only not mainstream, but was self-consciously antimainstream and anticorporate.

Gonzalez lost his mayoral run and now, to the chagrin of many who sup-ported him, has bowed out of municipal politics. His defeat offers a valuable lesson to both cultural innovators and political activists—the "communities" that the Gonzalez campaign sought to draw together. The campaign cham-pioned a progressive agenda addressed to nearly everyone in the city and the candidate presented himself as inclusive on both personal and political levels.

His campaign's active outreach to the alt-cult community—through the 130 parties—successfully fueled his electoral insurgence. Unfortunately, its apparently more limited appeal to others of the city's communities dogged the campaign and was surely one important reason why, ultimately, Gonzalez failed to win.

Nevertheless, the 130-odd parties reflected two critical developments, one essential for the surprising success of Gonzalez's insurgent campaign, the other pointing to far deeper changes remaking both cultural life and politics in the age of corporate globalization and the neo-cons' imperialist misadventures. First, these events provided a unifying language of "community" that framed Gonzalez's oppositional role in the election. This notion of community based on cultural identity not only gave voice to campaign issues, but expressed what some within the campaign referred to as the deeper "values" shared by Gonzalez and those who supported his candidacy. However, as shorthand, the events served as a substitute for rigorous political debate and formal organizing that may, today, be even more critically needed than ever before. The second aspect of Gonzalez's appeal points to a deeper development involving the restructuring now transforming the culture industry. This restructuring is as much a national as it is an international development, with San Francisco serving as North America's locus of creative fermentation. Together, these two developments raise important questions about the long-term viability of independent progressive politics in the U.S. as well as the sustainability of independent arts and media outside the hegemony of the marketplace—and the ability of these two developments to interpenetrate one another.

The Culture Industry and Alt-Cult

Alternative or independent culture plays multiple roles in a market-driven mass media society: it is an aesthetic shadow, an innovation incubator, a recruiting farm team—and a political guilty conscience. Today's alt-cult phenomenon, however, is driven by a historically new set of causal factors that just might enable the emergence of an era of sustainable alternative arts, culture, and media in the U.S. The twin forces redefining the culture industry—domestic consolidation and international globalization—are driving this possible change. They are imposing economic requirements on the giant conglomerates that reduce creative innovation to an aesthetic formula designed for a global market. Equally important, the underlying, enabling technologies of production and distribution—what is known as the digital revolution—are opening up unanticipated opportunities for independent media makers, changing what is created as well as who creates the new works. Finally, one cannot overlook the U.S.'s mounting social crisis, with its increasingly polarized social climate—involving the Iraq occupation, environmental degradation, and extremes of wealth and poverty, to name but three issues—as a factor fueling cultural innovation and its popular appeal.

Being "independent" or creating alternative art has been a distinguishing feature of the Western creative tradition since Rimbaud, Baudelaire, and the other great romantics of the nineteenth century. In similar fashion, Edgar Allan Poe and Walt Whitman offered America its first glimpses of the artist-as-outsider—an imagery that persists to this day. These and many subsequent artists embodied a sensibility that challenged America's increasingly class-defined cultural value system, contesting both established aesthetic standards and lifestyle conventions.

The artist-as-outsider achieved a new level of popular appeal among Americans in the post–World War II decades. This appeal grew as the consumer society took shape. In 1947, Max Horkheimer and Theodor Adorno published their classic work, *The Dialectic of Enlightenment*. With a prophetic vision that has now become a social truism, the two critical theorists outlined the coming half-century that would remake the conditions of Western cultural and intellectual life. In a chapter titled, "The Culture Industry: Enlightenment as Mass Deception," they clearly foresaw what was to come: "Film, radio and magazines make up a system which is uniform as a whole in every part ...The culture industry as a whole has molded men as a type unfailingly reproduced in every product." One of their most telling insights is for us today probably the most obvious but unremarked upon in a society obsessed by personal fulfillment through workplace "success": "Amusement under late capitalism is the prolongation of work."

In the decades between the Civil War and World War II, American culture was restructured along the lines of "highbrow" and "lowbrow," of elite and popular. This hierarchical structuring involved both the range and quality of the culture experience, of the types of artistic expression and how they were experienced. For example, during much of the nineteenth century, opera and Shakespeare were redefined as cultural experiences. Where once accessible to people from all walks of life, the demands of an intensifying class system removed them from popular cultural experience, recasting them as symbols of upper class, highbrow identity, as Lawrence Levine notes. (Few San Franciscans are aware that the Bay View Opera House was a popular performance venue in the late 1800s.) Equally significant, the period also witnessed traditional forms of live performance beginning to be replaced by technology-mediated forms of culture, prefiguring the new sensibility that would define the twentieth century—culture-at-a-distance.

In the half-century following World War II, mediated culture-at-a-distance became the dominant form of creative expression. During these decades, the culture industry grew increasingly hegemonic. It fashioned a very fluid, plastic cultural environment, one in which "highbrow" and "lowbrow" were subordinated to the consumer-driven mass market, the middlebrow. The mass market has become an expansive category, blurring with impunity the traditional segmentation—or system of hierarchical valuation—common to class society. However, as the new millennium takes root, cultural differentiation is being further restructured, but this time along different—and, potentially repolarizing—lines, "conglomerate" and "alternative."

Today, conglomerate culture is triumphant, nearly hegemonic in its drive to control the media in terms of both the creation and distribution of information and entertainment. Oligopoly rules! A half-dozen conglomerates run the world's mass media. Cultural hegemony is reinforced by similar structures defining the communications industry (wired and wireless, narrowband and broadband), the IC industry (multiprocessors and DSPs), and the operating-system sector (PC and server), to name but three.

A genius of the culture industry has been its ability to integrate the artist-as-outsider into mainstream, corporate culture. The commercialization of Elvis Presley signaled the formal triumph of corporate co-optation. His enormous—and unexpected—popular appeal transformed mainstream America. His appeal represented, simultaneously, a rejection of the former system of class-based ("high-brow") culture and the transformation of the consumer from a passive to an active force in social life. In an age of cold war patriarchy, Elvis's "new" masculinity incorporated two critical components: an explicit (and, some would say, more effeminate) sexuality not publicly celebrated since Rudolph Valentino and an explicit expropriation of black culture not paraded before white America since Al Jolson. This has been the culture industry's blueprint for popular taste over the last half-century.

At the same time, a more traditional, cutting-edge notion of artist-as-outsider was finding resonance in both the arts and the persona of such icons as Jackson Pollack, Allen Ginsberg, and John Coltrane. For them, commercial success was a by-product, a lucky outcome of the creative process. The next generation of cultural independents—Bob Dylan, Andy Warhol, and Francis Ford Coppola, among many others—drew inspiration from drugs, free love, civil rights, feminism, and still deeper creative passions. Not unlike those who preceded them, success for these artists was an afterthought to their creative life.

However, during the eighties and nineties, the entertainment corporations became global media conglomerates, undergoing structural changes that made things qualitatively different for media makers, mainstream or independents. These changes forced many artists to listen more to their lawyers than their muses. Behind a foreground of an apparent increase in the creative role of independent artists, the dominant culture industries were revising the ways they did business—doing so to better control the rapidly growing market. During the 1980s, the leading music labels, following the Hollywood movie-studio model, abandoned their traditional "closed system" to what Paul Lopes calls an "open system" of production. Entertainment companies aggressively established or acquired independent production companies or set up distribution agreements with nominally independent production companies. In movies, Disney acquired Miramax and Orion Classics became Sony Classics; in music, Motown was bought by MCA and TimeWarner gobbled up Rhino. The "open" system shifted control from production to distribution. In this shift, independent producers took over—at increasingly lower costs—the production process. This approach was intended "to incorporate innovation and diversity as an effective strategy in maintaining the viability of the market."

The open system is distinguished by a flexible relationship between corporate headquarters and the indie producer responsible for the production of new product. It allows media corporations to respond quickly to changing fads and trends by signing up innovative artists and producers. It also allows them to quickly dump those who no long perform at profitable levels. Such flexibility helps facilitate oligopolistic market conditions—with management insisting on increasingly tighter control over the bottom line.

Nothing more painfully reveals how this phenomenon has played out than the experiences of salsa and hip-hop. Both were, initially, insurgent cultural movements, combining radical nationalist sentiments with a unique musicality. They were, however, co-opted into mainstream culture. In doing so, each gained great market presence and contributed to the apparent integration of new minority cultures (Puerto Rican and African-American) into American society. But as this happened, these cultural movements lost their original, critical edge. As a consequence, the media conglomerates gained greater control over larger segments of both mainstream and minority taste. This marked much of cultural innovation of the eighties and nineties.

Co-optation enables the formal integration of innovation into the corporate system. Globalization, however, seems to be undercutting the apparent power of co-optation by forging an increasingly bifurcated culture market. Globalization requires conglomerates to push ever more formulaic products to satisfy the needs of a global market. Whether *Lord of the Rings* or Britney Spears, they are produced from the same cookie cutter; success is a function of packaging and distribution. However, globalization doesn't seem to know how to deal with the enormously rich, varied, autonomous arts, culture, and media emerging through worldwide local initiatives. Under global capitalism, "products" have to achieve a certain level of financial performance before the conglomerates seek to gobble them up. Beneath that level, a whole new world of creativity is taking root.

Over the last two decades, a movement for autonomous cultural innovation has begun to take shape—surviving and growing by remaining under the radar of the conglomerate culture industry. In the fits and starts common to uneven development, this new independent, alternative culture has emerged in pockets of creative fermentation. San Francisco is one of these pockets—and the city vibrates with this innovative culture, as a quick look at the *San Francisco Bay Guardian* shows. These pockets take innumerable forms, some quite accommodating, others breaking all molds, whether in music—world music, Michael Franti, DJ Spookie and Ani DiFranco; in movies—from Sundance to *Columbine*; in radio—Democracy Now, Radio Bilingüe, and dozens of pirate stations; in politics—MoveOn and Matt Gonzalez.

Today's multiform alternative culture appears to be growing in popular appeal. Ironically, it is doing so as much of the world is undergoing profound social and economic restructuring due to globalization. From its origins in Europe in the mid-fifteenth century, capitalism has finally become a fully integrated world system; the collapse of the Soviet Union marked the end to the last formal opposition to its reign. The U.S. government is seeking, simultaneously, to manage its dominant position in the new global market through the IMF, World Bank, and other trade pacts and to police development through its military force and, as needed, intervention. Consequences of this development are evident in the U.S.—class stratification is intensifying; the quality of life is declining; the military-police security state is expanding; and the culture industry is consolidating. All—international and domestic, military and media—are of a piece. Together, these forces are conspiring to narrow the definition of personal and social freedom that has characterized American democracy since its inception.

The new digital technologies introduced during the eighties and nineties fueled the development of both conglomerate and alternative cultures. These media were enabled by Moore's Law: impressive improvements in performance capabilities matched by equally consequential decreases in cost. These technologies have generated an unprecedented amount of original "content"—whether "good" or not is another matter. In addition, their adoption shifted the terrain of political engagement from production to the growing battle over the control of distribution; from who could own a printing press to who could speak to fellow citizens in the public commons. Today's media-reform struggle is succeeding in part by bringing together progressives and conservatives (especially old-school libertarians and small-media owners) in common cause with the public-at-large against global conglomerates.

Today's alt-cult movement has also benefited from the expansion of a sizable, receptive audience. Paul Ray calls this consuming citizenry the "cultural creatives"—the more sophisticated segment of the consumer society. Their consumerism is motivated by "tastes" and by "values." This audience consists of two critical demographic segments. One group consists the "nightlife people"—younger, urban dwellers, single or couples with no children, having jobs and money in their pockets, involved with all manner of digital devices and not afraid of new tastes (be they of the pallet or the flesh). The other are older, more affluent—often couples, empty nesters—looking to the city and young innovators to reinvigorate their creative sensibilities.

The alt-cult phenomenon is informed by insurgent political movements that formed in the mid- to late nineties. First emerging in support for the Zapatistas' imaginative struggle, the movement exploded onto the world stage in Seattle in November 1999 at the protests that halted the proceedings of the usually unchallenged World Trade Organization (WTO). Recalling the sixties slogan, "the whole world is watching," subsequent international gatherings of the world's rulers—whether in Genoa or Miami—no longer proceed without public scrutiny and outrage. These insurgent political movements make provocative use of media—be it the Web, satellite TV, radio, or print. Not surprising, many who backed Gonzalez participated in these events as well as the antiwar protests before the election. This radical political consciousness helped fuel the development of the city's alternative culture.

San Francisco Alt-Cult

San Francisco's cultural life is divided into the same tiers as the rest of society. On one level we have the opera, symphony, ballet, better-funded museums, and pricey galleries that regularly take the biggest ads in the *Chronicle*'s Sunday "Pink" section. Another tier includes the endless array of mass-market fare: commercial TV and cable channels, radio stations, blockbuster movie multiplexes, legitimate music and theaters, and the mass-gathering, outdoor performance venues like spectator sports and concerts. In addition, the city's very diverse ethnic, racial, religious, and national communities comprise a tier that further enriches cultural life.

Since the heyday of the Barbary Coast era, San Francisco has nurtured its own unique alternative culture. World War II revitalized the city, enabling it to recover from the long depression following the crash of 1929. The significant increase in locally-stationed and returning military personnel fueled the emergence in the fifties of an alternative cultural life that became not only a force in civic life, but one that gained national recognition as a beacon for the avant-garde, the outrageous, the outsider. It found expression in new literary movements, stand-up comics, gay and lesbian activists, and nude dancers. The "beats"—Ginsberg, Jack Kerouac, William Burroughs, Lawrence Ferlinghetti and Diane diPrima, to name but five of these figures—challenged the complacency of the fifties, set the stage for the counterculture of the sixties and seventies, and continue to inspire the insurgent arts and media movements of our new millennium.

Today, a growing alt-cult network enlivens city life. It is drawn from the vibrant music, theater, dance, spoken word, performance art, fashion design, and crafts scenes; strengthened by committed journalists, poets and writers, media activists, and film and video-game makers, and enhanced by Web designers, animators, video game makers, and open-source software proponents. Collectively, this network—and still others, for this is not an exhaustive list—gives city life its critical edge.

This is the culture of those who regularly visit City Lights, Adobe Books and Modern Times; who listen to KPOO, KPFA, and KQED; who watch public access and LINK-TV; who check out the hottest bands at Bruno's, Makeout Room, Hemlock Tavern, and the innumerable other bars and clubs that offer as much sociability as alcohol; who attend experimental film as well as music, performance art and dance festivals; who read the *San Francisco Bay Guardian*, blogs, and a zillion zines; who turn up at 111 Minna, 848 Community Space, and other venues promoting the visual imagination; and who regularly jam the streets on the monthly Critical Mass bicycle raves. These were some of the folks who came out for Matt.

This culture found unique expression in the Gonzalez-Newsom runoff. While both candidates appealed to constituencies based in part on an unstated but apparent cultural identity, Gonzalez's appeal seems to have been fundamentally different than the other mayoral candidates, including Angela Alioto and Tom Ammiano, the two other progressives.

Gonzalez genuinely identified with the youth-oriented alt-cult. Newsom appears less personally identified with "highbrow" culture than associated with the lifestyle of those who long have backed him. Alioto seems to have no explicit cultural identity, embracing a more generic, old-line San Francisco pluralism that embraces all cultures without identifying with any one. Ammiano seems to have drawn his cultural identity from the gay and lesbian community that expanded the city's cultural landscape, contributing an explicit sexual component to cultural identity. A politician's cultural identity, stated explicitly or not, served as a framework to address traditional civic issues. Gonzalez's political agenda reflected not only a progressive vision, but pointed to larger cultural shifts now taking place within the city and throughout the country.

Gonzalez's Cultural Agenda

Gonzalez's appeal was defined as much by his personal identification with the arts as by his campaign platform. Much of his commitment to the city's alt-cult community comes out of his personal support and identification with it. His close association as a member of the board of directors of the Brava Theatre is well known; his First Friday arts gatherings at City Hall are easy ways for ordinary citizens to meet and greet the president of the Board of Supervisors and see interesting art exhibits and schmooze with equally interesting people from varied walks of life.

The Gonzalez platform recognized the centrality of cultural life in the city's economy. Gonzalez cites the San Francisco Chamber of Commerce as to the important—if, as he says, "overlooked"—economic role of the arts. The chamber—using data derived from studies conducted for the San Francisco Arts Commission and San Francisco's Economic Summit—found the following:

- One in eleven jobs in San Francisco are related to the arts through employment in such sectors as graphic design, advertising, architecture, publishing, broadcast, and film.

- Arts organizations provide a $1.3 billion boost to the local economy.

- The arts are the fourth-largest growth industry in San Francisco.

- The San Francisco Bay Area has the largest arts attendance per capita among U.S. metropolitan areas.

Based on these underlying factors, Gonzalez's platform advocated three core propositions:

- Put the arts to work by increasing arts funding with a re-evaluation of the city's hotel tax, helping arts organizations acquire affordable space, and increasing the inclusion of arts components in public works projects.

- Recognize the centrality of art in a well-rounded education by supporting a regional blueprint for arts education, encouraging funding partners as well as artists and arts organizations to play a more active role in allocating resources to our public schools, and expanding the city's Visiting Artist program.

- Ensure a diverse arts community by pursuing a more demographically and geographically diverse membership on the Arts Commission, protecting neighborhood single-screen theaters, and ensuring higher rates of minority representation at the School of the Arts.

This was a progressive agenda for the arts.

Two features of his plan had special resonance. First, he hinted at new funding possibilities but did so without rocking the boat of existing arts support: "I will preserve the existing allocation of funds to large cultural organizations while seeking increases for funding small nonprofit arts groups." How would he have done this? He planned to "work to strengthen the city's commitment to integrating the arts into public infrastructure projects, expanding artists-in-residence programs at city departments, and creating an artist laureate program for the city." With the city's $300 million deficit, one can only wonder if this would have worked.

Gonzalez's platform aimed at enriching the life of the city's school-aged children. It was also a secret jobs program that challenged the tyranny of the prison-industrial complex. It recognized the tension between creativity and discipline at the heart of civic life. Its support for youth through education, sports, and the arts, while enriching the lives of younger citizens, challenged the powerful forces of social control—the prison-industrial system of police, courts, and jails. This is a battle that, since 9/11, progressive forces have been losing.

Gonzalez was well aware of the city's diversity and his program acknowledged complexity. Gonzalez clearly understood the role of traditional pork-barrel Democratic politics that rules San Francisco. His "arts" platform acknowledged the role of pork, but challenged the Brown-Newsom machine in how it was to be allocated. He saw it benefiting both the alt-cult community and the city's varied ethnic, racial, and national community cultures.

130 Events in 30 Days

Gonzalez's second-place showing in the general election caught everyone by surprise, none more so than the Gonzalez campaign. The victory filled his insurgent, rag-tag campaign with exhilaration—followed by dread. They were woefully unprepared to take on the winner-take-all, bare-knuckles political brawl with Newsom and the Democratic Party machine. They knew better than anyone that they lacked the money to pay for staff (especially professional campaigners), services, and outreach, let alone the organizational infrastructure to get voters attention and to the polling booths. Making matters even more intense, they had only thirty days to pull off their challenge to the city's entrenched power structure. During the general campaign, Marlena Sonn had established an Events group. In early October 2003, Windy Chien joined on as a full-time campaign volunteer and, because of her background in the music business, worked with Events. Chien typifies not only the alt-cult people who came out for Gonzalez, but symbolizes the deeper personal-social changes taking place across the country. How she integrates culture and politics suggests the new, radical sensibility that distinguishes many younger urban people today.

Windy ran Aquarius Records, an independent music store in the Mission District, on Valencia at 21st Street, for thirteen years before she sold it in October. Matt Gonzalez regularly patronized her shop and she got to know him before the election. After she sold the store, she was anxious about her life. "I was worried that I would never find something like my store; the sense that we were all working on something together that we truly believed in," she said. "I wanted to find a sense of family again." A friend recruited her to the Gonzalez campaign and she was hooked.

Chien was attracted to Gonzalez because "[h]e made it easy for people to feel comfortable to contribute in their own way." The campaign became a new family. She put in long, exhausting, but rewarding hours. She really was making something happen. So powerful was the experience that after Matt's runoff defeat, she jumped into Dennis Kucinich's California primary campaign and now is involved in the post-Gonzalez "NextSteps" progressive caucus.

Another campaign volunteer was Eddie Codel, a thirty-five-year-old unemployed dot.commer. He also joined after the general election, putting in twelve-hour days, sometimes six days a week because, as he says, "Matt shared our values, understood our culture . . . I believe that the social is the political," he reflects. "Matt was able to catalyze various social groups and the things they cared about ... homelessness, education, art ... was what he cared about." Codel insists that if "Matt hadn't addressed these issues and wasn't progressive, I wouldn't have gotten involved."

Like Chien, he joined first campaign. Gonzalez's run appealed to him because of the issues involved, but also because it was "something not traditionally political." Gonzalez's appeal to the alt-cult community suggested a different kind of politics: "Once we understood that Matt was into our culture, it was easy for us to come out for him."

Marlena Sonn came up with the original notion of "thirty parties in thirty days"—however, the enormous and unexpected outpouring of support for Gonzalez's run overwhelmed his mostly volunteer staff. In order to cope with the groundswell of popular interest, the campaign decided that the Events group would handle two types of "event" programs. One type included more formal occasions, like a Chinatown banquet organized by Walter Wong that drew 500 people. The other involved smaller fund-raisers, with individuals dropping $5 or $10 in the proverbial hat. It was this second type of event that quickly exploded from 30 to over 130 gatherings. "It just happened," Windy recalls, "people kept calling, ten to twenty proposals a day kept coming in, and we kept adding to the schedule. There was very little structure involved in planning the events. We kept the infrastructure to a minimum as to what would happen at the event." Eddie seconds this, "the campaign was very decentralized, not top-down. Things bubbled up." The events were initiated by individuals from varied backgrounds who wanted to get involved and were not directed by the campaign. "So many people wanted to do events that all we did was figure out, this event can make a difference," Chien admits.

The events ran the gamut from small lounge get-togethers and yoga sessions to citywide motorcycle rallies and "Moms in Glen Park" discussions to a soirée at the Great American Music Hall featuring Cake, Sonny Smith and a half-dozen other performers. The greatest number took place in bars, lounges, and clubs, and accounted for approximately 35 percent of all parties. House and loft parties accounted for 21 percent and gallery and art auctions added another 10 percent. The remaining 34 percent took place at bookstores, cafés, restaurants, community centers, churches, pilates studios, and still other venues; these also include outdoor events like bike rides and dog walks.

Bars and clubs were perfect settings for small, informal music events. And there were plenty of them, including karaoke sing-alongs, reggae fests, noise sessions, jazz jams, hip-hop raps, and rock sets. They were hosted all over the city, including the Attic (Mission), Club Cocomo (Potrero), Club Waziema (Haight), Slim's (SoMA), Werepad (Dogpatch), and the Red Rock Lounge (Glen Park). Bookstores like Adobe (Mission), City Lights (North Beach) and Bird & Becket (Glen Park) opened their doors to raise money and awareness. Arts auctions took place at the Loft (Western Addition), the Lab (Mission) and other venues. Many organizations sponsored events, ranging from Iranian-American Progressives and Greens (at Al-Fanous restaurant), an Independent Media Works fund-raiser, a National Lawyers Guild house party, SF Moto/Bike Coalition, Comedians for Matt, the Women's Building and Harvey Milk Institute. There was even a barbeque pig-out at the Uptown (Mission). As indicated in Figure 1, while events took place throughout the city, a third of the events took place in the Mission.

Most of the events were organized along a similar format. After an initial schmooze period of socializing and hanging out, the host or event organizer would introduce Gonzalez or, if he didn't attend, a representative from the campaign who would speak for five to ten minutes and then open up the event for a round of Q & A; the host or Gonzalez representative would then come back and make the "ask"—the request for support—and encourage those in attendance to pick up campaign literature, fill out a voter-registra-tion form, and drop off a donation at a designated table. ("Matt" t-shirts were sold. As Chien recalls, "they were white shirts with black sleeves that look like Van Halen rock tour shirts; we printed his face on the front with 'San Francisco Tour 2003' and listed many of the events on the back. We sold almost a thousand and raised about $20,000.") Then, the gathering would return to an informal get-together.

For a scrappy, grassroots campaign, these 130 or so events proved a very suc-cessful way to draw people into the campaign, register new voters, raise money, and encourage people to vote. Many of the volunteers, like Codel, were survivors of the dot.com era. They had either come to San Francisco as part of the nineties "digital gold rush" or were longtime dwellers; in any case, they had endured the great squeeze of skyrocketing rents, entrepre-neurial hype, and mounting homelessness that marked the decade. Now, as a post-dot-bomb sobriety was settling in and city life was returning to its overpriced but still offbeat normalcy, these nightlife people were coming out into the daylight of civic engagement.

Reflecting back on the campaign outreach experience, Chien understood the inherent contradictions the campaign faced. The night-life people were, as she half-jokingly says, the "campaign's dirty little secret." They were a discreet segment of the population, but were they a constituency? Was an alt-cult identity enough to be a force in political life? According to Chien, "I think there is a hunger among younger people, people more involved in cultural things, to engage in the political process—[but they] were never given a way to do so." For her, "Matt's campaign made it possible for younger people like me, people in their thirties, to get involved in local politics and make a change."

One of the campaign's unexpected developments was the support it received from Burning Man, the nation's foremost alt-cult event. According to Codel, it was extraordinary when Burning Man founder Larry Harvey endorsed Gonzalez. "Not everyone who attends Burning Man is political or, if political, not necessarily progressive," Eddie insists. "Up to then," he adds, "Harvey only addressed issues that directly affected the annual gathering itself. Coming out for Matt was unprecedented." Going further than a mere endorsement, Harvey spoke out on behalf of Gonzalez's candidacy at a pre-runoff rally at the Civic Center on December 7, 2003. Addressing many of the concerns of those in the alt-cult community, he declared:

You don't have to feel co-opted. You don't have to say that things have got too big, that money talks. You don't have to hide in a subculture and not speak to your neighbors. Big money doesn't have the power to co-opt us. Arnold Schwarzenegger's not the man to tell us what to do. We can collectively express

Figure 1	
GONZALEZ EVENTS DURING THE RUNOFF	
Location/District	**Number of Events**
Bayview-Hunters Point	2
Bernal Heights	2
Castro	2
Chinatown/North Beach	5
Civic Center/Tenderloin	3
Cole Valley	1
Embarcadero	3
Haight/Hayes Valley	8
Marina	1
Mission	38
Noe Valley/Glen Park	7
Pacific Heights	2
Potrero	3
Richmond/Presidio	10
SoMA	10
Western Addition	5
Others: City Wide	4
Others: Sebastopol and Berkeley	(1 each)
SOURCE: WINDY CHIEN EVENTS LIST	

ourselves. Now, at the beginning of the 21st Century, we, united as San Franciscans, can teach the United States of America what it can become.

Because of the campaign's catch-as-catch-can openness, there was wide unevenness in the quality of events. Most, like the events held at the Great American Music Hall, DNA Lounge, City Lights, 848 Community Space, and many house parties, were, according to Windy, "very cool—small, successful, [they] brought in people." But some, as she admitted, were "lemons." One unnamed bar held Gonzalez parties twice a week but seemed to want to tie itself to a Gonzalez bandwagon and use the events to promote featured bands. Still other events, like a planned party to be organized by the filmmaker Rob Epstein, never happened because of late notification or scheduling conflicts.

The campaign Events group principally worked to coordinate proposals and did not have an outreach plan to promote Gonzalez within the city's traditionally underserved communities. This was due to a very tight timeframe to pull it all together and a mostly voluntary campaign staff who seemed overwhelmed at times. Supporters organized their own events, and the campaign encouraged active grassroots participation. According to Chien, they were always playing catch-up: "We were dealing with an onslaught." One consequence was that, "We didn't say, hey, let's go to Chinatown or Bayview and put something together. People came to us who wanted to organize an event." The Gonzalez campaign tapped this hunger, but "the people who organized the events had their own built-in network of friends and comrades," and thus the events tended to be self-referential as to who attended. The outcome was a very high proportion of events in the Mission and SoMA and at bars and lounges and significantly fewer events in Bayview, Bernal Heights or the Castro.

The campaign, nevertheless, was successful in registering new voters. "We registered people at every single event," Chien said. She estimates that a few thousand people were registered at campaign events. Even more important, both she and Codel believe the majority of those who attended Gonzalez events—including new registrants—voted! As Eddie points out, "the campaign energized a lot of people who otherwise wouldn't have voted."

The Gonzalez Campaign and Restructuring the Culture Industry

Popular culture consists of two intertwined elements. One consists of the forms of *expression* of numerous media formats that saturate everyday life, the other involves the *experience* derived from these media. The unity of experience and expression gives culture its specific character. Today, live and prerecorded media merge into a false immediacy. Documentary and narrative media are becoming a deceptive TV-verité, a scripted "reality" indistinguishable from what passes as the news. Programming and advertising media are shrinking into a ceaseless commercial in which product placements, sponsorships, and endorsements blot out all recognizable differences between truth and fiction.

Culture is an industry of mass production and consumption. During the second half of the twentieth century, the same discipline exercised over production was imposed on the manufacturing of demand, the fetishization of desire. Culture—like nearly all other economic sectors—was subject to inexorable market pressure to standardize products and rationalize distribution. This process led to corporate consolidation and the dominance of a half-dozen or so global conglomerates over U.S. and, increasingly, worldwide cultural markets. Their collective output—the culture of distraction—produces audiences, their "product," to meet the profitability requirements of a global market. Culture is not only an industry in its own right, it is also that which lubricates the system as a whole with rationalized values, transforming the most intimate aspects of personal life—for example, self identity and sexuality—into commodity-mediated experiences.

However much the barons of the culture industry—yesterday's Louis B. Meyer and Jack Warner or today's Rupert Murdoch and Bill Gates—may want to impose industrial discipline on cultural production, they can never fully do so. Under late capitalism, culture has become a critical zone of creative practice. It is that zone where the market, seeking to impose predictability, is forced to make a pact with the devil of creativity, the unpredictable. The competitive pressures of globalization produce creative fissures, innovative interstices and, in doing so, let loose unanticipated consequences. One such consequence has been an increase in local, under-the-radar—and especially alternative—culture movements like those I've described taking place in San Francisco.

Into this complex moment of late capitalist culture entered the Gonzalez campaign. Gonzalez recognized the progressive role that the arts play in city life—whether as an economic force, a positive influence on the life of younger people, a defining feature of its history, or an undeniable aspect of San Francisco's overall livability.

The alt-cult coalition shared less an explicitly articulated ideological program than a common set of what was referred to as "like-minded values," be it about homelessness, the Iraq war, rent control, or jobs for artists. But more so, they—and Gonzalez himself—valued the cultural elements that drew people together. Nothing better expressed this shared sentiment than the parties themselves, which seem to have been organized to de-emphasize traditional ideological politics. Although Gonzalez was a self-declared Green Party member in a formally nonpartisan election, very little mention was made of the party and little or no party organizing took place. More rigorous discussion among event participants about broader social issues seemed only to have taken place informally, if at all.

Now that the election is past and Gonzalez has chosen to give up his supervisor's seat, the progressive movement that came out to the parties and backed his candidacy is facing a crisis. What will happen to these nightlife people as both a cultural and a political community? Some of the more hard-core veterans of the campaign, like Chien and Codel, are attempting to keep the insurgent political spirit alive through NextSteps, the Neighborhood Assembly efforts, indie-voter movement, and other initiatives. It is too early to know how successful their efforts will be. Clearly, the strong anti-Bush sentiment in San Francisco will help buoy their efforts through the November 2004 election. What happens after that is an open question.

In time, the Gonzalez campaign might share the fate of other one-shot insurgent campaigns. All too many independent political movements are epiphenomenal, dependent on the personal charisma of the candidate. Once he or she moves on, the "movement" disappears. Nevertheless, the deeper social impulses that empowered the candidate and the movement do not die but keep coming back, haunting the political status quo like a guilty conscience.

In this very specific sense, recent independent political movements share a fate similar to a hot musician or indie movie director who's just pulled off his or her first (and possibly only) hit. Some of these artists cultivate a strong following and even achieve commercial success without losing their independent identity. Others, like most small businesses, are doomed to simply disappear. A rare few get co-opted by media conglomerates and repackaged as global products.

Many independent political and cultural movements don't appreciate the need for sustainability, for building long-term presence. It remains to be seen if the energies, enthusiasm, and votes generated by the Gonzalez campaign can be harnessed to elect another progressive candidate. But more important, it remains to be seen if a grassroots movement can challenge the institutions of corporate and political power that run the city. In similar fashion, it remains to be seen if the alt-cult movement can generate alternative forms of distribution that permit an independent, nonconglomerate arts culture to sustain itself. If history is to be a guide, only very limited success will occur on either front. Nevertheless, the forces being advanced by globalization—and the great, worldwide refusal that accompanies it—just might provide the impetus for new cultural and political initiatives that can change the course of history.

Notes

Adorno, Theodor. "The Culture Industry Reconsidered," in *The Culture Industry*, ed. J. M. Bernstein, pp. 98–106. New York: Routledge, 1991.

Burnett, Robert. *The Global Jukebox: The International Music Business.* New York: Routledge, 1996.

Bynoe, Yvonne. "Money, Power and Respect: A Critique of the Business of Rap Music," in *R&B: Rhythm and Business—The Political Economy of Black Music*, ed. Norman Kelley, pp. 220–34. New York: Akashic Books, 2002

Chien, Windy. Interview, March 31, 2004.

Codel, Eddie. Interview, April 6, 2004.

Matt Gonzalez for Mayor: The Arts. See www.mattgonzalez.com.

Harvey, Larry. December 7, 2003, speech. See www.burningman.com.

Horkheimer, Max, and Theodor Adorno. *The Dialectic of Enlightenment.* New York: Herder and Herder, 1972.

Levine, Lawrence W. *Highbrow/Lowbrow: The Emergence of Cultural Hierarchy in America.* Cambridge: Harvard University Press, 1988.

Lopes, Paul D. "Innovation and Diversity in the Popular Music Industry, 1969–1990," *American Sociological Review*, 52 (1992), pp. 56–71.

Marech, Rona. "Galvanized by a Reason to Believe Three Supporters of Gonzalez United by Message and Trust." *San Francisco Chronicle*, Sunday, December 14, 2003.

Miller, Karl Hagstrom. "Crossover Schemes: New York Salsa as Politics, Culture, and Commerce," in *R&B: Rhythm and Business—The Political Economy of Black Music*, ed. Norman Kelley, pp. 192–217, New York: Akashic Books, 2002.

Neima. "Matt Gonzalez Campaign Benefit Concert." See www.BAMboozled.org.

Pirenne, Henri. *A History of Europe*, vol. II. Garden City, NY: Doubleday, 1958.

Ray, Paul H., and Sherry Ruth Anderson. *The Cultural Creatives—How 50 Million People Are Changing the World.* New York: Three Rivers Press, 2000.

Furthering the Divide
Gay Shame and the Politics of Resistance
Mattilda, a.k.a. Matt Bernstein Sycamore

The Golden Age

As a radical queer fleeing to San Francisco in search of hope, the early nineties were a formative time for me. Nevertheless, I would not have guessed that scarcely a decade later, people would look upon that period with nostalgia bordering on delusion. No one is immune to such lapses in judgment. I too remember a time of cheap rent, artistic possibility, and radical direct-action activism, a time when there were almost as many freaks as yuppies, and "community" felt more like a possibility than an advertising gimmick. But I also remember that, even if no one I knew in 1992 paid more than $300 rent, this felt exorbitant and unaffordable.

Everyone was way too depressed and/or strung out on drugs to do much art. Direct action was certainly far more prevalent than today, but in the early nineties most queer activists looked back wistfully to the late eighties, when a hundred people would show up at an ACT UP meeting (of course, that was because all their friends were dying). In 1992, the city was still filled with freaks of all sorts, but we felt overwhelmed and desperate—we saw the gentrification of the early nineties as a tidal wave we'd unwittingly helped cause, but nonetheless did not know how to stop (little did we know what was to come).

And community? In the early nineties, there was more interconnection between activist groups, as well as more coordination across divides of race, class, and sexuality. With so many queers dying of AIDS, drug addiction, and suicide, there was a sense in outsider queer circles that we were bonded together. I felt a palpable sense of potential in embracing a sluttiness infused with the romance of collective desire. But all of these possibilities dissolved quickly when tensions erupted. Small questions of process cracked most activist coalitions. Radical queers betrayed each other as quickly as the families who raised us, and the sluttiness I cultivated left me more heartbroken than healed.

I fled San Francisco just before the hypergentrification that wracked the mid–late nineties (I fled despair and drugs, not gentrification). I came back for eight months in 1996–1997, then left again (the same demons). For three years, I lived in Giuliani's New York, which offered little more than a rabidly consumerist, commodified, careerist monoculture that drained and disgusted me. In the winter of 2000, I returned to a San Francisco that mimicked all the worst aspects of New York. Entire neighborhoods had been bulldozed to make way for the ugliest luxury housing I'd ever seen. The radical outsider queer culture that I craved, which had nurtured, scarred, and transformed me in the early nineties, had suffered demolition as well, replaced by high-fashion hipsters looking for the coolest parties.

The winter of 2000 was still the height of the dot.com frenzy, at least as far as the rental market was concerned. I found myself entering Tenderloin buildings with no front doors, walking up bare hallways lit by exposed bulbs, to enter dank thousand-dollar studio apartments filled with numerous preppy blond women all vying for the manager or realtor's attention: Is the neighborhood safe? (not for you). Is there anything nearby? (a ticket out of town).

When I finally did get an apartment (yes, a thousand-dollar Tenderloin studio), everything on my rental application was fake—references, former addresses, current job—except my name and social security number. I was magically transformed into a "technical writer" who made $4,800 a month.

At the crest of the dot.com boom (or just before the fall, depending on how you look at it), my technical writing consisted of giving blow jobs in plush off-white hotel beds (you can buy the bed at the W!) while TV sets flashed stock prices (I'm serious). I remember one Tuesday night, after my third trick and on my way to a fourth, stepping into the W Hotel and finding so many people in the lobby that they spilled into the elevators to make deals on their cell phones, cocktails in hand. Outside the Ritz-Carlton one night, there was a couple no older than twenty-five stepping out of a Rolls. The guy wore a waist-coat and held a cigar in one hand and an attaché in the other; the woman wore a full-length fur and gold slip-on heels—they were dressed like someone's ruling-class grandparents. Stepping into a taxi, all I could think was: *at least I'm making cash.*

At the height of the dot.com boom, hordes of drunk yuppies crowded the sidewalks in front of posh bars, restaurants, and clubs in "fringe" neighborhoods. It became all too clear who controlled the streets. Hummers sped down side streets like they were at Burning Man (once a neo-hippy festival in the desert, now featured in lavish spreads in *Men's Fitness* and *Details*). The suburbanization of San Francisco was not just a transformation of attitude, it was a decimation of the urban imagination.

Against this disheartening backdrop, in March 2001 I found out about a "squat party" on Market Street between Fifth and Sixth Streets. I was laughing all the way there: a squat party on Market Street, who were they kidding? Would it last longer than ten minutes? Coming from Guiliani's New York, where activists could hardly march in the street without getting beaten up, I couldn't imagine a squat on Market Street—in an area filled with boarded-up buildings, yes—but still just blocks from the financial district.

I walked up a flight of stairs into a cavernous room full of brightly painted murals and hundreds of people dancing to live music. Many people I knew from different circles were there, including people I hadn't seen for ten years. The crowd, mostly young and white, was nonetheless populated by numerous weirdos dressed to the nines in mix-and-match glamour. There was a wide range of class aspirations and social skills. I couldn't remember a squat party like this in San Francisco. It lasted for hours, without interruption, and without the arrival of the cops. I felt a heady sense of potential that I hadn't experienced since I'd moved back to San Francisco, and I wondered what else might be possible.

Gay Shame

At some horrible party in the spring of 2001, Oakie, a new friend, asked me, half-joking, what I was doing for Pride.

That was all I needed to hear. Pride? Hiding inside my apartment—what else was there to do? I talked (somewhat wistfully) about Gay Shame, a radical queer alternative to Pride that a bunch of us threw in New York for three years at a collective living/performance space called dumba. I wanted to take it further, hold it in an outdoor public space like Tire Beach, a rotting industrial park on the San Francisco Bay where discarded MUNI streetcars are dumped and a concrete factory borders a small grassy area.

Oakie was excited—let's do it, he urged. He was drunk. We had three weeks until Pride. I'd embarked on way too many projects in which my co-conspirators were flakes, yet I'd come back to San Francisco to find home and all I'd found was a new desperation. I explained what it would take to put on the event—scouting the location, making flyers, wheat-pasting and flyering all over town, getting all the performers and speakers together, finding a sound system and DJs, and so on. That sounds great, Oakie said. I was skeptical, but Oakie's enthusiasm turned on my manic button and we were a pair.

Oakie and I called everyone we knew, and about ten of us—queer freaks of all genders (but mostly white and all in our twenties and thirties)—met for three weeks, and then a week before Pride, we held our alternative. Our hand-written flyers were grandiose—over a photo of the San Francisco general strike of 1934, we proclaimed, "Are you choking on the vomit of consumerist "gay pride?"—*Darling* spit that shit out—*Gay shame* is the answer." We encouraged people to "dress to absolutely mesmerizing ragged terrifying glamorous excess," and to "create the world you dream of."

Several hundred people trekked out to Tire Beach and made it our queer autonomous space for the day, which included free food, t-shirts and various other gifts, bands, spoken word, DJs (and dancing), a kid space for children, and speakers on issues including San Francisco gentrification and the U.S. colonization of the Puerto Rican island of Vieques, as well as prison, youth, and trans activism. We encouraged people to participate in creating their own radical queer space and culture instead of just buying a bunch of crap (like at Pride), and people argued about political issues, painted, poured concrete and made a mosaic, dyed hair, and mud-wrestled naked.

In spite of our efforts to create a politicized space, many participants were rude to the speakers and seemed uninterested in anything beyond partying and socializing with their friends. We realized that, as organizers, by separating the "politics" from the "partying," the speakers from the bands, we unwittingly helped participants ignore our radical intentions. We resolved to be more confrontational in the future, to make our political agenda clear.

Ten months later, we came up with the Gay Shame Awards, where we would reward the most hypocritical gays for their service to the "community." We sought to expose both the lie of a homogenous gay/queer "community," and the ways in which the myth of community is used as a screen behind which gay people with power oppress others and get away with it.

We held the Gay Shame Awards in Harvey Milk Plaza, at the center of the white-washed gayborhood of the Castro, and bestowed awards in eight categories, including "Best Target Marketing" and "Making More Queers Homeless." We served free food and gave out homemade patches and artwork, Gay Shame buttons with the image of Rosie O'Donnell or George Michael, and various other delicacies. As requested, people dressed to excess, in exaggerated, smeared makeup and glitter, torn ball gowns, and crumpled dress shirts—one participant wore a dress made entirely out of shopping bags—the Gap, Starbucks, Abercrombie and Fitch, and other gay mainstays—and stiltwalkers dressed in garbage bags added to the festivities.

We burned a rainbow flag after each award was announced, and the climax of the event occurred when we moved sofas and the sound system into the streets for a dance party. This was a fiery moment—I think we were a little in disbelief that it all went so smoothly. As police negotiators handled the cops, we held Castro and Market Streets for several hours before packing up, with no arrests. The crowd included many queers both a generation older and a generation younger than us, and even straight tourists gaped in disbelief, and wondered: is it always like this?

The Gay Shame Awards inseparably connected spectacle and politics. We started to think seriously of Gay Shame as a direct-action group that fused the theatricality and pageantry of the seventies drag troupe the Cockettes (*The Cockettes* movie was premiering at the Castro Theater), the militance of late-eighties/early-nineties ACT UP, and the anticapitalist direct action of Reclaim the Streets.

The Pride Parade adapted the Budweiser advertising slogan for its official theme: "Be Yourself—Make It a Bud" became "Be Yourself—Change The World." We prepared to confront this assimilationist monster by installing our festival of resistance inside the barricades. Two months of planning culminated in volunteer parade marshals instigating violence against us, and the bashing and arrest of two Gay Shame participants. We placed our official Budweiser Vomitorium outside the parade gates and resolved to be more prepared in the future.

If Gay Shame's first major transition moved us from festival of resistance to direct action extravaganza, our second transformation involved broadening our scope, from focusing primarily on Gay Pride to challenging all hypocrites, and specifically to confronting the racist policies of a "gay-friendly" politician. This politician was none other than the illustrious Gavin Newsom, soon to catapult to national fame, but at this point merely your average straight, white ruling-class city council (Board of Supervisors) member busy criminalizing homeless people for getting in the way of tourist dollars.

Just before Halloween 2002, Gay Shame went to Newsom's Marina district with a Haunted Shanty-town, which we installed on the block alongside his campaign headquarters and four businesses he owned (a bar, a café, a restaurant, and a wine store). We then rolled down a "bloody" carpet and held the Exploitation Runway in the middle of bustling Fillmore Street. This was a scripted event in which impersonators of key exploiters walked the runway in several categories, including Gentrification Realness (Old School and New School), More Blood for Oil, Displacement Divas, Gavin Authenticity, Luxurious Liberals, and Eviction Couture.

The Marina action was another example of how our spectacle served to draw spectators in rather than alienate them. Marina yuppies gathered around to observe our glamour and we distributed a pamphlet exposing Newsom's antihomeless policies. The cops harassed us so we made an emergency decision to take the runway up to Pacific Heights and confront Newsom at a nearby campaign function. Our frantic decision turned out to be the most beautiful and symbolic moment of the evening, as 150 of us pushed the sound system and our shantytown up a steep incline to Pacific Heights, the richest part of San Francisco.

Months later, in February 2003, Gavin Newsom held a lavish fund-raiser for the LGBT Center, a blatant (and successful) attempt to pander to San Francisco's gay elite in order to bolster his looming mayoral campaign against several gay candidates. Our banner read, "Gavin Newsom Comes Out of the Closet—As a Fascist!" We gathered not only to protest Newsom's closeted right-wing agenda, but to call attention to the hypocrisy of the center for welcoming Newsom's dirty money instead of taking a stand against his blatantly racist and classist politics.

We found out about the event at the last minute, and therefore had little time to plan much more than a banner drop and a flyer. In a flourish we handed out hot-pink bags of garbage to smiling patrons. Attendees, thinking perhaps we were part of the festivities, even agreed to pose for pictures while holding the delicately arranged trash. In spite of the tame nature of our protest, police officers called by "our" center began to bash us as soon as they escorted Newsom inside. One officer hit a Gay Shame demonstrator in the face with his baton, shattering one of her teeth and bloodying her entire face. Four of us were arrested; one arrestee was put into a chokehold until he passed out.

The press loves blood, and the spectacle of the SFPD bashing queers outside of San Francisco's LGBT Center was not lost on local media. Police violence became a cover story in local gay papers and even corporate newspapers, as well as on network news channels. With the arrest of antiwar protesters ten days later, we were unable to use this public outcry much to our advantage in indicting either the police or the center. Those arrested at the center were held in jail for up to three days and faced charges as ridiculous as assault on a police officer (four counts for me) and felony "lynching," an antiquated term for removing someone from arrest. Our court cases lasted eight months and charges were only reduced to infractions after our publicized subpoena of Gavin Newsom.

Just preceding the official start of the U.S. war against Iraq, Gay Shame meetings swelled from around a dozen participants to thirty or forty. We participated as an affinity group in the mass direct action organized for the day the war against Iraq began. Our goal was to block a specific exit ramp from the highway, and on March 20, 2003, we gathered furniture, a refrigerator, huge pieces of metal, and construction barricades for this purpose. Nonetheless, we were unable to secure the ramp for long, and instead turned into a roving band of marauders, supporting various affinity groups throughout the city. The next several days were a volatile time of public protest and arrests of 2,100 protesters—though perhaps these arrests would have been more effective if they'd occurred *before* the official start of U.S. aggression. The crackdown was shocking. Police helicopters flew overhead all night and protesters were thrown into police vans for marching on the sidewalk. It seemed war had broken out in San Francisco as well.

By the time of the Second Annual Gay Shame Awards, we were back to less than a dozen at meetings. Perservering, we added several new awards, including the Wargazm Award and Best Front-Row Seat to Watch Police Brutality (the center). We held a Walk of Shame, where we marched to the Castro and bestowed our prizes, including a rainbow phallus as the Gender Fundamentalism Award, and a framed picture of Dan White, the murderer of Harvey Milk, as the Auntie Tom Award. The highlight of the ceremony occurred when we burned an effigy of Newsom in the middle of 18th and Castro Streets (the location of numerous Newsom for Mayor signs). People danced in jubilation as the effigy burned to the ground and a fire truck arrived to disperse us.

Pride once again involved arrests, as Gay Shame participants who attempted to enter the parade ahead of Newsom were attacked by Newsom staff, and then sent to jail with felony charges—only dropped after intense pressure. As the mayoral election loomed, and Newsom held an enormous lead in public opinion polls, Gay Shame came up with the Mary for Mayor Campaign, in which a new candidate—Mary—entered the mayoral race and delivered a truly radical platform that included converting members of the SFPD to nutritious compost, supporting terrorism in all forms, and advocating forced relocation of loft condominium owners into the San Francisco Bay. In addition to a fictitious candidate with grandiose plans, we created numerous organizations who wholeheartedly supported Mary in her campaign: Terrorists Against Gavin (TAG), Fashionistas Against Gavin (FAG), and Riff-Raff Against Gavin (RAG). TAG resurrected the image of Patty Hearst, a.k.a Tania, in the 1970s Symbionese Liberation Army, gun in hand, and FAG pronounced: "Gavin Newsom is so last season."

The Mary for Mayor action included all of the Gay Shame hallmarks. First, a festival of resistance, this time outside a Newsom fund-raiser in the heart of the theater district. Second, a ceremony, in this case the delivery of Mary's platform, including a campy theme song resurrected from mid-nineties club culture ("Tyler Moore/Mary"). Third, elaborate and disastrous costumes that included construction site material, bloody underwear, and a stuffed snake. Fourth, a 'zine that detailed both the vicious platform of Gruesome Newsom and the liberatory absurdity of Mary's largesse. Fifth, the usual assortment of hand-painted signs, free food, banners, and buttons. And sixth, an event that markedly differed both in scale and scope from our original intentions.

The Mary for Mayor Campaign Kick-Off commenced down the block from the Newsom fund-raiser. The police had already arrived in order to prevent us from moving closer, and immediately threatened to confiscate the sound system and arrest anyone who disobeyed their orders. Of course, we quickly took to the street, blocking traffic in front of the gala. When cops began to surround us we moved a block away, in front of the luxurious and fashionable Clift Hotel, and finished our ceremony in the middle of the street. We occupied the whole block for over an hour while burning effigies, delivering Mary's platform, attempting to enter the Clift, and—of course—dancing, prancing, and romancing.

The Mary for Mayor Campaign Kick-Off was both more and less participatory than any of our previous events. We recruited people on the spot to improvise Mary's campaign pronouncements, and encouraged the crowd to join us in everything from blocking the street to doing runway outside the Clift Hotel. We organizers wanted the crowd to engage in the same level of risk-taking as we did. But by the time we marched through the Tenderloin to City Hall, our numbers had dwindled from about 150 to 40. The Mary for Mayor Campaign arrived at City Hall to a rude rebuff by members of the sheriff's department. Of course, Mary had plenty to do outside.

The Divide

Gavin Newsom was annointed mayor way before the official campaign had begun. Both the *San Francisco Chronicle* and the *San Francisco Examiner* ran story after story about how Gavin Newsom was "solving" the homeless issue (that is, getting rid of homeless people). Newsom's high-fashion wife, Kimberly Guilfoyle-Newsom, former Victoria's Secret model and assistant district attorney, appeared as a "legal expert" on *Fox News, Entertainment Tonight* and *CNN*. As the election approached, *Details* ran a glowing appraisal of San Francisco's ascendant first couple. National news focused on how wacky it was that a candidate such as Newsom, who was in favor of gay marriage and medical marijuana, could be cast as "conservative"— only in San Francisco, they cooed. It's conventional wisdom in the mainstream press that politicians considered "moderate" or "conservative" in San Francisco would be flaming liberals anywhere else. This ignores the reality that big-money, prodevelopment candidates have dominated the mayor's office for the entire history of San Francisco.

As gay "progressive" Tom Ammiano moved swiftly to the center, prodevelopment "moderate" Susan Leal (Willie Brown lackey—*and lesbian!*) entered the race in order to split the "gay vote." When former supervisor (and daughter of a former mayor) Angela Alioto entered the race, she portrayed herself as a more "serious" (read: rich) challenge to Gavin Newsom. But the candidate portrayed as the savior of progressive causes was the last to enter the race, Board of Supervisors president (and Green) Matt Gonzalez.

After the mayoral election was whittled down to two candidates—Gavin Newsom and Matt Gonzalez—progressives, hipsters, and formerly apolitical fringe types all united behind the banner of Matt for Mayor. Bars throughout the city became sites of voter registration drives, and scenesters usually intent on getting their cheap liquor into a bar unseen were suddenly frantically adoring Matt. In the month leading up to the election, every night there was a different fund-raiser for Matt Gonzalez at some hip (but not too hip) venue. Matt for Mayor buttons became the new fashion statement for the downwardly mobile. Punx Against War, the same people who had thrown the squat party on Market Street two years earlier, organized their own Matt for Mayor get-out-the-vote drive at UN Plaza.

While some championed this new interest in electoral politics by usually "apathetic" nonvoters, it depressed me to see activists I admired and respected (for trying to create outsider culture) encouraging people to vote. I planned to vote for Matt Gonzalez, but had no illusion that this would lead to any lasting change. Seeing the fringe *hipoisie* uniting with such fervor around the alleged possibilities of voting exposed the lack of commitment in "anti-establishment" subcultures to actually challenging mainstream morals and the sham of electoral politics.

Gavin Newsom barely defeated Matt Gonzalez at the polls—in spite of outspending him 10 to 1 and uniting every big-money Democrat across the country in a desperate quest not to "lose" San Francisco to a Green (Bill Clinton, Al Gore, and Jesse Jackson all campaigned for Newsom). On the eve of the election, Gay Shame put out a call for a mobilization at Gavin Newsom's victory party. This was an informal call, and not an official Gay Shame action. Still, we fliered several hundred people at the Matt Gonzalez for Mayor party and also posted on Indymedia. In total, only twenty people showed up—two from the Matt Gonzalez "victory party. " It was depressing to realize that doing something as basic as protesting the election of a ruling-class hypocrite had now become so marginal. As Gonzalez supporters "celebrated" Matt's loss by boozing it up (free beer!), we stood out in the rain and attempted to harass the luminaries as they basked in the reflected glow of money and power.

Gay Shame has always had an uneasy relationship to hipster culture. To be sure, we have benefited from a certain cachet among the taste makers and deal breakers of the indie white Mission scene. Nonetheless, by Gavin Newsom's election, our initial popularity among the jaded had essentially collapsed—we were seen as too bitter, too judgmental, too white, too confrontational, too serious, too young, too cliquish, too angry, too whiny, too disorganized, too elitist, and too extreme. Our brazen challenge to "community" lies was seen as brash and unnecessary when the "community" was closer to home than the wealthier and more blatantly hypocritical targets in Gaylandia. As we consistently faced police harassment and brutality, participants at our demonstrations became increasingly jittery. When Gay Shame wasn't quite so new, and once we started taking bigger risks, we were no longer a hot commodity in a subculture attuned to the latest trend. Perhaps, as well, it became clearer just what Gay Shame actually was: not so much a movement as a small group of alienated queers trying desperately to do something.

If the fringe was divided, then so was the city. While Gavin Newsom's election was no surprise to me, his slim margin of victory blatantly revealed the existence of two San Franciscos that rarely meet. I confess that I've spoken to only one person who expressed any intent to vote for Gavin Newsom, and that was someone I met on a phone sex line. The beauty (and danger) of San Francisco is that you can choose to interact only occasionally with people you hate. I'm sure I've sucked off plenty of Gavin Newsom supporters, but I've rarely interacted with them otherwise (except, of course, at protests).

When Newsom immediately began talking about bridging the gap between two cities, everything could have exploded. Instead, Gonzalez demonstrated his "skills" as a politician, and echoed Newsom's rhetoric. Other than a small "funeral" Gay Shame held at the Newsom inauguration, no one seemed to care—Gavin Newsom had won fair and square, right? Even when it was exposed that city workers were paid to walk precincts for Newsom, Gay

Shame was called "immature" for daring to challenge Newsom's rule.

Three months after the election Newsom pulled the ultimate risk-free political stunt and "legalized" gay marriage. Throngs of gay people from across the country descended upon City Hall day and night, camping out, sharing snacks and wine, and toasting Gavin Newsom as the vanguard leader of gay civil rights. This was a brilliant maneuver by a ruling-class politician with national ambitions and enough capital to hire only the best political consultants (many of them gay). What had formerly been a divided city was now a city united around marriage "rights."

The gay marriage hoopla paralyzed Gay Shame. If we already felt marginalized for continuing to protest Newsom after his election, now we felt like pariahs. It was obvious to us that if gay marriage proponents wanted real progress, they'd be fighting for the abolition of marriage (duh), and universal access to the services that marriage can sometimes help procure: housing, healthcare, citizenship, and so on. Instead, gay marriage proponents want to fundamentally redefine what it means to be queer, and erase decades of radical queer struggle in favor of a sanitized, "we're-just-like-you" normalcy (with marriage as the central institution, hmm . . . sounds familiar). Just the fact that challenging the gay marriage bandwagon became immediate heresy exposes the silencing agenda of gay marriage proponents as they move steadily toward assimilation into the imperialist, bloodthirsty status quo.

As Newsom's popularity surged, Gonzalez announced that he would retire from public office after his term as president of the Board of Supervisors. One can only assume that Gonzalez felt he'd gotten as far as he could, and it was time to call it quits—*fuck "the movement"!* Some argued that he was never a "real" politician, that he'd been recruited just a few years earlier (by Tom Ammiano) to run for the Board of Supervisors, and that he'd become caught up in a system he viewed with increasing distaste. Yet Gonzalez's acceptance of contributions from some of the city's most notorious slumlords, and his immediate capitulation to Newsom's call for "unity," suggest that Gonzalez was far more seasoned in the less savory aspects of politics than his most ardent supporters would like to imagine.

If the dot.com era left outsider queers, artists, and activists feeling helpless and hopeless, then the crash opened up a window of opportunity as rents lowered (slightly) and resistance felt (slightly) less futile. The Matt Gonzalez campaign/Gavin Newsom victory may be closing that window. With Newsom continuing the Willie Brown legacy of hyperdevelopment and the dismantling of systems of care, gentrification continues unabated, especially in the Bayview, Mission, and Tenderloin, and things look a lot less rosy.

For non-mainstream queers, these are especially dangerous times. Just two blocks from my apartment, a block of Polk Street known for street hustling and speed dealing has been transformed into the site of not one, not two, but four yuppie straight (or "mixed") bars—all replacing lower-end gay bars. My Place, a South of Market gay bar known for decades as a cruising hole, was shuttered by the Department of Alcoholic Beverage Control, sending shock waves through South of Market leather bars that now police their premises to root out sex deviants. As gay people of all political affiliations, ethnicities, and social backgrounds (including the publisher of my novel and my ex-boyfriend) rush to tie the knot, what is being discarded is a queer identity that demands *fundamental changes* in the dominant culture, *not inclusion.*

The debate over gay marriage presents only two sides to the story: foaming-at-the-mouth conservatives who think gay marriage marks the death of Western civilization (I wish), and rabid gay assimilationists who act as if gay marriage is the best thing since *Will and Grace.* When anti-assimilationist queers are mentioned (which is rare), we're presented as rebels within the "community." But when gay landlords evict people with AIDS to get higher rents, when Castro residents fight a queer youth shelter because it might get in the way of "community" property values, when gay bar owners call the cops to arrest homeless queers—this exposes the lie of a queer "community" that serves only those in power.

The fight between pro-marriage and anti-marriage queers is not a disagreement between two segments of a community, but a fight over the fundamental nature of queer struggle. When Newsom weighed in on one side, he gained not only the loyalty of the rich gays who got him elected, but the support of liberals across the sex-and-gender spectrum (especially straight lefties who were suddenly happy to support gays, even though they've never had much interest in queer lives). As former foes of Newsom capitulate to this newfound "unity," resistance can seem all the more useless.

The Matt Gonzalez campaign demonstrates what anti-establishment activists get when we compromise our values and vote for change: nothing. The real potential of the election was not that a Green Party candidate might get elected, but that conflict might erupt. In a divided city, hope lies in embracing, sculpting, and furthering the divide. We can always build houses in the ruins.

Queerly Shifting Affinities

Notes on the Ever-Diversifying Queer Political Classes in San Francisco, the Gayest Little City in the World

By Keith Hennessy

Tom Ammiano is as queer as a $3 bill. He flames. There are homophobes, and others who fear difference, who couldn't get past Ammiano's voice. The rest of us would have been proud to have him as mayor, partly because of that queer voice. But he's a tough sell, especially to the wannabe upper classes. They are terrified of losing unearned privileges to the policies of an unapologetic leftist and community-based politician. Resistance to Ammiano among many well-employed and propertied homos is rooted in a messy fusion of internalized homophobia and neocon class terror. Ammiano's "voice" outed all who identified with it, linking us proudly to San Francisco's history of radical sexual politics and progressive socio-political agendas.

A veteran of gay comedy (and public classrooms), Ammiano always begins his speeches with a joke, often a silly sexual innuendo. He flaunts himself as a sexual libertine but not as actively sexual. In contrast, Willie Brown is a ladies' man, doubly more masculine than Ammiano because he's not only hetero but also dating in public. Brown flaunted being a bachelor. A smart dresser with a big budget for stylish suits and hats, Brown could easily mix with financial district executives, opera house socialites, and leaders in African-American communities. With a girlfriend by his side, we might imagine that he's got an active sex life, something we don't assume for most politicians, many of whom struggle to appear happily married. Virility gets votes. Unfortunately, even the toughest nelly isn't perceived as virile. In a homophobic culture we miss the courage, wisdom, and power in a queer queen's wit.

If San Francisco had a more sizable black community, and if Brown was an identified member or ally of that community, he would never have been elected mayor of San Francisco. White fear of black power is too massive (yes even in Subaru-liberal San Francisco). Fortunately for Brown, a cruel history of city planning, gentrification, and police harassment had reduced the African-American population by 40% since the 1970s, making San Francisco safe for a black mayor. During Brown's tenure as mayor this steady population decline continued, despite the economic boom which marked his first few years, and despite the number of people of color appointed by Brown to manage city bureaucracies.

Black and queer male sexualities are projections of a mainstream culture heavily invested in racism and (hetero)sexism. Usually they are found at opposite ends of the male sexuality continuum, framing the idealized masculinity of the middle-class, white, married man. This ideal is sporty yet tame, neither too macho nor too effeminate. In four short years the mayor's contest went from the sexual margins, Black King against White Queen, to Gavin Newsom's election, which marked a return of the chief's job to the sexual center.

In the 2003 mayoral race between Gonzalez and Newsom, the attractiveness of the candidates inspired media stories, volunteer recruitment, citywide gossip, and even real votes. Regardless of their class, political, ethnic and marriage status differences, there seemed to be a similarity in how they were viewed sexually. According to the press and to my own informal surveys, both men were attractive not only to San Francisco's legendary underclass of "poor" single women ("Woe is me, all the good men in SF are gay!") but to gay and bi men as well. It didn't matter that the rest of us thought they both needed serious hair, body, and wardrobe makeovers, because that meant we were still talking about what they looked like! Up against these post-gay metrosexuals, Ammiano's gayness seemed almost quaint, passé, and definitely not sexy. It's beyond me that anyone of any sexual preference could waste a minute on the sexy quotient of these guys—but I haven't considered any politician to be sexy since Trudeaumania swept my homeland in 1968. (Pierre Trudeau was a young, single, artsy, bilingual intellectual who always wore a rose and promised to keep Canada from dividing into two nations—and I was eight years old!)

After the 1999 election in which Ammiano galvanized a progressive voter movement but didn't succeed in toppling the Brown regime, many of us, including Ammiano, assumed that the following four years would be one long campaign to "take back San Francisco" and elect Tom as mayor. Of course, Brown, the corporate media, and many of San Francisco's richest citizens spent every day of those four years humiliating and marginalizing Ammiano, who not only went on his own divisive offensive but got caught in the compromises of building consensus—something he didn't do in his short, fiery campaign. I was one of many who felt like the next election ought to put Tom Ammiano in the mayor's office but what seemed like an obvious outcome became more and more unlikely.

Gay Shame, a Virus in the System

It is a global consensus that San Francisco is the gayest city in the world, even if Stonewall & ACT UP are phenomena of New York City, gay marriages happened in Europe first, and Sydney's Mardi Gras might be more fabulous. Nonetheless, San Francisco's biggest public event is the annual Lesbian, Gay, Bisexual and Transgender (LGBT) Pride Parade and San Francisco is known around the world for its queer pride, culture, and politics. LGBT people can be found in all the major corporations headquartered here and City Hall has not been without queer representation since the landmark victory of Harvey Milk, our most famous martyr.

Tension between radical and reformist queers is older than recorded gay history. A visible chasm seemed to open up during the AIDS years between the multi-issue, poly-gendered, anarchist-inspired politics of Queer Nation and the more established gay and lesbian organizations and politicians. Assimilation of radical currents into the mainstream is an ongoing process. In recent years a new post-gay radicalism has emerged to challenge assimilationist tendencies in queer culture and activism. Fusing anarcho-class war tactics with camp fabulousness and sexual liberationist ethics, Gay Shame made a splash challenging Gavin Newsom's war on homeless people, that is, Care Not Cash, when he first proposed it as a member of the Board of Supervisors in 2002. The rise of Newsom's visibility was met with increasing resistance from, and therefore visibility of, Gay Shame. Their actions, which call for participants "to dress to terrifying excess" have included genderfuck, trash fashion shows outside Newsom's properties (do millionaires have homes or just properties?), interventions to the Pride Parade protesting corporate sponsorships, and postering the city with the Right to Have Sex in All Bars. Just when we thought that all the freaks and innovators had left town due to the rising costs and decreasing joy of everything, Gay Shame proves that San Francisco continues to evolve lineages of artist-activist provocateurs.

When some anti-Ammiano LGBT citizens hosted a fund-raiser for Newsom at our new center (that's the LGBT Center to non-queer people), Gay Shame showed up to protest. The cops instigated a police riot, violently attacking unarmed queer activists, resulting in hospitalizations, a dislocated shoulder, and broken teeth. In their own way Gay Shame had already "declared war" on Newsom (and the state), but this was an unjustifiably brutal response from the city. Responses in the queer community revealed strong ambivalence not only to Gay Shame but also to "politically correct" or "street activist" queers. The lack of solidarity revealed the lack of queer consensus in the upcoming mayoral elections . . . and Gonzalez had not yet entered the race.

Further Political Divides within Queer and Progressive Constituencies

We had advance notice that all was not consensual in the Castro-centered queer political scene. In the 2002 District 8 election for Board of Supervisors (representing the Castro and Noe Valley), Bevan Dufty, the favored candidate of Willie Brown and a supposedly deteriorating Democratic Party machine, defeated two progressives, Tom Radulovich and Eileen Hanson. All of the candidates were queer (only in the Castro!) so the election was won and lost on the politics and affinities of class and gender. Hanson, Radulovich, and their friends, advisers and funders failed to predict that they would split the Left/progressive vote. Their political shortsightedness lost the opportunity to build the anti-Brown, anti–big money solidarity on the board. I think Radulovich should have stepped down and helped to elect Hanson, a dedicated activist and uncompromising critic, to a board that has only one woman. But he didn't (and neither did she) and they split the vote. Dufty won and queer solidarity in LGBT San Francisco seemed weaker than ever.

Before Gonzalez had entered the race there was already discontent about Ammiano at both ends of the queer political Right/Left spectrum. This surprised me. I had expected everyone from Republican queers to the Alice B. Toklas Democratic Club and even the NIMBY clean queens (the ones who tear down club and performance posters, resist queer youth shelters, and try to illegalize panhandling) to oppose Ammiano. But I hadn't anticipated San Francisco's more dedicated street and community-based activists abandoning Ammiano, especially when it was clear that Newsom's campaign was growing in dollars and influence. I could smell the shift but I couldn't pinpoint it. A couple of months before Gonzalez entered the race I encountered him at a juice joint in the lower Haight. While waiting for his two shots of wheat grass he asked me what I thought of Ammiano and his chances at beating Newsom. I shared with him my queasy and confused prediction that even though I had expected everybody I knew to enthusiastically back Ammiano, maybe it was too late, that he no longer had the mass community support he would need to inspire his campaign. I assume that many others must have similarly answered this question because two months later, Gonzalez was running for mayor against Newsom. With the backing of board progressives, he declared that he was the only hope to beat Newsom.

Gonzalez garnered grassroots support from many communities within the queer political spectrum. Queers previously affiliated with Ammiano, including liberal progressives and direct-action radicals, joined the

Gonzalez campaign while Ammiano was still in the race. Ammiano's affiliation to the Democratic Party was a nonissue when all candidates were Dems but suddenly it seemed hopelessly pre-Seattle, last-millennium-stale compared to Gonzalez's risky and passionate switch to the more visionary yet marginal Green Party. The Gonzalez campaign mirrored and then exceeded the thrill of Ammiano's movement-building campaign four years earlier. In the final month of runoff there were house parties for Gonzalez touching many queer constituencies and subcultures. In reaction to both Bush and the recent win of Schwarzenegger, Gonzalez supporters sought to differentiate San Francisco from right-wing corporate apologists.

There is a relatively new phenomenon that I call the "Burning Man factor," which is having a significant influence on Bay Area (and beyond) art, culture, and now—maybe—politics. The Gonzalez mayoral campaign benefited directly from the e-mail network and affinity group subculture of Burning Man, an annual, noncommercial, desert art fest and gathering that attracts over 25,000 people from around the globe (yet the majority of whom come from the Bay Area). Gonzalez, by age, subculture, and neighborhood (lower Haight), matches the Burning Man demographic. The late summer "Burning Man" gathering is one of several emerging strains of alternative culture that helped to fuel Gonzalez's fall campaign.

Despite the thrill and the promise of something completely different, there were Ammiano supporters who felt betrayed by Gonzalez and his supporters. They accused the Gonzalez campaign of homophobic and secretive tactics, which undermined public confidence in Ammiano. Although these core Ammiano people were willing to be quiet in their objections, participating in a progressive/Left unity against Newsom, most refused to participate in the Gonzalez campaign during the runoff. Ammiano disappeared for a couple of key weeks during the runoff and delayed endorsing Gonzalez until after rumors of conflict and mistrust had spread widely. This feeling of broken trust, although it peaked during the election, continues to divide some queer and progressive activists.

Newsom, Queer Basher or Gay Superhero?

When Gavin printed out real wedding licenses in April 2004 he instantly became an internationally famous gay activist. I overheard and read about gay men declaring that they would support Newsom for the rest of their lives, which is pretty scary, considering Newsom's youth and ambition. It was a shrewd move, but this adopted son of the ruling class didn't care about queer people, any more than he cared about homeless people. His "compassion" is not distinct from either his political ambition or the assumptions of his class and community.

Many would agree that Newsom's marriage action was an attempt to win support from the nearly 50% of San Francisco voters who had supported Gonzalez. I don't think Newsom was going for the Gonzalez "people," most of whom did not have gay marriage high on their priority list. Nonetheless, Newsom had been exposed by the Gonzalez campaign as a conservative lacking compassion and he needed to regain some of San Francisco's socially liberal center.

Spending time with my boyfriend on Valentine's Day outside City Hall among at least 1,000 homos wanting to get legally married, it was odd that I only knew one person in line. The vast majority of the wedding crowd were neither street activists nor campaign volunteers. The cars of the couples doing victory laps included new SUVs, a Jag, a BMW sports car, and other fancy new cars. These were mostly well-employed, comfortable Americans who happen to be queer. There was an element of subversion and historic justice to the proceedings but it was not a radical crowd by any means. Still, it was euphoric. We also waited in line for an hour or so the next day, Sunday, before being turned away again. I heard that the lines Monday were the longest of the whole weekend, in the rain!

At worst, the whole thing was a stunt without legal spine, not dissimilar to the "Care Not Cash" initiative: a wild and probably illegal, or legally inconsequential, move that galvanizes a particular aspiring and security-obsessed constituency. The queerness of this constituency is much less a rallying point of solidarity than their desire for the right to make money. Newsom's advisers knew that the opposition to gay marriage by right-wing Republicans and religious extremists did not represent significant votes or funds in San Francisco. The opposition to cutting homeless welfare checks by over 80% also lacked electoral power, in spite of its vocal visibility. With both of these political stunts, Newsom's team displayed a crafty ability to manipulate public symbols—much more strategically important to Newsom than long-term change.

A Downward Spiral Before the Next Uprising

We'll never know what would have happened if Gonzalez had stayed out of the race and if all the progressives on the Board of Supervisors had backed Ammiano. We do know that the once-upon-a-time inevitable trajectory toward a progressive gay mayor, which began with Harvey Milk's election in 1977, was now on hold. The lineage of progressive gay politicians on San Francisco's Board of Supervisors will end, at least temporarily, when Ammiano's term is complete.

Public "queerness" is defined these days by consumer queers on network TV teaching the world to conform, or at the other end of the spectrum by anti-assimilationist queers puking in the streets about corporate sponsorship. Queer visibility and engagement is both more pronounced and more nuanced than ever before. An entire generation is coming of age with many more options for political affinity, within and beyond queer cultures and identities. Our newest generation of sex and gender radicals suggest that San Francisco will continue to be a pioneering home for experiments in sexual and gender liberation, symbiotic to the city's large minority of progressive, anarchist, and Left activists. Despite class and nationalist tensions, queer culture and politics have the potential to inform and inspire a politics of solidarity, sensitivity, pleasure, and justice. Whether this will result in a significant challenge to a politics of cuteness and comfort remains to be seen, especially within a context of increasing economic and psychological fear.

Postscript

When straight folks marry, the license has no role in the ceremony. After the wedding, the couple retires to some back room and takes all of thirty seconds to sign a piece of paper that will live the rest of its life (until death or divorce) in a file or drawer. At City Hall on Valentine's weekend 2004, each married couple would exit City Hall waving their blue-trimmed, officially stamped paper. Many couples posed for photos with their paper and others paraded around City Hall in cars (often with dogs or kids) holding their licenses up to the window. Traffic stopped. Horns blared. Bystanders cheered and cried. The magic of this moment will have political reverberations for years to come. Rarely has a municipal document carried such weight.

Another Postscript

Seth Eisen and I never did get married—because we never got up early enough. We made an appointment but the state ended the joyride before our date arrived. Now, instead of being one of the 4,000 couples in limbo, we're one of millions around the world whose partnership remains legally invisible.

McFrisco

Quintin Mecke

The effects of Mayor Willie L. Brown Jr.'s land-use policies will be felt for generations. Due to his fast-food approach to land-use planning, production, convenience, and conformity reigned over a "balanced and healthy" planning diet. As a result, the city became increasingly obese, with high-end developments that only served the upper class and privileged, with working-class people being forced out of their workplaces and homes. Brown's answer? "If you don't make $50,000 a year in San Francisco, then you shouldn't live here," he said on national television. It was the most direct assault on the demographic soul of this city since the 1960s era of redevelopment and Justin Hermann. Reshaping the city in his own inflated self-image gave Willie the moniker "da Mayor," but gave the city big-ticket developments that will wreak havoc on the quality of life in years to come.

A noted sociologist, George Rizner, coined the phrase "McDonaldization" in the 1990s, which for him represented a *"process by which the principles of the fast-food restaurant are coming to dominate more and more sectors of American society as well as the rest of the world."* Historically, development issues have often divided San Franciscans, but the transformation during Mayor Brown's administration of what was once the Department of City Planning into a Department of Development Facilitation stunned even the most jaded observers. It quickly began to resemble the famed golden arches—new projects were approved as fast as developers could propose them. For example, from 1997 to 2001, during the height of the dot.com boom, the Planning Commission of the City and County of San Francisco approved over 2,500 live-work units throughout the city, the vast majority in neighborhoods like the South of Market, Mission, and Potrero Hill. This does not include the vast number of dot.com offices that were placed throughout the city in areas not zoned for office use. During that same period, *not one proposed live-work project was ever rejected*, a record so frighteningly perfect that to this day it can make any sane planner still working for the Planning Department cringe when it's mentioned. That was a time when San Francisco reveled in being a hip playground for the up-and-coming. It was also a time when San Francisco's McDonaldization was at its peak, simplifying and commodifying the elements that make our city unique, and packaging them for consumption.

With its inaccessible lexicon of phrases, terms, and concepts, the language and discourse of land-use planning represents the epitome of Michel Foucault's belief that not only is knowledge power, but that power is at its strongest (and most invisible) in the simple structures of language. Terms like "conditional use," "discretionary review," "PDR," and 'nonconforming use' are the everyday tools that shape and mold our neighborhoods. They are found within the planning code, the bible of land use, and if you don't know what they mean, then you are not alone.

But when plans threaten to demolish or radically alter your neighborhood, time is of the essence and you will have just weeks to learn these terms. Just imagine a new project is being proposed in your neighborhood and you happen to be one of the lucky neighbors within 300 feet who is deemed worthy of a public notice by the Planning Department. On the off chance that you actually read the posted notice on your way to the coffee shop, were able to vaguely decipher it, and found yourself masochistic enough to follow your curiosity, you now have made your first step into the world of land use, and quickly down the rabbit hole you will go.

In this world where language is power, there is no greater example of the power behind two words than "conditional use." "Conditional use" is the term used to define the idea that the use being proposed is not allowed "as of right" and will only be permitted with "conditions." Depending on the size of the project, these conditions can include specific hours for delivery of goods, parking limitations, pedestrian safety measures, noise restrictions, and affordable housing units. For activists, "conditional use" represents the stone in David's sling relative to a neighborhood's power to fight or alter a proposed project, and it guarantees a hearing at City Hall in front of the Planning Commission, which will decide whether to grant the permit. This is not to say that neighbors or activists win every conditional-use permit hearing, but it does mean that there is at least a chance to do so, and importantly that there will be a dialogue about it.

Deploying this language are the translators and native speakers, the real players and dealmakers who are found every Thursday in City Hall's room 400 for the weekly meetings of the Planning Commission. Within that room social engineering is allowed by law and is driven by language that reinforces and strengthens our society's historical divisions of race, class, and gender. The typical San Franciscan doesn't realize that, of the numerous issues that people here argue about, only a few issues truly have the power to fundamentally affect who and who does not live here. For those in the loop, land-use planning and zoning decisions represent the most effective way of encouraging and—more important—*discouraging* certain types of people. Not only is zoning used to dictate what uses will be permitted, it also determines economically who and who may not live in a given area. While the idea of social engineering may conjure up strong images of a Brave New World future society for some, this is the heart of land-use planning and a stark reality. The decisions of who will live in San Francisco are made by a select few who can use and manipulate this complex system of specialized and coded language. Only by learning and explaining it will activists and neighbors be able to expose the wizards behind the curtain who determine the shape of our city with their weekly planning decisions.

Aside from language, the other obstacle to challenging the dynamic of land-use planning is an institutional one. Until the passage in March 2002 of Proposition D, the mayor had complete control of appointments to the Planning Commission and also appointed the head of the Planning Department. This gave him enormous political power and that power was used without pause or regret. Upon assuming office in 1996 and with the economy of the Bay Area growing steadily, Brown (who had extremely close ties with developers during his career in Sacramento) made land use his signature priority. And with his appointment of then midlevel planner Gerald Green as director, the Planning Department shifted from land-use planning to development facilitation. Unfortunately for the city, Brown's tenure happened to coincide with the largest influx of capital into San Francisco since the Gold Rush. Another great battle for the city had begun.

Those most directly affected were slow to react at first, as they tried to come to terms with the magnitude of what was happening. With his "build it and they will come" mantra, Brown made it absolutely clear that no dissension from his plan was to be tolerated (portending Bush's "you're either with us or against us"). Significant public casualties foreshadowed the political struggle that was to come, and left no doubt about who was in charge and how Brown would deal with dissent. In December 1999, the then-zoning administrator of the Planning Department, Mary Gallagher, ruled that all of the roughly 177 antennae on the Sutro Tower atop Twin Peaks (owned by the major media outlets) did not have the necessary permits. She ruled that they would all need new conditional-use permits, sustaining the concerns of the surrounding neighbors. However, within days of her decision, she was relieved of her duties as zoning administrator and her decision was reversed by Director Green. One of the first public shots across the bow had been fired. The second came in September 2000 when Brown fired longtime planning commissioner Dennis Antenore because he refused to support Proposition K, the mayor's pro-development ballot initiative. In a letter to Antenore, Brown told him that "this issue is simply too important for there to be disagreement at the highest level of government," and with that, he was gone.

Resistance at this point began to gather steam. Neighborhoods that were late to catch on began to muster coalitions for an effective counterattack. In 2000, I was a community organizer in the South of Market, and a virgin to the world of land use. However, as I watched longtime small businesses, nonprofits, and artists forced out by higher rents due to bad planning decisions, necessity drove me and many others in the neighborhood to take action. We took our cues from better organized neighborhoods like the Mission and organized the South of Market Anti-Displacement Coalition, also known as SOMAD. (Of course, given what we were facing, SOMAD could have easily been known as SO-STUNNED or SO-PISSED but then our catchy acronym wouldn't have worked.) We tried to stop the flood of live-work projects and dot.com offices that were moving in faster than we could protest against them. Over the course of the following months, we organized protests at the Planning Commission, held rallies at City Hall, and tried desperately to direct the media's attention toward what was happening.

By the summer of 2000, the battle took on a fevered pitch and the media began to cover the stories more regularly. In June the neighborhood protests grew louder and developers called for decreasing the limitations on new commercial office buildings. Brown held a meeting at City Hall with members of the Chamber of Commerce, SPUR, and other groups to see what changes could be made to 1986's Proposition M, which had created annual limits on office-space development in the last major land-use battle. The meeting ended without agreement, but it spawned the framework for Proposition L, a ballot initiative favored by neighborhood activists and community groups that limited new office development in parts of the Mission, South of Market, and Potrero Hill districts, while also redefining the controversial live-work lofts as residential units, subject to infrastructure fees for transportation, schools, and affordable housing. Support for Proposition L quickly became the dividing line between whether you were a friend or foe of Mayor Brown. With the return of district elections in November 2000, land use had now become the single defining issue and it eventually led to a slate of "progressive" supervisors being elected. After suffering from years of Brown's cronyism and McPlanning, this was the political change that activists had been waiting for.

The initial shock of our political victory in the fall of 2000 lasted well into 2001 and the first months after the election represented the best days of

SOMAD's existence. We had regular well-attended meetings and, in Chris Daly, a voice who listened to us in City Hall. It felt as if we had some power.

Slowly, however, things started to settle down into routine politics. Differences among groups that were glossed over during the campaign began to emerge again. Once united in their opposition to Brown, neighborhoods began to reclaim their individual identities around the issues that were important to them. On the land-use front, issues of race and class began to emerge again, as the reality of the work that lay ahead of us became clear. We were left with the daunting task of empowering and enabling residents to participate in a game that was fundamentally stacked against them. Quickly it became clear to me that SOMAD, as a volunteer grassroots coalition, was not up to this task. We had a few individuals who could speak the language of land use, but they did not have the ability, time, or patience to transfer and pass this knowledge onto others. Add to that the fact that with the new Board of Supervisors and the sudden crash of the economy, many people believed that the danger had passed. There seemed no longer a need for them to participate, and they felt free from the obligation of doing the less dramatic and more grueling work of developing our community's resources.

The neighborhood dynamic shifted from active resistance to solution creation, and our relevance and influence waned when we couldn't break out of being SOMAD to become SOABLE. Other groups began to form, such as the South of Market Community Action Network, that were more adapted to the new landscape. Additionally, SOMAD discovered in itself the same divisions of race, class, and gender that we had projected onto the dot.com businesses. We were slow to realize this, but once we did, it was clear to me that SOMAD's days were numbered. We managed to hold things together until early 2003, primarily because our name still had some minor political influence—always hard to acquire. SOMAD did manage in a brief period of time to become an established player in the world of land use, but in the end, we too McDonaldized community development in that we tried to be a quick fix to a problem that actually required a long-term diet of investment, organizing, and empowerment.

Even with SOMAD's limitations, good work did come out of this tumultuous time and healthier options did arise. In the Mission, MAC (Mission Anti-Displacement Coalition) was able to gain substantial funding and succeeded in organizing the neighborhood, later guiding it through a rezoning process. This represented a hopeful example to other activist groups that it was possible to lead not only by being against something but to also be *for* an idea as well. In the South of Market, a commercial printer by the name of

Jim Meko recognized the desperate need for dialogue regarding land use and took on the responsibility of convening people from all over the neighborhood once a month to discuss land use, planning, and rezoning. The response was better than expected, and the forum has now become a regular venue for residents to vet their concerns and hear new updates about what is planned for the area. On an individual level, because of his persistence and knowledge, Meko has also cultivated important relationships with planners, developers, and commissioners. He has now become a political force large enough to ensure that residents have an opportunity to be heard and consulted before attempts are made to further McFrisco the neighborhood.

What I didn't realize at the time is that the change for which we had fought so hard and long was only an illusion. Despite our political efforts, we found no Rosetta Stone making the language of land use planning suddenly accessible to thousands. The Planning Commission continued with its weekly meetings and Gerald Green continued as director. Room 400 was still packed with land-use attorneys every Thursday. The local election results of 2000 were satisfying on the surface, but I began to see that the game itself had not changed, nor had the institutions and power that shape it. We had substituted different players who supported our positions, but the rules and referees were the same. (It reminded me of the first presidential election that I was eligible to vote in, in 1992. I had somehow survived a Republican upbringing, and Clinton's victory made me believe that the world had shifted. But then the inaugural chords of "Don't Stop Thinking about Tomorrow" faded into typical political gamesmanship.) We want to believe that change can come quickly. That is the ultimate tease and temptation of political campaigns, especially candidate-driven ones. We transfer collective power onto an individual who we believe will rise above his or her own humanity and change *our* lives. All we have to do is pull the lever.

This cult of personality was never more evident than in the recent mayoral election between Gavin Newsom and Matt Gonzalez, with supporters from both sides projecting values and qualities onto the candidates that expanded them beyond normal human boundaries. As one of the original campaign workers on the Gonzalez campaign, I can remember sitting with the campaign manager in the cramped Horseshoe Café in the Lower Haight in early August, thinking to myself, "What in god's name are we doing?" And no sooner had I said that than we were in the December runoff. Yet despite the energy, new relationships, and successful efforts that developed during that campaign, I still feel empty. Once again, instead of developing our community, instead of investing in the long and tiresome work of grassroots organizing, of empowering our neighborhoods, we allowed ourselves to fall into the predictable dead-end of a political campaign as our preferred method of change.

What became of all that energy, excitement, and talk of a movement after the campaign ended? It was quickly deflated as the chosen progressive vessel, Matt Gonzalez, bowed out of public life only months after proclaiming that he, or rather *he-representing-us*, would act as loyal opposition to the Newsom administration when needed. And with that simple decision, the Left was presented with a self-reflective, scathing critique of why communities need to invest in themselves and not in politicians. In the end they will stay while the politicians come and go. I felt especially burned because we had learned this lesson in countless previous election cycles, and specifically after the 2000 elections.

I will not miss the San Francisco of Mayor Brown, but I know that unless we learn the lessons from what happened during his tenure, we will be faced with a similar situation in years to come. I have often thought of wisdom as the ability to learn something without having to directly experience it, a talent based on observation and intuition rather than visceral reaction. Now, having experienced Mayor Brown and the disappointment of winning political campaigns, I want to discover new alternatives to old paradigms. As a result, I do not hope for a utopian solution to fundamentally alter the framework of land use. But I do believe that we can change the menu and the process behind it and we have examples of the recipes that can work. Both MAC and Jim Meko represent exactly the type of home-cooked alternatives that can begin to provide better fare than the developer-led, politician-facilitated, and genetically modified meals cooked up under Brown and current director Green.

To advance this, our neighborhoods must reclaim our forgotten power. We will not succeed with a singular focus on electoral politics as a means for change. How we use our land is a direct reflection of our values, and as such, is worth fighting for. With these ingredients we can build the foundation of a healthier existence and gain the wisdom that has eluded us so far. A community realizes its potential only through a balanced program of organizing and empowerment. If we continue to fall for the temptation of exclusively channeling our limited energy into electoral politics, then we will be as guilty as Willie Brown of McDonaldizing the city.

San Francisco is not alone in this fight against cultural homogenization; it is a battle that it is taking place across the globe as people have begun to recognize the growing threat of McDonaldization to all aspects of our lives.

Taking our cue from French farmers like José Bové, who has led direct-action campaigns against McDonald's and corporate agribusiness, we can find inspiration to stand up to the golden arches of convenience that are deemed as progress. Here at home, we know that there are countless José Bovés among us and it is time to empower and encourage them to continue struggling for a genuine community, a life worthy of we the living; a life worthy of San Francisco.

Put Your Head in It!

Dr. Ahimsa Sumchai

I grew up in southeast San Francisco. We lived at 27 Dakota Street in the Potrero Hill housing projects, 1726 Sunnydale in the Sunnydale housing projects and in a house on Thomas Street in Bayview. After graduating from Woodrow Wilson High School and San Francisco State University, I attended medical school at the University of California at San Francisco.

In 1982 I became the first African American woman to train in UCSF's prestigious department of neurological surgery. I am forever left with the memory of a recommendation during the stress and frantic hurry of my surgical internship on how best to stop a closing elevator . . . put your head in it!

In the beginnning the Muwekme Ohlone Indians lived in harmony with the land on the promontory extending eastward into the Bay in southeastern San Francisco. They called it Sea Shell Point. The Ohlone Indians thrived on a diet rich in shellfish and decorated the burial mounds of their departed loved ones with sea shells. These shellmounds are documented in the archeological history of the region. The Ohlone Indians have survived for 2000 years and today are locked in legal battles over the ownership of the federal lands on which the modern day Bayview–Hunters Point district is situated.

In the 1800s Spanish explorers sailed into the Bay and named that promontory of land Point Avisadero. By the mid-1800s the California Gold Rush had ushered in an era of economic prosperity and a boom in commercial sea transport. The southeast peninsula became a vital seaport for the arrival and departure of goods, merchandise and supplies on Clipper ships for the "49ers." The Alaska cod fish industry flourished as did the Chinese shrimping industry.

Hunters Point operated as a commerical drydock from 1869 to 1939. In 1939, eleven days before the attack on Pearl Harbor, the U.S. Navy acquired the land and until 1974 used it for shipbuilding, repair, maintenance, and submarine servicing.

One fateful morning in April 1945 the Hunters Point Naval Shipyard was thoroughly evacuated for the arrival of the *USS Indianapolis*. According to the ship's captain, the components of the atom bomb that was ultimately dropped on Hiroshima were picked up and transported to an island in the South Pacific.

By the mid-1950s, 8,500 civilians were employed at the Hunters Point Shipyard. Many of these shipyard workers were African Americans recruited from the southern states to work in the shipyard industries during the World War II era. The navy deactivated the shipyard in 1974. In 1989, following extensive environmental investigations, the U.S. Environmental Protection Agency placed the shipyard on the National Priorities List, thus designating it a federal "Superfund" site, making it eligible for federal funds to clean up toxic waste.

There are three generations of longshoremen in my family. My father, George Donald Porter, was a college-educated "walking boss." A handsome guy with a bright smile and a zany sense of humor, one morning in February 1992 I walked into his bedroom and found him dead. He was fifty-six years old. He had pulmonary asbestosis; with his chest Xray as evidence, a class action civil suit was ultimately settled. I was very angry for about five years. My father's death changed my life and changed my career direction.

In 1997, as an attending physician in the emergency department of the Palo Alto Veteran's Administration Hospital, I took charge of the Persian Gulf, Agent Orange, Ionizing Radiation Registry. The VA Hospital's health care network boasts the nation's largest and most comprehensive toxic registry. My background in emergency toxicology, civil litigation, and environmental sciences, coupled with a two-year research fellowship at Stanford University prepared me for what was to become the most challenging experiences of my professional career, volunteering as an environmental activist in the Bayview–Hunters Point District of San Francisco (BVHP). The community I grew up in, the community I love.

Environmental Racism

The first health study of San Francisco's heavily polluted Bayview-Hunters Point found that chronic illness hospitalizations were nearly four times higher than the state average. Doctors from the University of California at San Francisco and the city health department studied records from 1991 and 1992 and found that hospitalization rates for asthma, congestive heart failure, and emphysema were 138 per 10,000. The statewide average was 37 per 10,000. Rates of hospitalization and premature death for children were found to be markedly high and according to Dr. Kevin Grumbach, a UCSF researcher who headed the study, "I would not be adverse to saying the environment is a smoking gun."

Bayview–Hunters Point contains four times as many toxins as any other city neighborhood, according to a 1995 city health department study. The area has 700 hazardous waste facilities, 325 underground petroleum storage tanks, the state's oldest and most polluting power plant—the infamous PG&E Hunters Point Power Plant. A second power plant located in near-by Potrero Hill is operated by the private corporation Mirant. Additionally, BVHP is the site of the sewage treatment plant for the city and county of San Francisco; it is a state Superfund site and one of the most extensively polluted federal Superfund sites in the nation.

I serve on the Restoration Advisory Board of the Hunters Point shipyard and chair the Radiological subcommittee. The Hunters Point Naval Shipyard was the site of the premier military radiological laboratory in the United States during the post–World War II era. The Naval Radiological Defense Laboratory used over 100 radionuclides. Shipyard environmental studies document a vast array of toxic chemical contaminants, including heavy metals like arsenic, mercury, manganese, lead, and the asbestos that contributed to my father's premature death. Moreover, studies confirm the presence of petroleum products, pesticides and numerous airborne contaminants and toxic gases.

The Wizard of Oz

Two people aptly personify the traits of pathological narcissism, the ficti-tious Wizard of Oz and the very real former mayor of San Francisco, Willie Lewis Brown Jr.

According to the *Diagnostic and Statistical Manual of Mental Disorders,* people with Narcissistic Personality Disorder have a lifelong pattern of grandiosity in behavior and fantasy, and an unquenchable thirst for admiration. They are arrogant, self-important individuals—usually men—who commonly exagger-ate their accomplishments to make themselves seem bigger than life. Narcissists fantasize about wild success and envy those who have achieved it. They choose friends who can help them get what they want. Their job per-formance may suffer due to interpersonal problems or be enhanced by their incessant drive for success. Despite their grandiose attitudes, narcissists have fragile self-esteem and fundamentally feel unworthy. Psychologists call this the "impaired real self" and its emergence is often provoked by minor insults called "narcissistic fractures." Even during times of great personal success they may feel undeserving. As sensitive as they are, they may have little authentic understanding for the needs and feelings of others but may feign empathy in attempts to extract compliments or to further their belief that they are special.

Because they tend to be overly concerned with grooming and their youthful looks, they may become increasingly depressed with age. They may display cruelty, anger, dangerous rage or icy indifference in job settings and social situations where they are subjected to unflattering or unfavorable criticism.

State and local conflict of interest laws prohibit a public official from participating in public actions in which he has a private economic stake. One section of the state government code puts it this way: "No public official at any level of government shall make, participate in making, or in any way attempt to influence a governmental decision in which he knows or has reason to know he has a financial interest."

The Hunters Point Naval Shipyard has been called "one of the most valuable pieces of soon-to-be-developed real estate in San Francisco." While the site of massive environmental pollution, the former naval base offers impressive views of the Bay. The contract to develop the 500 acres of decommissioned land was awarded by the San Francisco Redevelopment Agency to Lennar Corporation of Miami, Florida. The redevelopment contract became politically controversial in 1998 because some of Mayor Brown's close associates were hired as consultants by the companies competing for the contract, including trucking contractor Charlie Walker, lobbyist Billy Rutland, and local Democratic party chair Natalie Berg.

A *San Francisco Weekly* investigation revealed that Mayor Willie Brown Jr. was an investor in Live Oak Associates III and that this firm is a secondary investor in Whitney Oaks development project, a 1,000-acre golf course community north of Sacramento. A subsidiary of Lennar Corporation is paying the owners of Whitney Oaks for the right to build one section of the Whitney Oaks development.

The San Francisco Redevelopment Agency Commission, appointed by Mayor Willie L. Brown Jr. gave development rights for Hunters Point Naval Shipyard to a team led by Lennar Corporation, abandoning the recommendation of an outside consultant. The city retained Peat-Marwick to analyze three development proposals for the shipyard. The Lennar team, which is also developing Mare Island in Vallejo and had also won development rights for the Treasure Island development under Brown's mayoral reign, won a unanimous vote by the seven-member commission, beating out Catellus Corporation and the Peat-Marwick consultants' pick, Forest City Enterprises. They said Lennar had done a better job of mustering community support.

The Job Myth

On November 7, 2000, a declaration of policy was passed by 87% of San Francisco voters. Proposition P was formulated by a committee chaired by Hunters Point Shipyard Restoration Advisory Board community cochair Lynne Brown. Its original wording enshrined the mandatory requirement for community acceptance of environmental clean-up standards under the Federal Superfund law.

"The United States government should be held to the highest standards of accountability for its actions . . . the Bayview–Hunters Point community wants the Hunters Point Shipyard to be cleaned to a level that would enable the unrestricted use of the property—the highest standard for cleanup established by the United States Environmental Protection Agency."

On November 2, 2000, Mayor Willie Brown and Secretary of the Navy Gordon England signed the HPS Memorandum of Agreement between the city and the navy. This action triggered an avalanche of debate among a vast array of community, government, and private interests regarding the health risks, economic benefits, and legal authority of the proposed phased cleanup and development of the shipyard.

In 1992 the Navy, state and federal regulators divided the Shipyard into six parcels to facilitate the environmental clean-up process. The parcels are sequenced A through F based on information available at that time and by the anticipated level of clean-up that would be required. Parcel A was touted as being the least environmentally challenged. Since that 1992 agreement extensive evidence has surfaced negating the navy's claim that Parcel A meets standards for unrestricted residential development and reuse. Six radiation-impacted buildings are sited on the parcel and challenges have been filed to the original clean-up standards that led to the 1995 "no further action" determination of the Parcel A Record of Decision.

Most significant, two years after the August 2000 fire on the Parcel E industrial landfill, flammable and explosive methane gas was detected in concentrations exceeding 80% in air less than 100 feet from the Parcel A boundary with the extensively contaminated Parcel E.

Even more seriously contaminated than Parcel A is nearby Parcel B, where a former submarine base was found in a 1992 navy investigation to harbor soils that emitted gamma radiation more than 1.5 times greater than background. On analysis these soils were found to contain elevated levels of the radionuclide radium. This region of Parcel B has been designated for mixed use and community development under Lennar's HPS Phase I Development Plan. It has been preposterously proposed as the future site for homes, "health care services," and artist studios in the Environmental Impact Report surreptitiously generated by the Planning Department in November 2003, and adopted by the Redevelopment Commission as a "negative declaration" in April 2004.

A Civil Grand Jury investigation of the Hunters Point Shipyard was conducted and its findings and recommendations were issued in a 2001 report. Perhaps its most astute finding centered on the need for immediate implementation of Redevelopment Agency, navy, and city contract policies and programs that prioritize training and hiring in shipyard clean-up and development agreements.

Vehement dissatisfaction was expressed by community residents with regard to the passionless, visionless, directionless leadership and oversight of District 10 supervisor Sophie Maxwell. The most legitimate concerns focused on Maxwell's blatant and negligent disregard for shipyard remediation and pressing health and safety concerns. She has paid little attention to measures that would create immediate job opportunities in the shipyard clean-up process.

The public has demanded that HPS remediation and development transaction agreements with the city and the Redevelopment Agency incorporate equal opportunity programs, nondiscrimination contracts, prevailing wage, minimum compensation programs, health care accountability, and the city's First Source Hiring Program. According to the San Francisco Redevelopment Agency, "the HPS Conveyance Agreement requires to the maximum extent allowed under federal law that the Navy use its best efforts to give preference in contracts for remediation of the Shipyard to locally owned and minority- and woman-owned businesses in the Shipyard vicinity."

In reality these goals were never met. A navy-sponsored economic development workshop was held in March 2004. A navy representative provided a dismal economic report. In fiscal year 2003, the navy spent $38 million on the shipyard and $700,000 locally. In 2004 the navy will spend $28 million on the shipyard, $2.5 million to local truckers and $144,000 to local businesses. In 2004 only twenty-eight local hires were made. In 2003 only thirty-nine local hires were made. Contrast this to the naval shipyard of the 1950's where 8,500 civilians were employed, people like my father.

Newly elected Gavin Newsom perpetrated the shipyard development job myth and narcissistically credited himself with "breaking the log jam of the

HPS Conveyance Agreement" in an article he authored in the local media. Peak homicide and unemployment rates among African American men in the southeast sector during the early months of 2004 further fueled the neighborhood's willingness to be taken in by the Job Myth.

An analysis of the HPS Phase I Development by Arc Ecology planner and economist Eve Bach challenged the shipyard plan's realization of job opportunities. In the years since the plan was first proposed by home-builder Lennar Corporation, light industrial and maritime development was phased out of the plan in favor of building additional housing units. In Bach's words, "Although the project description observes that non-residential uses would be reduced by two thirds, it needs to be pointed out that this reduction would be achieved by eliminating all industrial and maritime development from Phase I. We believe that the city should be clear that in revisions to the Reuse Plan the Community's job-creating strategy that prioritized light industrial development has almost completely vanished from Hunters Point Shipyard Phase I development."

Under the proposed BVHP Redevelopment Plan Amendment, blighted portions of the BVHP Redevelopment Survey Area would be arbitrarily added to the Hunters Point (Hill) Redevelopment Project Area. The basis for the addition of these private homes and properties in the neighborhood surrounding the shipyard was the designation of the existence of deterioration or blight. Arbitrary "blight designations" like this have been used repeatedly by the Redevelopment Agency to remove specific populations. This same bureaucratic mechanism was used in the 1960s to target the African-American Fillmore district when it was at its peak of vibrancy as a West Coast Harlem. It was also used to remove the retired longshoremen and seamen from the area now known as Yerba Buena Gardens.

The San Francisco Redevelopment Agency and Mayor Gavin Newsom tout the BVHP Redevelopment Plan and the Shipyard Conveyance Agreement as the answer to joblessness and a boost to the local economic vitality of the southeast corridor. But the community is not "buying in" to the development process and the reality of forced relocation of multigenerational inhabitants. There is a growing belief among residents that the BVHP Redevelopment Plan is fundamentally a grand exercise in ethnic cleansing and in the words of *SF Bayview* publisher Willie Ratcliff, "negro removal."

Breath of Fresh Air

It was easy to fall in love with Supervisor Matt Gonzalez. He was a Green

Party activist and potent political force whose message resonated harmo-
niously with my personal and political philosophies. He was a breath of fresh
air. I had never met an elected official who was passionately concerned about
the plight of animals, genuinely supported same-sex marriage, and was universally opposed to the death penalty. He was the Sir Lancelot of environmental protection. He was a respectful and enlightened man. Additionally, he
was fiercely honest, humble, unpretentious, sensitive, and one of the most
articulate and intelligent men I had ever met. His temperament was remarkable in the face of extremely stressful, long committee meetings.

It was easy to fall in love with mayoral candidate Matt Gonzalez. He was a
man of ethnic and cultural heritage who always looked as if he needed a
girlfriend to iron his suits, massage his back, prepare his lunch, and make
sure he got plenty of exercise. He also enjoyed a good glass of wine.

The juggernaut of the 2003 Matt Gonzalez for Mayor campaign was
launched in the basement of the Horseshoe Café one Saturday morning in
August. I was there. It spread like wildfire throughout the Mission and
Bayview–Hunters Point districts where two additional campaign offices were
soon situated. Willie Ratcliff, publisher of the *S.F. Bayview* newspaper— the
only paper that endorsed Matt in the primary race—donated the space for
the Gonzalez for Mayor campaign office on Third Street and Palou.

Matt Gonzalez became the prodigal son and darling of the progressive left
and galvanized a ragtag army of left-wing enthusiasts, many of whom had
been pushed to the sidelines of San Francisco politics for decades. Another
battalion of troops emerged from the freshly inducted new generation of
young political thinkers and idealists who saw Gonzalez as the champion
of leadership for the new millennium.

The Gonzalez for Mayor campaign took on a religious fervor and with
every media attack or political slight his core group of apostles broadened.
The Gonzalez for Mayor campaign was fueled by a People of Color coalition. Early on, the campaign drafted an Environmental Justice platform that
drew mainstream media attention to issues in the Bayview, including the
closure of the Hunters Point Power Plant, the clean-up of the Hunters
Point Naval Shipyard and the need for clean, alternative, renewable energy
sources including Gonzalez's own proposal for tidal energy.

When Matt Gonzalez lost the mayor's race and announced his decision not
to seek a second term as supervisor it was as if the circus had left town
without us. Left behind were the colorful remnants of a political fairground

that once promised to bring redress to a host of political, social, ecological, and economic injustices we have endured under the arrogant machine of Democratic politics in San Francisco.

An avalanche of disasters hit Bayview–Hunters Point in the months following the corrupt inauguration of Mayor Gavin Newsom. The homicide rate reached a zenith. Newsom announced plans to site three additional peaker plants in Potrero Hill, and the Hunters Point Power Plant was granted a five-year reprieve for continued operations. Newsom announced the signing of the Conveyance Agreement to transfer the heavily polluted Hunters Point Shipyard for residential development. Using eminent domain, the Redevelopment Agency threatened to bulldoze the private homes and businesses of the dwindling and endangered African American community's final political stronghold in San Francisco.

The community fought back. Legions of attorneys showed up at community meetings to volunteer time and consultations. The submissive District 10 supervisor faced two recall efforts. The Project Area Committee members for the Bayview–Hunters Point Redevelopment Agency were served with subpoenas for recall. The Conveyance Agreement and the shipyard transfer were held up by threats of legal action. The siting of the new peaker plants as well as the continued operation of the polluting Hunters Point Power Plant were met with fierce political opposition and legal challenge.

The fight continues but the elevator door is closing on the neighborhood I grew up in and on the friends and family and people I love. I am left with the saying from the stress and frantic hurry of my surgical internship, "the best way to stop a closing elevator is to put your head in it!"

A Decade of Displacement
San Francisco's Hidden Housing History
James Tracy

The housing crisis doesn't exist because the system isn't working. It exists because that's the way the system works.   —HERBERT MARCUSE

Whether fleeing from a death squad in Latin America or a homophobic family in the Midwest, many have sought refuge here. Those who consider San Francisco an "island," offer ample evidence: the sizable protest culture, gay marriages, and the municipal minimum wage. Certainly we live in a beautiful city, worth fighting for. However, cold, hard reality demands that we acknowledge the ways that San Francisco is nearly identical to every other city in the nation.

Segregation? Here? Maybe not apartheid or "separate but equal" but let's just say that here two people can walk down the same street and experience it in completely different ways. One person can look at Valencia Street and wonder where the best crêpes are, the other can wonder if she can make it to the bus stop without being stopped by the police.

Consider the depths of a decade of displacement: nearly 17,353 formal, "no-fault" evictions filed with the Rent Arbitration and Stabilization Board. Ted Gullicksen of the San Francisco Tenants Union estimates that this number is doubled if all those who moved at the mere threat of eviction are considered. These estimates don't cover evictions as a consequence of simply not being able to make the high rent: on the average 5,000 evictions a year. The grand total hovers around 90,000 evictions for the years from 1990 to 2000. This number does not even include housing lost in government-subsidized buildings, immigrants who leave when threatened with a visit from *La Migra*, or residential hotels lost to suspicious fires. The eviction wave was intensified, of course, by the dot.com boom (1997–2000), but persists to this day.

Thanks to decades of economic assault, "racial cleansing" initiatives such as urban renewal/removal, African Americans make up about 15% of the city's overall population but nearly half of the clients in the emergency homeless shelter system.

The 1990s also saw the high profile police murders of people of color, notably Mark Garcia, Aaron Williams, and Sheila Detoy. In most cases, those responsible suffered little consequence and families were confronted with absolute indifference from San Francisco's liberal political establishment. Far from the image of a progressive island, from this vantage point, San Francisco continues a long love affair with the venerable Jim Crow.

The electorate is hypocritical when it comes to class-consciousness. While consistently defending rent control and bucking the national rightward trend, the same voters have an appetite for persecution of the poor. Voters overwhelmingly approved gutting general assistance checks; even though recipients were forced into workfare to "earn" those "benefits." It is now possible to clean a city bus, fold towels at General Hospital, or do "alternative" workfare at a nonprofit for $1.81 an hour! The same voters also outlawed panhandling in the subsequent election. Support for anti-poor legislation was so broad that many a "progressive" voter also supported near-slave labor. Our Left shuts down the streets in protest of war but notable corporate war profiteers, such as Bechtel, still find our island hospitable enough to call home.

Nevertheless, every step of the way there has been pitched resistance, some of it quite effective, to attempts to rebuild San Francisco in corporate America's image. The city's potential dissident populations have never gone out without a fight. The concerted effort to displace, segregate, and discipline these groups out of existence has never been entirely successful. Toward this end everyday people have turned to a variety of tactics, both at the ballot box and the barricades.

The Hidden History of the 1990s

Some observers have commented that it seemed as if San Franciscans took the nineties' displacement assault lying down, that no real fight back occurred until the end of the decade. In fact, everyday San Franciscans led a variety of campaigns confronting evictions, exclusion, and the criminalization of homeless people.

The case of 83-year-old Lola McKay became a symbol of the eviction madness and helped to galvanize political opposition to displacement. McKay's home of forty years was bought by the John Hickey brokerage. Hoping to sell each of the four units in the building separately, the firm moved to evict her (homes delivered vacant to new buyers increase in value). With virtually no support network or family, McKay vowed to fight to the end for the right to live in her home.

A loose collection of groups including the San Francisco Tenants Union and the Senior Housing Action Collaborative began a campaign with only one demand: a lifetime lease for McKay. Although it would have been easy to grant this, and still make an enormous profit on the three vacant units, the brokerage did not relent until activists occupied the offices of their lawyers, Weigel and Freed. Television coverage shifted between McKay and a protest that resulted in a broken window and an altercation with a security guard. The occupation took sympathetic attention away from "first-time homeowners" fulfilling the American Dream, and exposed corporations that wouldn't think twice about evicting your grandmother.

"Lola McKay's case stood for seniors who have to fight for their rights in this city, and unfortunately Lola died for these rights. Her case ripped the mask off of the evictors and revealed them to be property speculators, not just small property owners trying to exercise their property rights," explained Barbara Blong of the Senior Action Network.

The McKay actions were simply the most visible of many spirited protests and "landlord visits" pulled off by tenant activists in the 1990s. Other actions shut down landlords' places of business, such as when the owner of a flower shop attempted to evict a person in the latter stages of AIDS. At one protest a 92-year-old woman who had spent time in the French Resistance against Nazi occupation declared "I have shot fascists dead in the streets of Europe so I will not let a petty landlord drive me from my home."

On another front, the Mission Agenda, a poor people's organization, was on the frontlines in another key housing battle. Throughout the latter part of the 1990s suspicious fires swept through residential hotels, destroying several hundred units of housing. Residential hotels often provide the last line of defense against homelessness. Many speculated that the fires were set by slumlords, but it was impossible to prove. The Agenda worked directly with fire survivors, often meeting people in makeshift shelters. Typically the city, along with the Red Cross, would offer limited relief and relocation assistance in the form of a small rental voucher.

After forming a new tenants union, the residents and the Agenda aggressively confronted public officials every time a batch of housing vouchers expired. This forced the city to extend the subsidy until permanent replacement housing was found for each tenant. The organization coordinated with caseworkers to make sure that services were also provided. Many people avoided homelessness by refusing to settle for crumbs. The relocation campaigns made anger visible at slum conditions within the hotels. As a consequence, the Board of Supervisors passed long-overdue legislation mandating sprinklers in residential hotels, outlawing the practice of extract-ing bribes for guests, and increased city attorney attention to the already illegal practice of evicting hotel tenants after a twenty-eight-day stay in order to prevent them from gaining rights as residents.

Taken together, such in-your-face tactics were extremely effective at beat-ing back specific evictions, yet failed to provide a sustained and focused counter-attack against evictions and displacement. Tenants also went to the ballot to strengthen rent control four times during the 1990s, with half the victories diluted or defeated by a pro-landlord Superior Court.

Dot Colonization and Resistance

If San Francisco's heart still beats, it is despite the "new money" that arrived during the 1990s. The fabled boom-time economy, fueled by the dot.com explosion, cannibalized the housing stock and the last blue-collar jobs. During this boom, one of San Francisco's oldest neighborhoods, the pre-dominantly Latino Mission district, bore the brunt of the eviction frenzy.

The Mission Anti-Displacement Coalition (MAC), a collection of groups such as People Organized to Demand Environmental and Economic Rights (PODER), the Mission Agenda, St. Peter's Housing Committee, the Day Laborers Program, and Mission Housing and Development Corporation formed the core of the new grouping. Each organization had done respect-able community organizing separately—defending the rights of residential hotel tenants, fighting immigrant discrimination, and evictions, or building low-income housing. MAC represented a more coordinated, broader attempt to work together toward a different vision of the city.

MAC recognized that the fight was on all fronts. Direct action against spe-cific targets (for example, a developer of unaffordable housing) was part of the tactical arsenal. MAC could also turn out hundreds of people for plan-ning commission meetings. As nonenforcement of city regulations monop-olized much of the available land for luxury condominiums, unequal devel-opment became the focus. MAC's demands were:

- An immediate moratorium on new market-rate housing and live-work lofts in the Mission.

- An immediate moratorium on office conversions and new con-struction of dot.com office space in the Mission.

- An immediate end to all illegal conversions.

- A community planning process to rezone the Mission District.

The coalition grew in the wake of an apparent corporate takeover of the gentrification process. After the Mayor Brown–controlled Board of Supervisors approved the Bryant Square project, a gigantic office development in the middle of the Mission, residents mobilized in unprecedented numbers. The Southern California–based Stein Kingsley Stein Corporation pushed for approval even though it was acknowledged that planting such a development in the middle of a residential neighborhood would fuel displacement.

A community "accountability session," with planning department director Gerald Green produced a surprising 500 angry attendees. MAC launched an energetic year of direct actions aimed at exposing the Planning Commission's complicity in displacement. One time MAC occupied Bigstep.com, a company that displaced dozens of community-service agencies when it moved into the Bayview Building (purchased by the Cort family). Outside, a community dialogue on displacement was ignited through a banner-hanging event while bilingual agitators passed out flyers for the next MAC meeting.

On numerous other occasions, planning commission meetings were stacked, and many times shut down altogether. A "caminata" procession throughout the neighborhood attracted over a thousand people. While the Lola McKay actions had helped to put a human face on displacement, MAC took the debate a step further as a collective movement willing to work both within and outside the formal legislative system.

The San Francisco Print Collective's partnership with MAC set a wonderful standard for how artists can make themselves useful during times of political strife. While many other groups of artists spoke up only when their own art spaces were threatened with eviction, the SFPC collaborated with MAC to create awesome silkscreened antigentrification posters promoting the struggles of the neighborhood's working classes. One poster in particular summed up the conflict, the slogan "They Plan for Profits, We Plan for People," over a picture of everyday neighborhood folks.

"MAC had an impact because it meant that the Mission District community attempted to take control over its own destiny around critical issues such as housing and community planning. MAC created an optimism that you could fight and win," remarked Renee Saucedo, executive director of the San Francisco Day Laborers program, "Also, it was significant that immigrant day laborers, some of the most excluded members of society, participated."

Contestation also erupted at the ballot box. Inspired by the return of district-based elections, neighborhood groups fielded independent candidates to directly challenge the Board of Supervisors members installed by Mayor Brown. Of the eight candidates endorsed by MAC, seven were victorious, winning on platforms that were explicitly antidisplacement. One MAC coalition founder, Chris Daly, took District 6 (which included part of the Mission) by a landslide. Matt Gonzalez, a public defender and poetry patron easily won the Haight and Western Addition after switching party affiliation from Democrat to Green in midstream. Proposition L, which encapsulated the spirit of MAC's demands, was defeated thanks to a large infusion of corporate cash and a decoy measure, Proposition K, placed on the ballot by Mayor Brown.

After the progressive sweep, participation in MAC dipped dramatically. Many individuals held the mistaken impression that with electoral success, the housing crisis would simply be taken care of. Years later, rents are still extremely high and evictions common.

Antonio Diaz of PODER summed up the MAC experience. "When we were talking in the late nineties about the dot.com boom, it became obvious that the single-issue groups had to come together. Fighting gentrification wasn't going to be a short-term campaign. It would mean effective organizing, mass mobilizations, and more. MAC brought together groups that were already doing work and created a force that could counteract the displacement push."

Still, even with significant gains Diaz knows that there is still much to be done. "Since the dot.com bust MAC has been trying to dig deep into our constituencies. In the beginning we needed to make a swift impact. Now we're making sure that we pay attention to bringing in new activists and doing popular education. I think that if we had incorporated more of this in the beginning we would have made more of a change."

Keeping the Public in Public Housing

Public housing often serves as the last line of defense against homelessness for low-income workers. Neither resident or neighbor would argue that these ancient developments didn't need rehabilitation. San Francisco became ground zero in the battle against another wave of urban removal, through the federal HOPE VI program. The program is ostensibly progressive, demolishing and rehabilitating dilapidated buildings. But the program also reduces the quantity of housing. The first two projects to be rebuilt were reconstructed with fewer dwellings. Many residents were not able to return due to a labyrinth of new federal regulations designed to make sure that public housing wasn't so public anymore. Add to the mix the local partnership with private developers (well connected to Mayor Brown) and you have a recipe for disaster.

The residents of North Beach Public Housing (NBPH) weren't about to let their community be destroyed by the wrecking ball. Many of them had come to live in subsidized housing after having their neighborhoods and homes demolished thirty years prior in the so-called "Urban Renewal" push. Residents went through a complicated process of resident meetings, street protests, petition drives, and legal action in partnership with the Eviction Defense Network (EDN) before coming upon the trump card: voting with one's butt.

Residents found their strategic advantage: the San Francisco Housing Authority (SFHA) might have had to return over $20 million to the federal government if residents did not move quickly. This meant that it would be risky for the agency to second-guess the residents' willingness to engage in civil disobedience by refusing to move, or by putting up legal obstacles.

The residents demanded cooperative ownership of the development, revitalized through a community process. When they got nowhere, they refocused on other bread-and-butter issues. Their ten-point-program spelled out one-for-one replacement, the right to return, and various safeguards designed to make sure the development was rebuilt swiftly and that residents were not disqualified for technicalities.

Another simple tactic helped build tenant unity. Many issues between Chinese and Black tenants were settled by simply recruiting translators. Also, tenants who faced evictions were protected by the advocacy work of the EDN, helping to build a willingness to stay in the larger fight.

The residents morphed their program into a contract. Soon, nearly the entire development signed cards stating their refusal to relocate unless the contract was signed. Orange signs simply demanded "Sign the Contract!" in English, Chinese, and Spanish. Faced with the prospects of a protracted fight, resulting in the loss of funding, the agency relented, and signed the contract.

Today, the development is nearly reconstructed *according to the demands of the residents*. The residents stayed organized, even from their temporary homes, and all signs point to a successful reoccupancy. Today, the SFHA doesn't even talk about "revitalizing" a development without stepping to the table with the guarantees won by the North Beach residents.

Homelessness and the Civil Disobedience of Everyday Life

Forget what you might have been told about homelessness. Ronald Reagan didn't cause the homelessness epidemic by de-institutionalizing mentally ill people. Homelessness is linked to two main causes—the economy and the destruction of the social safety net. Mental illness, addiction, veteran's status, and domestic violence intensify the homelessness cycle for many. Homelessness expands when living-wage jobs are replaced by service-sector ones, when welfare-to-work programs lead to no work or low-wage work without child care.

In step with the rest of the nation, San Francisco, through five administrations, has been stuck in an endless rut of policing the "visible" homeless population. The cycle goes something like this: business people begin to complain loudly about homeless people, then a torrent of "exposés" come out in the media blaming tolerance for the presence of people on the street. Soon after, laws prohibiting "Quality of Life Crimes" (read: sleeping or panhandling) are proposed by a mayor or mayoral candidate.

This is invariably accompanied by massive police sweeps, incarceration, and ticketing of homeless people. For those sleeping on the streets, sleeping is an act of civil disobedience. During this time, groups such as Homes Not Jails and Religious Witness With Homeless People led high-profile takeovers of vacant housing. Such actions rarely yielded permanent gains but often provided a stark contrast to the media stereotypes. As a result, homeless people were portrayed repairing homes instead of the usual images of drug-addled scam artists.

Our society fetishizes private property, but apparently this fascination does not extend to the personal property of homeless people. The Civil Rights Workgroup of the Coalition on Homelessness has recorded numerous incidents between police officers and un-housed person that would be hilarious if it weren't right out of *Catch-22*.

In this scene an officer points to a shopping cart filled with bundles of clothes and other items. He asks, "Are these things yours?" If the answer is "yes," then the property is confiscated and a citation issued. If "no," then the property is confiscated anyhow.

When historians start to write the biography of Big Brother, they may very well conclude that he started his political career in a homeless shelter. Those using emergency shelters must be fingerprinted, as all single adult welfare recipients have had to be since 1993, under Mayor Frank Jordan. In 1997

Mayor Brown borrowed a helicopter, equipped with infrared night vision, to identify homeless encampments in Golden Gate Park.

Now many thousands of tickets later, homeless people are more visible than ever, yet there seems to be no end in sight to the scapegoating. Homeless people did not take the assault on their sleep lying down. Police sweeps have triggered numerous sleep-ins at the homes of public officials. "Camp Agnos" occupied City Hall plaza as a protest against the push to expel visibly poor people from the central city during Art Agnos's mayoralty (1987-1991).

As a supervisor, our current mayor Newsom added a slick new tool to the mix: his successful Care Not Cash campaign, Proposition N, convinced voters that the way to show caring was to cut general assistance checks down to $59. The campaign promised housing and services in lieu of cash. A report by City Controller Ed Harrington pretty much established that such care was not unlike weapons of mass destruction in Iraq: missing. In addition, homeless people will now pay for the privilege of sleeping on a two-inch thick shelter cot.

The poetic irony is that Care Not Cash not only harnessed both hatred and sympathy but also sounded like Food Not Bombs, the activist group persecuted by Mayor Jordan for its ongoing felony conspiracy to commit lunch.

The campaign gave Newsom a lot of face time in the local media, conveniently circumventing campaign laws. The next election, Newsom, with the backing of the chamber of commerce, convinced voters to outlaw "aggressive" panhandling. In a parallel effort the hotel council began to take out advertisements implying that giving spare change to homeless people would spread sexually transmitted diseases and shut down small businesses. It doesn't take a degree in health or economics to figure out that STDs are spread by unprotected sex and small businesses sink when the economy does.

When Mayor Newsom, or anyone else for that matter, proposes poor laws, they are simply repeating a bad script first written in England 400 years ago. Is this much different from being sent to the gallows for the crime of begging? Have we come far from the days when an unemployed Londoner could be conscripted into slavery by any willing master? Ask the person making $1.81 an hour cleaning the MUNI bus you rode to work this morning.

Cities and the Future of Community Organizing

Like any other city, San Francisco has a simple choice: inclusion or exclusion? Will our city complete the turn toward a gated community, where citizenship is defined by class status?

Cities often function similarly to factories. They are places where diverse people must live next to each other, take public transportation, and wait in line for the same public services. Like factories of old, this holds potential for community organizing and building unusual alliances. This is not to suggest that workplace organizing should be a thing of the past. On the contrary, this concept merely expands the idea of the labor movement into additional arenas. Wherever market forces take away resources needed for working-people's survival, there exists a potential for transformative social struggle.

Community organizers can draw another lesson from the history of the labor movement. Turn-of-the-century labor radicals agitated against narrow unions based on trades and for industrial unions. The logic was that if workers in the same industry were in different unions, bosses could easily pit trade against trade. In tenant and community organizing, tenant groups are often hopelessly segregated between subsidized-housing tenants and those living in private apartments. At one tenant convention in the middecade, public housing residents were even told by movement "leaders" not to come!

As James Baldwin pointed out "If they take you in the morning, they will be coming for us that night." As public housing was demolished, the ripple effect fueled additional evictions in the surrounding areas.

Effective models of resistance can be many and varied, but probably share the following in common: a willingness to take action, outside of formal electoral and legislative channels, engagement at the ballot box only on strategic terms, nurturing participation from those most excluded from power, and resource sharing.

Our Vision Thing

One should have no illusions that the housing crisis will go away without a radical restructuring of an economy that encourages property speculation and a cultural shift away from the idea of housing as a commodity. Before that day, reforms that combine practical survival with an alternate, community-based vision of urban life, are worth working toward.

The chamber of commerce has plenty of long-term vision. They spawned Proposition J in March 2004 to turn over the entire central city to market-rate housing development, creating a distinct class-segregation pattern, skewering the electorate further rightward. This was done by promising to create "affordable housing" available to households with an annual income of

$77,000. Fortunately, San Francisco voters defeated it by a two-to-one ratio.

If the elites have a vision of a city of elites, how best to counter it? Community activists have proven that we can defend many people from evictions, and win at the ballot box occasionally. Despite numerous organizing successes, the gated community expands at the costs of all others. Most of the truly interesting proposals share some characteristics in common: a redefinition of public goods that doesn't necessarily involve state-owned forms of public ownership, a clear vision of economic uplift rooted in challenging race and class inequities.

Imagine if any of the community struggles described above went beyond their inherent limits and led to a truly mass upheaval of San Franciscans, resolved to not only end the current wave of community displacement but drastically alter the way people relate to land and housing?

In this alternate future, say that in addition to the populist electoral upheaval, a parallel citywide rent strike led to massive renters' defense, reminiscent of the Unemployed Worker's Movements of the 1930s. In this future, landlords would not only be picketed, but families un-evicted through collective direct action. In this scenario, eviction courts would be unable to operate as everyday people regularly blockaded the courthouse when eviction cases were heard.

In this future, San Franciscans build the type of power to challenge not only evictions but change the assumptions of housing for profit. An aggressive strategy of housing decommodification could take place.

This would take many forms, including traditional models of nonprofit ownership found in many cities today. However, a key demand would be social housing managed collectively by the residents themselves. In any case, the aim would be to insulate large sections of neighborhoods from the boom-and-bust cycles of the housing economy.

Tired of only acting defensively, many housing activists are working toward a community land trust to provide housing without landlords, therefore without the threat of evictions for profit. Under this model, community members own an interest in the building they live in, but the nonprofit land trust retains stewardship of the land. When a unit is vacated, the resident receives a return, but equity is limited in order to preserve permanent affordability. While residents maintain democratic control, safeguards exist to prevent breaking equity caps and speculation.

Recently in New York, the city turned over dozens of buildings to squatters who had lived in them for years, using a model very similar to the land trust. Advocates see an opportunity to concretize "no displacement" demands made through the organizing process as a way of moving beyond landlording—an outdated holdover from feudalism. Similar approaches could stabilize homesteaded, or squatted, buildings. It should be no surprise that residents of two demolished public housing developments had proposed cooperative ownership of their reconstructed homes.

Such a program should not give governments cover to slash spending on housing and human services, asking residents to manage their own austerity. In an ideal situation, as displacement ended, preserved communities could turn their attention toward building innovative institutions of resistance, and of course, spend a little more time on things that high housing costs steal from us all: creative pursuits and time with each other.

By experimenting with forms of cooperative social relationships we can provide a real challenge to the notion that private profits are sacred and that the marketplace is the only way to distribute housing and other vital goods. To paraphrase the turn-of-the-century radical union the Industrial Workers of the World, "building a new world inside the shell of the old." We can at least get a glimpse.

A city worth living in cannot be won solely at the ballot box or City Hall. It requires a constant push from below, on community, not corporate terms. As San Franciscans confront the next wave of displacement, most likely fueled by demolitions to skirt the rent ordinance or the looming biotech boom, we would do well to remember that entering into a fight for survival without direct action is the same as tying one's arm behind one's back.

Despite our losses, the future is still thankfully up for grabs.

The Race Card

Bianca Henry

Willie Brown, San Francisco's first black mayor, was a disaster for the Black community. Blacks continued to exit the city thanks to a landlord-friendly agenda and mishandling of the HOPE VI demolition of public housing. He refused to support a real cleanup of the toxic Naval Base at Hunters Point. His "solution" to runaway gang violence was to assign more cops to the neighborhood, increasing the tension and oppression that fuels gang formation in the first place. Mayor Brown hired and appointed so-called "leaders" to positions of power, turning the San Francisco Housing Authority and the San Francisco Redevelopment Agency into his own personal plantations. The Brown regime reached unprecedented levels of nepotism and crony-capitalism, starving the black community of badly needed resources, while expanding the airport, the convention center, and unleashing developers to build "lawyer lofts" throughout the city.

On his way out of office due to term limits, Brown anointed Gavin Newsom as his heir apparent. When Newsom's campaign was faltering in the face of the remarkable grassroots surge for Matt Gonzalez, Brown called a meeting of African-American pastors where he called Gonzalez "a racist." But he knew that race was not the issue. He just knew what cards to play in the black community to get votes for his candidate. Playing the race card also diverted attention from the fact that he had just spent eight years trying to sell Bayview–Hunters Point to the highest bidder. It's marketing in the 'hood.

Brown needed the Bayview community one more time to put the final nail in our own coffin, allowing him to solidify his financial power in the black community long past his time in office. Calling Gonzalez a racist was just a distraction, and part of his standard operating procedure whenever he faced meaningful opposition.

Willie Brown was not the first mayor to fail Bayview–Hunters Point; however, we had hoped for more from him. But he lived in the world of the rich and powerful. His San Francisco was remote from mine. My San Francisco isn't a Disneyland or a playground for the well-to-do. My black San Francisco is a war zone. The value of human life in my neighborhood, the Bayview, is sometimes zero. Between the guns, drugs, evictions, police brutality, and lack of access to good education, my community isn't a community anymore—it is a commodity.

This is a story about another San Francisco, which shaped the person I am. Who am I? Just another black statistic that society thought wouldn't make it out of the ghetto. I grew up on the hardest street in San Francisco's Bay View–Hunters Point where you're lucky if you make it to puberty. But my story really starts in the Western Addition, the Fillmore.

My first memories were of shooting galleries, where people shot drugs, of not having enough food and being hungry. That was a normal part of life. I remember my mom as a beautiful woman in those days, but she wasn't really cut out to be a mom. During my childhood, she overdosed all the time. She took beatings regularly from the men she got involved with. I wanted to become invisible, or to get out of there. By the time those scenes ended we had moved to the Sunnydale area at San Francisco's southern edge in Visitacion Valley. New problems began immediately. Crack became mom's drug of choice and I was beginning to feel like killing myself. I wondered what I had done to God in my short life to deserve this.

I started looking at myself from outside—I realized I could be anyone as long as I was true to myself. I got through this period thanks to my thick skin and by imagining what I wished my mother was. I tried to the best of my ability to be what I wanted to see in my mother.

I never had any home training so I really didn't have much to work with. I learned as I grew. By the time I turned eleven, I'd had enough of this reality. One day I asked my mother a question, hoping that she would say "no," because I wanted her to want me. "Can I go live with my aunt?" She said "yes," and that same day I left and went to live with my favorite aunt in Double Rock, a crowded public housing project in the Bayview. It was all that I wanted—to be part of a poor but surviving family. My aunt worked her ass off just to feed and clothe us. We were five kids—she had four of her own—but she made it work. In those four years I got straight A's in school and visited my father in the summer. That was the best time I ever had (I was safe). But it didn't last long because then my aunt and uncle got involved in drugs too.

Some say you have choices. You don't. You either go with the system or you go with the system. I could not go back home because my mother was too far gone. And she was having a new baby, my brother. I worked summer jobs to pay for my school clothes, but I now had to pay rent. I couldn't tell my aunt at the end of the week I didn't have her money. I couldn't get out of the game even if I wanted to by this time. It was either sell drugs or go through the Child Protective Services into a foster home and you never wanted that as an option. The money I made selling drugs had to support me, my mother, aunt, and uncle, and sometimes my sister too.

I went to jail the first time when I was seventeen. I thought my life had been bad until then, but I was not prepared for that. This was one of the worst experiences in my life!

The day I got out I went right back to what I knew. That was the game. Me and my best friend at the time, Lisa, were two misfits hanging together. We both thought our families didn't want us, or just didn't know what the fuck we were going through. When you're at that stage you don't give a fuck! You can do anything and commit any crime and not even know why you're doing it, because everything in your life has brought you to this point. In other words, you're numb, your heart is shut down, and you cannot remember how to feel.

I had been through so much destruction in my life by this time. I made a promise to myself that if I made it through this, I would change my life, for myself and for my son, who witnessed me in prison while I was continuing the cycle that my parents passed down to me. So when I got out, I kissed the floor of the Hall of Justice, prayed to God, and never looked back. And then I found the Coalition on Homelessness, and they turned on the lights I needed to see my way and to find my voice.

I want to say to people who never think about what life is like in my San Francisco:

This is what it looks like when your neighbors get evicted. When property values go up and there are less and less people willing to form a community. It's no longer a community, but a self-interested neighborhood controlled by corporations whose only interest is to make money. They say, fuck the people living life in those places. If you have issues, talk to an answering service!

This is what it looks like when the city government tears down homes and gentrifies your neighborhood. More and more families become homeless or simply disappear. I never knew what happened to my neighbors because I was so worried about what was going to happen to me. The government turns a blind eye to red-lining, making it impossible for black families in the neighborhood to qualify for credit. Creditworthiness is further jeopardized by a vicious cycle of "crimes" of survival. Most black families have at least one member carrying felonies because of the things they have had to do to survive.

This is what it looks like when your childhood friends go to prison. Where I come from going to jail is like setting the table for dinner. We have a harder time getting a job than going to jail. From your first day in school you're being set up to go to jail. Schools are underfunded, starved for resources, and run like prisons. At our schools we find no books, no homework, no computers—we have the oldest teachers in the district, who haven't even learned computers. Parents are seldom notified by schools about their children unless they are on the way to jail or Child Protection Services. Our high school graduates have little chance of attending college. So the next stop is prison. You can get a better education in prison than on the streets. By the time you get out you're likely to end up in another institution or have so much hate for yourself that you are now a menace to society. After all, you still don't have a job, your family life is wrecked, and now you're homeless because of your record. This is the vicious circle trapping many of us.

This is what it looks like when Child Protective Service takes your kids. It's as if your kids have a felony strike against them. I have a cousin doing life because of what all the years of foster care did to him. The CPS is set up as an institution for babies. But most of the time they are not protecting the children. Most black families here live in poverty and the CPS uses misfortunes that happen to people in poverty to justify taking their children. I'm not saying some kids shouldn't be removed from their homes but curiously the system often doesn't remove those kids because they are already considered too fucked up to be helped. Instead CPS bureaucrats look at the struggling parents that might need a little extra help and call them "unfit." CPS makes it harder for single mothers who may have made a few mistakes but are still loving mothers—sometimes they take their children from them permanently.

This is the black San Francisco that existed when Willie Brown became mayor in 1995, and it has only gotten worse since then. When Brown was first elected, there was a lot of hope that he would make a difference, but he turned out to be a wolf in sheep's clothing. Sometimes you run into false prophets and that's what he was. He used the black community to get what he wanted. He basically pimped this city. He was like a cannibal that sucked his community dry, leaving nothing for future generations. He left the situation graver than it was before he took office.

He could have helped us put the community back together after three generations of "black removal" under the guise of redevelopment. Instead of helping he put us back years, and his parting "gift" to Bayview is a sweetheart deal with the Lennar Corporation to be master developer of the decommissioned Hunters Point shipyard—leaving the community, local businesses, and the 40% unemployed in the neighborhood out in the cold. Instead of a new unity, we're still fighting among each other, calling names, and even using guns.

At least two years before the campaign for mayor began, Gavin Newsom came along with some of Willie's people to Bayview–Hunters Point. They knew they couldn't win the election without the black community, so they made all the promises and the back-room deals before the campaign even started. They used funding that the community was already entitled to in order to divide and conquer. They gave it to a small group of self-proclaimed "community leaders" who sold a bill of goods to the uninformed men and women in the neighborhood. It was a process that shut the door on true leadership.

On the other hand, it took the Gonzalez campaign a while to figure out that my community had to be dealt in. It took them too long to figure out that the black community was a political force. I worked with him but I felt a little cheated and played out because we were only given a few weeks to get the Bayview organized around his campaign. I really felt like we didn't get the attention that other neighborhoods got.

If politicians really cared about bringing change, they would ask the communities how to implement policies that would work. The first step toward solving Bayview's problems starts in the Bayview. We need to rebuild our own community—without "help" from all those false prophets and outside "father-knows-best" types who claim to have all the answers. We need to rebuild the families that have been knocked down by drug use and a lack of self-worth. We have to reconnect ourselves with our history of unity and believe in what the Civil Rights struggle was all about. We need to start to respect ourselves and stop looking for respect from others. Start looking at who we are and why we are dying and who is making the profits off destroying our communities.

A Vision for the Neighborhood

Replace the banks that redline our community with community-controlled institutions that will help us develop community-owned resources, cooperatively-owned housing, and develop jobs.

In a ghetto, we have so many people with talents that are misspent, but don't tell me that the OGs don't have the ability to handle money! We need to channel that energy into something positive. Take, for instance, a drug dealer. When a dope fiend comes into the neighborhood there are a hundred dealers waiting to sell the same drugs to him. If you can convince that dope fiend to come back only to you, you've done a great job of marketing. Imagine that energy and intelligence set loose in City Hall, or organizing our communities.

Depending on lawmakers to stop gang violence is silly. Going down to City Hall and begging for a change only results in more police. People need to step up and heal the community through cooperative efforts such as raising children of imprisoned parents.

As for housing in our community, we need more community ownership and limited equity ownership. When people don't own a thing in their community they will let anything be dumped in it. Take a ride through the community. The cooperatives are in pretty good shape but the projects are messed up. It's the difference between building a community and living on a modern-day plantation.

Black people, like everyone, have to have something to believe in. Crack and heroin in our communities generates despair. So many kids who grew up during the crack epidemic don't believe in tomorrow or that there will be opportunities to do better. If you grow up not respecting your parents, how can they expect you to live in a just society? After all of the struggling we have done, we deserve a lot more peace than we have. We must carry the load of the people that are blinded by slave talk. Educate them about what our grandmothers and grandfathers know about a better day and what Martin Luther King meant when he said he had a dream. Remember Judas sold his soul for a few pieces of silver. We can't let our movements be destroyed by people who had a chance to do good in their community but use their knowledge of the community to make money for themselves.

The World at My Feet

D. S. Black

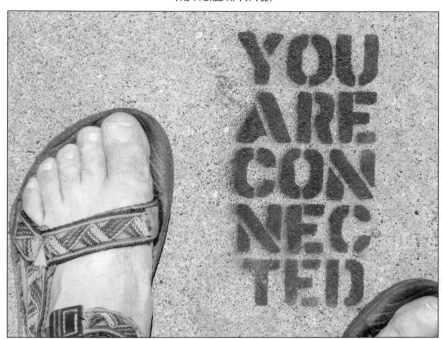

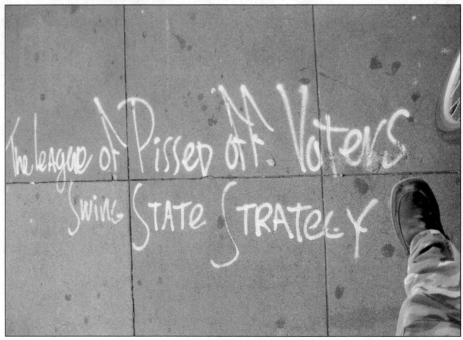

A City for Idiots

Iain A. Boal

"Idiot" derives from the Greek word meaning "private person," that is, someone barred or absent from the public life of the city. "Private," likewise, is etymologically kin to "deprivation," though any memory of why that might be—namely, that privacy was a prideful abstention from a life in common—is long gone.   —The Devil's Glossary

From any point of view other than that of police control, Haussmann's Paris is a city built by an idiot, full of sound and fury, signifying nothing. Today urbanism's main problem is ensuring the smooth circulation of a rapidly growing number of motor vehicles.

—Guy Debord, *Les Lèvres Nues* 6, 1955

Sometime this year humanity will cross a watershed. For the first time in history, the majority of people on the planet will be city dwellers. Despite a deep strain of anti-urbanism running through North American culture, which comes in several varieties of reverse puritanism— rural militias, the Unabomber, Earth First!ers, back-to-the-land rusticators ("city bad, wilderness good")—the fact is that the human future is bound up with the fate of cities. They are strange and fascinating artifacts, though poorly understood. In particular, the megacities produced by structural adjustment programs and the new enclosures of capitalist globalization are, sociological-ly, UFOs. That was the phrase used by the urban historian and critic Mike Davis to describe these new sites of unrecorded and heroic improvisation in the Global South, many of whose inhabitants are engaged in a struggle for sheer existence. In the cities of the North too, in the midst of great plenty, millions are forced to improvise an impoverished and marginal livelihood. San Francisco is no exception, but thanks to the critical biographies that "everyone's favorite city" has inspired—Hartman's *City for Sale: The Transformation of San Francisco*, Brechin's *Imperial San Francisco*, and Brook, Carlsson, and Peters's *Reclaiming San Francisco* come to mind—it is possible to grasp something of the dynamics that have shaped the place, including the history of struggles on the terrain of transportation across its various modes— trains, trams, buses, bicycles, automobiles, and, okay, cable cars.

The chronic shambles of Bay Area transportation—a daily insult to the work-ing population, and above all to those poor, elderly, and young who depend on buses—means that nobody in recent memory has been able to run for public office in San Francisco without having to make some noises about improving public transit. It was true of Willie Brown, and no less true of the candidates in the 2003 mayoral race. They all have to deal with the fragmented nature of urban government (of which there are more than a hundred in the greater Bay Area) and the dominance of suburban and auto interests. The subway system is occasionally fought over but in reality is in thrall to exurban developers, leaving most of the inner Bay Area underserved. The Metropolitan Transportation Commission failed for thirty years to create an integrated transport system; they doled out the lion's share of funds to freeway construction, leaving some for the subway, and a pittance for the buses. What needs to be explained, however, is the extraordinary galvanizing of transit and local community activists by the Matt Gonzalez campaign, when in reality his "transit-first" manifesto on transportation was not radically at odds with Gavin Newsom's own "transit-oriented" position. The Gonzalez phenomenon must ultimately be set within a deeper history of the San Francisco region and its politics.

The peninsularity of the city and the severity of its hillsides are at the same time a condition of its glory and an element in its chronic transportation woes. The breathtaking physiography of the bay, together with a crustal geology that fortuitously extruded huge mercury deposits to complement the gold and silver in the Sierra Nevada, constitutes the physical setting, though sadly San Francisco turned its back on the bay long ago, except for high-premium views. The contrast with, say, Sydney—its flotillas of water taxis, ferries, sailing craft, and vibrant waterfront life—is a standing embarrassment. The reasons are manifold; first, as with Manhattan and its relation to the Hudson and East Rivers, San Francico's bay was, from the beginning, predominantly used for industrial and military purposes. Second, the building of the Golden Gate and Oakland Bay Bridges in the 1930s evacuated the bay of most of its ferry traffic and consequently of pedestrian traffic moving through the Ferry Building, to the permanent detriment of life along the city's main axis, Market Street. Thirdly, the paucity of deep natural anchorages within the bay combined with the barrier of railroad (and later freeway) corridors, created by eminent domain along the shore, to sever communities from the water. In the East Bay the Southern Pacific and Santa Fe railroads had acquired most of the waterfront and it was only in 1911 that the city of Oakland was able to pry it loose. In San Francisco itself the merchants and shippers intentionally walled off the bay to control it and to keep down customary appropriation ("theft") at the dockside; the assault on the longshore—a matrix for radical politics and labor solidarity in the city—went back at least to the building of the Embarcadero itself after the earthquake of 1906.

The extraordinary energies released by Gonzalez's run for mayor were pre-figured by the lightning three-week write-in campaign for Tom Ammiano in 1999. By no stretch could either candidate be called your average machine politician. Ammiano's improbable headquarters was Josie's Cabaret and Juice Joint, a small gay comedy club in San Francisco's Castro district. He had led the opposition to City Hall on behalf of tenants and neighborhood activists, agitated for an $11 an hour minimum wage for workers on city contracts, and refused on principle to deal with paid lobbyists. "Taking back the city"—from downtown money and the Willie Brown machine—was how many grassroots volunteers described what they were doing during those frenzied days, though it would be hard to claim that the city was ever in the hands of the people in the first place.

The Gonzalez campaign contained many echoes of Ammiano's run in 1999, and tapped the same reservoir of latent energy. Like Ammiano, Gonzalez was a regular rider on San Francisco's MUNI Metro system. Though a lawyer with a Stanford training, he continued to share a rented group house and could be seen walking around town. His brand of "antipolitics"—to be sure, a venerable American political tradition—could not be dismissed as a pose. He seemed unlikely to behave like Diane Feinstein who as mayor had fired Richard Sklar, head of the Public Utilities Commission, when he insisted on downtown developers paying larger fees for public transit. Charismatic in a quiet hunched way, Gonzalez became the darling of organized transit activists such as the San Francisco Bicycle Coalition, as well as pedestrian and motorcycling lobbies. More broadly, he mobilized "alternative" and subcultural elements, and appealed to thousands of young unaffiliated city dwellers seriously alienated from electoral politics. The campaign was quickly boosted by significant numbers of residents of the inner neighborhoods, particularly the Mission, Potrero Hill, Haight-Ashbury, and Bernal Heights, as well as South-of-Market denizens, who were on the rebound from almost "losing the city" in the dot.com gold rush. Luckily the gloomier implications of *Hollow City*, Rebecca Solnit and Susan Schwartzenberg's anatomy of gentrification during the silicon boom years, were averted by the collapse of infotech stocks in 2001. Wall Street's bagmen quit town, leaving Mayor Brown to settle the succession and candidate Gonzalez, as reticent pied piper, to lead what an old friend of his from law school sardonically called a "children's crusade" against the Democratic establishment. A motley crew of all genders, colors, and sizes—bohemians, artisans, greens, assorted wage-slaves, and alarmed liberals looking for a local buttress against the atavistic turn in state and national politics—went canvassing with a will.

This temporary and ragged-arsed coalition of volunteers was further energized by the recent and vivid memory of a series of extra-electoral actions. In particular, the massive peace and antiglobalization demonstrations, which have been bringing hundreds of thousands into the streets of San Francisco since the spring of 2003, gave many their first taste of a highly charged public sphere ("public" being a deeply suspect and unfashionable notion in an era of neoliberal individualism) in which serious business—more than getting to work or shopping—is conducted in the spirit of Eros. On such occasions people glimpse the possibility of doing politics—and of living—differently. The crowds were noisy and full of banter, the mood was carnivalesque. One longtime chronicler of popular struggles in the city noticed above all "the civic feeling of the event—'everyone' in SF seemed to be there or wish they'd been there."

The memory of the city as a vibrant public sphere—albeit fleeting and partial—is, I believe, one reason for the remarkable energy thrown into the Gonzalez campaign by the transit activists, many of whom poured into the streets to protest the invasion of Iraq. Furthermore, the antiwar movement was making the connection between imperialism abroad and automobilism at home, between the massive military expenditures ensuring the flow of oil and the interstate highway system as a Defense Department project. What must also be recalled is the crucial role played by transit activists during the 1990s in nurturing hopes that a popular victory might just be possible despite being vastly outspent, and that a more livable city—one not given over to cigar-smoking traders and content providers driving Armadas—was not just a dream. After all, was it not an evanescent, anarchist, monthly, open-air, moving assemblage of San Francisco cyclists who had, *mirabile dictu*, inflicted the first serious damage to the Willie Brown administration?

In 1997 the mayor, representing the interests of downtown capital and its smooth flow, suffered a political defeat when he found that he could not co-opt, buy off, discipline, or otherwise domesticate Critical Mass, which has joyfully transformed the Friday commute home for some, while revealing the exquisite tedium and irrationality of traffic dominated by privatized transportation. The mayor apparently was unable to grasp that Critical Mass was an idea about urbanity and the possibilities of collective life, not an organization that might be destroyed by a police riot. If there was coordination, it was not because there was an executive committee or leadership that conspired to cause traffic jams. There were only the antinomian merlins of Market Street, who smiled and said quietly: "We are not blocking traffic; we are traffic."

In fact, recent political battles about transportation in San Francisco must be understood in terms of the production of space under capitalism, its priorities (in particular, the political economy of transit as servant of land values), its uneven development, and not least the contradictions of the circulation of its workforce. As early as 1896 there was a police riot on Market Street during a demonstration by thousands of cyclists, on that occasion demanding better roads (ah, the dialectic of history!). The owners of the tram companies felt threatened, as well they might, by this new mode of freewheeling personal mobility. But by 1900 the human-powered high-wheelers and safety bicycles were being challenged as "kings of the road," and the long reign of the automobile was dawning. (Bicyclists in the United States seem never to have forgiven motorists for their eclipse and many today even claim to represent the antithesis of the automobile, even though historically they share with car drivers an ideology of personal mobility and absolute entitlement to "freedom of the road.") We continue, at the outset of the following century, to live in the part-built, part-demolished utopia of 1930s car company executives, who gave fair warning in the GM pavilion of the 1939 New York World's Fair. And it's not over yet. The U.S. consulting firm of McKinsey recently produced a document titled "Vision 2020" for the city of Hyderabad in India, proposing a state subsidy of $100 million so that Hyderabad could become a "world class futuristic city with Formula 1 [car racing] as a core component."

Nevertheless, the so-called San Francisco Freeway Revolt of the 1950s and 1960s marked a turning point of sorts. It was the vanguard of resistance to cold war urban planning, which had been more or less handed over to highway engineers. Cities are in the best of circumstances ecologically dubious, as Gray Brechin shows in his Mumfordian account of San Francisco's parasitic relation to its enormous hinterland. But the immense costs, social and environmental, associated with the motor car, as a result of the zoned disconnection of domestic and productive life, make matters far worse, and perhaps ultimately catastrophic. But all this was hardly obvious to the residents of the city at the time of the postwar masterplans of 1948 and 1951, which laid out proposals, without any consultation whatever with the people to be displaced, for ploughing freeways through the city to connect the Golden Gate and Bay Bridges as part of the interstate highway system. They were to be routed where possible along existing rights of way, across public land, and otherwise through neighborhoods of least resistance (read: poor and black communities). Moreover, the city rushed the process in order to qualify for massive (90%) funding under the Federal Highway Act of 1956. The construction of the first section of the double-decked Embarcadero Freeway passing in front of the Ferry Building, and the virtually simultaneous opening of the Central Freeway in the spring of 1959, showed San Franciscans the full horrors of a city designed by highway engineers. The fight was on to prevent the juggernaut demolishing the Panhandle, cutting a swathe north-south across Golden Gate Park and bulldozing through the wealthy Marina district. The proposed Western Freeway, which was slated to run parallel to 19th Avenue and would have bisected both the Sunset and Richmond districts, turned the working class and petit bourgeois of the city's west side, notoriously conservative, into the avant-garde of a worldwide freeway revolt.

In the course of the struggle, neighborhoods and communities normally indifferent or even mutually hostile, found common cause. The sheer scope of the destruction planned by the highway bureaucrats forged citywide alliances strong enough to have the maximum scheme withdrawn in 1965. The federal funds were transferred to the building of Interstate 280, and city planners now trumpeted a Bay Area Rapid Transit (BART) system as the answer to getting about the city. (Actually, BART had been conceived as early as the 1940s by the new Bay Area Council and the Bechtel Corporation as part of San Francisco's effort to maintain its centrality as the suburbs spun out of control; the plan was to keep white-collar workers and executives downtown.) It is unclear whether planners anticipated BART's centrifugal effect, raising land values at the core and on the periphery, eventually allowing Chevron and PT&T to move their headquarters away from downtown. Part of the problem

1948 freeway plan by the San Francisco Dept. of Planning.

The Embarcadero Freeway had by 1958 put a wall along the waterfront, separating the Ferry Building from the foot of Market it had once served so well.

was that in 1947 40% of U.S. workers relied on public transportation to get to and from their job; by 1963, only 14% did so. This precipitous decline was not unrelated to the conspiracy by General Motors, Standard Oil, Phillips Petroleum, Firestone Tire and Rubber, and Mack Truck to dismantle mass transit and to replace it with private cars, buses, and trucks. They systematically bought up and closed down over 100 trolley lines in forty-five cities (often ripping up the tracks and selling the rights of way); they were indicted by a federal grand jury and eventually fined a nugatory $5,000 each.

Daniel Burnham, who might have had highway engineers in mind, once said: "Make no small plans: they have no magic to stir the blood, and probably themselves will not be realized." Tom Ammiano and Matt Gonzalez were both surprised by the surge of enthusiasm and civic energies generated by their modest plans. It is striking that such mild proposals to mitigate the irrationalities of the city's transit systems and to enhance public space (including undeniably useful schemes such as an Office of Streetscape Design, the encouragement of sidewalk business, and the rationalizing of rail, bus, and tram links) were enough to galvanize the transportation activists of San Francisco. It is, if the Gonzalez manifesto is any measure, a safe prediction that even the youngest of San Franciscans will be living out their lives in the long twilight of automobilism. Apart from the demolition of the Embarcadero Freeway structure, efforts so far to undo the damage citywide have been absurdly inadequate, or illustrate the adage "Be careful what you wish for." The Octavia Street rehabilitation, part of the agonizingly long fallout from the Loma Prieta earthquake, may end up with an outcome actually worse than the original condition, a classic case of half-baked solutions. Bicyclist and pedestrian activists pushed hard for the Octavia Boulevard Plan, finally prevailing in a third local election. Now that the plan is being built, many cyclists are dismayed to find their beloved Valencia Street bikeway once again covered by an ominous freeway overpass, on its way to a nearby touchdown at Market Street. Market Street cyclists, pedestrians, and bus riders in turn will have to wait through extraordinarily long traffic cycles designed to give priority to the movement of cars on and off the freeway.

Of course, nothing short of the abolition of current priorities—of a world organized around the wage form, exploitation, and the production of commodities by commodities—will be able to turn cities into livable places for all their inhabitants. Community-based resistance in its current form, and measures such as transit subsidy fees imposed on big developers, color-coordinated bikeways or showers in corporate offices, to mollify the tide of commuters in their daily ebb and flow—while reasonable enough, are themselves symptoms. They serve only to reveal the poverty of modern cities.

The question, then, is, given that totalizing blueprints, both liberal and stalinist, are for good reasons discredited, how do we truly get out of this mess? Mike Davis has proposed a retrieval of nineteenth-century urbanism, of the utopian writings of Geddes, Bellamy, and Morris. In another medium, and homegrown at that, Mona Caron's Market Street Railway mural on Church Street inspires the imagination in the spirit of P.M.'s *bolo'bolo* or the Goodman brothers' *Communitas*, an anarchist prospectus for the island of Manhattan. These visions of a renovated urbanity are not to be confused either with white ecotopias à la Sierra Club or the piecemeal mitigations and social engineering of capitalist urban planning, which is, under present conditions of re-ghettoizing and incarceration, a branch of criminology. Such artful and utopian poetics needs to be conjoined with ruthless analysis, laying bare the logic that connects automobilism at home to the imperial base-world abroad, that sees the linkage between gated communities in the cities and the prison gulag in the hinterland, that insists on the relation between the dedicating of so much space to private vehicles and the impoverishment of our collective life.

The current state of things will not endure. Still, Gramsci was proved right when he wrote in his notebook that "the crisis consists precisely in the fact that the old is dying and the new cannot be born: in this interregnum a great variety of morbid symptoms appear." Who can deny that this captures the situation of modern cities? Gridlock, SUVs, smog, epidemics of asthma, road rage, carnage. Yet, in this long interregnum, materials for the reappropriation of daily life are to hand, and they must be combined with slow, hard, imaginative work by groups such as the Mission Anti-Displacement Coalition and neighborhood activists across the city. Matt Gonzalez, San Francisco's remedial urbanist, may have left the stage, but we cannot in any case hope for the construction of a better world as long as we continue to surrender popular power to "representatives" in rituals of periodic ratification by ballot. Any democracy worth the name is direct and participatory, and yet the very configuration of capitalist space does not invite public assembly. On the contrary, land use under modernity makes circulation the highest priority. What that means is that struggles over roads and public space will always be at the political edge. The huge open-air demonstrations of 2003 and the Gonzalez campaign, materialized—however briefly—the dead percentages in the polls, took life for a moment off the flickering screen and interrupted business as usual. They imprinted the senses with a reminder of what the public realm could be.

This essay draws on material from a chapter on automobilism, bicycles, and the spaces of modernity in *The Long Theft: Episodes in the History of Enclosure*, to be published by City Lights Books. For helpful comments, thanks are due to Summer Brenner, James Brook, Christina Gerhardt, Joseph Matthews, Michael Weber, and especially to Gray Brechin, Chris Carlsson, and Richard Walker.

What Does Green Mean?

Steven Bodzin

Across the United States, the headlines were breathless. In November 2003, the Green Party was suddenly an aggressive political force. A party known mainly as (nonmember) Ralph Nader's sponsor for the presidency had launched an attack on the Democratic stronghold of San Francisco. Hitting from the left flank, the Greens had come in ahead of a Republican and three Democrats, forcing a runoff for the mayor's throne.

Democrats need not have worried. The Green Party doesn't have a lot of alternatives to offer. Even in its electoral style, it imitates the Democrats to the extent that the "party" is little more than a Democratic environmental club. The local Green Party reflects a political culture in which people refuse to discuss long-term visions, strategies, and tactics, or formulate a specific program. The huge number of San Franciscans who call themselves environmentalists find it easier to stick with short-term goals and small battles rather than figuring out what "green" means.

Volunteers swarmed to support the Green Party's Matt Gonzalez, apparently attracted more by the candidate's cultural markers than by a Green program with specific plans. The fogginess of Gonzalez's platform was clear at the campaign parties. There, one found a diverse crowd: tenant activists who liked Gonzo's stance for rent control, a major loft developer, Joe O'Donoghue, who felt threatened by Democrat Gavin Newsom's plan to attract national big-bucks developers to build large residential high-rises downtown; low-income social justice advocates who hated Newsom's hallmark program to eliminate most cash grants to the poorest residents; and art collectors who liked Gonzalez's monthly salons.

But somewhere in the excitement, the word "green" lost its real-world referent—chlorophyll. Plants. Making the world safe for living things. In fact, the only detailed environmental platform in the campaign was released by Newsom.

In theory, the Green Party embodies an alternative set of values, basing its politics on a healthy environment and social equality. But as individuals, environmentalists have a bad habit of assuming that their personal definition of a "healthy environment" is a shared set of premises; that their vision of the ideal future is identical to that of others in the community of ecological activists.

This has led to internal dissonance and chaos, not just in the San Francisco Green Party, but in other environmental groups, from the Milquetoast San Francisco Tomorrow to the sometimes fiery San Francisco Bicycle Coalition. They all avoid discussions about specific visions of the future, or how to achieve practical goals, or about the tradeoffs people will have to make to achieve a better world. It's more comfortable to have the car-haters and car-drivers, the bosses and workers, the organic gardeners and Costco shoppers all in the same club. What's needed is to adopt, stick with, and evangelize for a clear set of values.

Environmentalists who take part in the city's politics settle for provisional alliances toward small goals that everyone can accept. The Gonzalez campaign was an example of one of these sprawling, inclusive, diluted coalitions. The mass of volunteers who sacrificed for the campaign probably hoped their tall, thirty-something white guy from the Haight would be able to deliver something like fairness and equality for all people. Democrat Gavin Newsom, a tall, thirty-something white guy from Pacific Heights, had been part of the influence-peddling, economic cleansing machine of Mayor Willie Brown. But Gonzalez did little to explain how his Green values could be put into action, given the real political and economic environment of the city.

What would he do about the planning code that requires every new dwelling to provide a car parking space, regardless of expense, even in neighborhoods with tremendous transit availability? Would he call for walkable urban neighborhoods at Hunters Point and Treasure Island, rather than suburban-style vehicle destinations? Would he call for a stricter energy code for new construction? Would he push for better indoor air and more sustainable downtown buildings by allowing openable windows in high-rises?

What about transportation? There is almost no intentional traffic calming in San Francisco. The west span of the Bay Bridge—the section connecting downtown San Francisco to Treasure Island—has no bicycle or pedestrian access, even as the new east span is being built with a multiuse path.

How about economic development, parks, and agriculture? Golden Gate National Recreation Area, a national park in San Fransisco, is the national poster child for parks privatization, with a Lucasfilm studio under construction within the park boundary. The city's biggest new development, Mission Bay, has hung its financial future on the biotech industry, which relies on hazardous materials for research and production. The only large agricultural effort in the past fifteen years, the San Francisco League of Urban Gardeners' five-acre plot on Alemany, has reverted to weeds.

The only environmental platform that Gonzalez put forward on any of these issues was for tidal energy generation. The campaign called for tremendous turbines in San Francisco Bay. The proposal was doomed from the start, sure to be blocked by the regulators that protect endangered salmon, migratory birds, the bay ecosystem, and safe navigation. Not to mention the problems of silt, salt, and barnacles. The absurdity of the proposal only made more distressing the campaign's silence on other, far more achievable, environmental policies.

However, no one seemed distressed. Despite a city full of self-proclaimed environmentalists, elections in San Francisco have never been decided on green issues.

The reason is that no one knows exactly what environmentalism is. There are those who consider air, light, and green space to be environmental priorities—so they support low-density housing, grassy space around public buildings, and "access" to parks. They fight other environmentalists with equally impressive credentials who say that low-density housing forces potential city dwellers into urban sprawl, that many urban green zones are useless except as urinals for people and dogs, and that "access" is a code word for parking lots in city parks.

Still, environmentalists have won victories on water, energy, and transportation in recent years. In 2001, they convinced the local water authorities to work on a decentralized wastewater plan, rather than continuing to pour billions of dollars into the stinking central plant in the largely African-American Bayview neighborhood. The city is moving to close down its existing power plants and replace them with a mix of renewable energy facilities and small cogeneration plants that generate energy while providing steam for large facilities like the airport. And bicycle and pedestrian improvements creep forward citywide.

City policy is supposed to reflect the public's shared values, but the closest the city has to principles for the environment are in a Sustainability Plan, adopted in 1997. But even that plan doesn't provide guidance about how to deal with current issues. Plenty of public policies could be guided by environmental values once they were discussed, understood, and decided on. Car sharing is a perfect example.

City CarShare is a private nonprofit corporation that buys cars and rents them to members by the hour. In addition to rental fees, it charges a monthly membership fee and a high mileage rate. Its founders argue that it allows city dwellers to get rid of their cars, freeing up space for more humans. On the strength of this environmental argument, the company has gotten a valuable subsidy—the city provides free parking spaces at city-owned garages.

There is an environmental argument *against* this group, as well. For one thing, by making car rental more convenient, it could turn people who currently rely on BMW—bike, MUNI, and walk—into drivers. The argument that the group reduces driving overall fails—given the latent demand for vehicle space in the city, anyone who gets rid of a car just makes room for someone else to drive and park one. More important, no one has identified the measurements by which City CarShare can be judged. So no one can analyze whether the city subsidy is being used in the most effective way possible. If the standard were, say, energy savings, would it save more energy to spend city money insulating apartment buildings in low-income neighborhoods? No one knows—no one has even defined standards for environmental spending, much less tried to measure whether CarShare fulfills them.

There are cities where the public has gone through intense community workshops to develop shared visions for the future. Some of the biggest have been in surprising places, like the metro region around Salt Lake City. At these events, urban planners, landscape architects, community leaders, and, in Salt Lake City's case, many thousand members of the public all take part in looking at how different policies could affect the future, what trade-offs would follow from different sets of environmental values. These discussions are usually biased toward local elites and they favor people who like meetings. San Francisco could do even better.

The city has plenty of infrastructure for civic discussion. There are myriad official city bodies with a hearing every night of the week. There are various print publications that are open to op-eds and letters. There's ceaseless on-line discussion of everything from lipstick colors to cracks in the sidewalk. And there are the best-qualified leaders of all, the advocacy groups and political parties.

All over the world, when government leaves a gap, advocacy groups and deviant political parties—so called "civil society"—fill it. San Francisco is a paradox when it comes to civil society. On the one hand, the Sierra Club started here and maintains its headquarters on Second Street. Groups including the Rainforest Action Network, Friends of the Earth, Earth Island Institute, Amazon Watch, and Global Exchange all influence ecological discussions around the world from their offices in the city. The Nature Conservancy, the Natural Resources Defense Council, and the Trust for Public Land all have major branch offices downtown. The New Urbanism movement in urban design and regional planning was born here, descended from the region's 1970s pioneers in off-the-grid and solar energy, such as Sim Van der Ryn, the *Whole Earth Catalog*, Governor Jerry Brown, and the University of California–Berkeley's energy and architecture schools.

Despite this wealth of expertise, there are no local groups that provide effective forums for discussion and debate on the full range of environmental issues. The Golden Gate chapter of the Sierra Club, the League of Conservation Voters, and the League of Women Voters all issue slate cards at election time. Various local environmentalists have at times tried to craft coalitions of local groups, but these coalitions of coalitions have never generated any grassroots excitement.

The Green Party looks like the ideal place for this melding to happen. Environmentalists were attracted to the Gonzalez campaign like squid to a light stick, and there seemed to be a general sense that he was on our side. He would listen to *us*. With a party called Green, *someone* must be writing the environmental policy.

But at this writing, the Web site of the San Francisco Green Party has no *environmental platform*. On one point after another—energy, land use, water supply, water disposal, garbage, and even the hectic, productivity-obsessed workaholism of urban life—there is no official position. Even the land-use platform is vague at best. The national party is just as bad. At least the California Green Party has reasonably specific policy points on its website. For example, "Encourage appropriately higher-density communities and urban infill development as two possible solutions to prevent urban sprawl into agricultural and wilderness areas."

The local party's silence might reflect the same disease that has destroyed the Democratic Party since Vietnam. Rather than recruiting people to a set of principles, the Democrats have pursued the mass of voters. Meanwhile, the Republicans have built a network of talk radio shows, preachers, and ideological nonprofits that recruit people rightward. The Greens seem to be following the Democrats' pattern of chasing voters rather than converting them.

It's unfortunate, but environmentalism in San Francisco is, to use the old phrase, a mile wide and an inch thick. Everyone wants clean air, quick transportation, and nice scenery—for herself. But when push comes to jostle, people still prioritize their conventional values—real-estate value, political power, and convenience—over the greater good. What might be the single biggest thing that a city can do to save the world, providing more housing for people who would otherwise live in sprawl, attracts little support from open-space advocates, affordable-housing activists (who oppose the construction of almost any new market-rate housing and the demolition of even the most anti-urban affordable housing), and legions of NIMBY homeowners. Few environmental groups unambiguously favor such infill. The only large one that does is San Francisco Planning and Urban Research, or SPUR, which continues to take heat for providing intellectual cover for the 1950s and 1960s policy of Negro Removal in SoMa and the Western Addition. The smaller groups that support such policies, Transportation for a Livable City and the Housing Action Coalition, are foundation-sponsored groups with limited grassroots memberships.

What will it take for people in San Francisco to change? We have seen utopian visions in literature and murals. But organization and leadership have been missing, even in the supposedly green Green Party.

There are opportunities for bottom-up discussion and decisionmaking for anyone in San Francisco who wants to be part of it. In addition to the overtly political parties and clubs, the community gardens, the neighborhood emergency response teams, and the over 400 neighborhood associations could all be venues for these discussions. These could be places where people figure out what is meant by "green" and push the environmental discussion ahead for the world. Over a century ago, San Francisco was where the conservationist environmental movement got off the ground, with John Muir and the Sierra Club. The world is ripe for new environmental values. Will San Francisco once again take the lead?

San Francisco's Clean Little Secret

Joel Pomerantz

Surrounded by the salty ocean, San Franciscans take as a given the need for fresh water drawn from mountains on the far side of the state. Hetch Hetchy reservoir, located in Yosemite National Park on the Tuolumne River, is our main source. The Tuolumne, combined with creeks in counties nearer San Francisco, supply 95% of the water we use for our residences, industries, and irrigation. We have this water in our taps as a result of more than a century of San Francisco's political dominance over an arid region, where control of water is indeed the key to life. Spending billions, we take the water 165 miles from a mostly dry area to distribute among ourselves.

The oddest part of this arrangement is not the extravagance of our resource grab, but the redundancy. It is not clear that San Francisco needs this water as much as we claim to. Unbeknownst to most San Franciscans, our little seven square miles contain a remarkable geologic feature, a significant wellspring of quality water. At one time, local sources were our only supply and were taken for granted in their own right. Now, the gushing output of San Francisco springs is diverted into our sewers, replaced in our homes by other sources of water that are more susceptible to central control. Our relationship to water has been determined as much by revenue streams as by streams of water.

As world population surges beyond the levels that planetary fresh water can provide for, the groundwater of San Francisco will quickly become more valuable than oil. If we look closely at what we have and use our "native" creativity, we could establish our city as a self-sufficient user of sustainable local resources, accomplishing the transition over a relatively short period of time. We could restore some of San Francisco's natural lakes and expose buried creeks to the daylight. We could possibly even return Hetch Hetchy Valley—which environmentalist John Muir compared favorably to the beauty of Yosemite Valley—to its original condition.

Water resources have been notably absent from the platform planks of election campaigns, even those of recent progressive candidates. Yet we do not need to start from scratch. Best practices are already codified, many studies have been done, a master plan has even been written (and then shelved) by the Public Utilities Commission. At this point, we need a broader education about our heretofore secret water options, and a cooperative path into the fragile future. It is time to insert this pivotal issue into the local political agenda. Then we need to fight like hell to steer our new policies past the pitfalls of profit and corporate control, which have so thoroughly poisoned our present system.

Aqueous Ubiquitous?

Here, in our peninsular paradise, we see, feel, and use water daily in a hundred forms. The tide caresses our shore, three-fourths of our border with the outside world. Fishing lines, swaddled in damp fog, are dangled off generations of piers into the salty bay. With each winter storm, surf pounds Ocean Beach leaving patterned blips on the seismograph at the Randall Museum. On sunny days, the mists and sounds of fountain spatter make our public spaces seem grander. Parks and golf courses are coaxed green by old rain sucked from the ground.

Rain washes oil, left on the concrete by manifold thousands of dripping cars, into the sewers. Clay skeet falls dayglo and shattered from the Pacific Rod and Gun Club into fresh Lake Merced, once an estuarial inlet of the sea. Gurgling through colorful pipes, water extracts acrid and metallic chemical discard from refineries and circuit board manufacturers, mostly now banned from direct release into the bay by policies developed in the past few decades.

A Chinatown fishmonger sprays down the scented sidewalk at closing time. Meanwhile, inside, the president appears on a television floated from its Asian assembly line in an airtight container over rising seas. He disingenuously declares a national effort to harness hydrogen energy from "abundant" water.

We charge ourselves monthly to draw clean water into our homes. It swirls to the left or right down our toilets, sloshes grime off dinnerware in our sinks—water used once and then thrown away. By opening the faucet, we pull it effortlessly from distant reservoirs through aging pipelines and brittle concrete aqueducts snaking miles over active faults and under bay sediments. Convinced our taps are contaminated, we suckle expensive "pure" water from bottles made with estrogen-mimicking plastic contaminants. We somehow derive a sense of purity from famous springs named on the label, though it is often simply trucked in from distant spigots dispensing worse water than our own municipal taps.

But do we really understand the water around us? While plentiful, most of it presents a great challenge to use, because of sea salt. To drink and manufacture, irrigate and bathe, we require low-saline fresh water—traditionally extracted from rivers. It would seem that all we need to do, if we wish to drink fresh water, is find a sweet water source such as a river.

Where is the nearest river? If you live in San Francisco and want to escape the pressures of city life, you have probably gone north for a visit to the Russian River region, or east to the Stanislaus River in the Central Valley. Probably you have seen the Delta of the Sacramento and San Joaquin Rivers, where High Sierra snow melt meanders at sea level through drained tracts like Bethel "Island." These two rivers, the Sacramento and the San Joaquin, join forces and flow through the Carquinez Straits, bringing most of Northern California's precious fresh surface water to commingle with the salty tides of San Pablo Bay and the San Francisco estuary itself, which we refer to as simply "the Bay."

And, indeed, many Bay Area municipalities draw their drinking water from these rivers, always threatened by salt incursion as reduced river volume brings salt water farther upstream.

Some of that reduction of flow is due to San Francisco's use of Hetch Hetchy. Our municipal water leaves the river system high in the Sierra Nevada, where three 75-year-old dams arrest the Tuolumne headwaters. These reservoirs gather water from a prime watershed more than twelve times the size of San Francisco. They pool the annual cycles of snow melt into drowned granite valleys now called Lake Eleanor, Cherry Lake, and Hetch Hetchy.

In a sense, we have exactly what we need; a fresh sweet river can be found by simply turning the faucet. When we do this trick, we get even more than that river, because the nearer Pilarcitos Creek and Alameda Creek watersheds make their contributions to our system from San Mateo and Alameda Counties, respectively. Turn the tap, get a river and two creeks. Spared the journey they once took along winding, lush banks, "our" water is diverted into the artificial rivers of the Hetch Hetchy Project before being distributed within San Francisco through 1,200 miles of water mains.

On the way, it slakes the thirst of about 4 million households and businesses in dozens of Bay Area municipalities—and millions of other users in other parts of California. Residential and industrial users of northern watersheds have addresses as far away as Los Angeles. A statewide system of aqueducts brings Central Valley water to the foot of the Tehachapis, hundreds of miles south of San Francisco, where it is pumped over the mountains into the even drier and far thirstier L.A. basin.

Money and power motivated entrepreneurial engineers to establish the complex Hetch Hetchy system. However, the earliest water sources for our peninsular village-turned-boomtown were right here in our lowlands and along the slopes of Twin Peaks. Some of these sources are easily perceptible—and some are thoroughly hidden. In fact, San Francisco has a remarkable native water source that is so out of sight and mind that we may as well call it a secret.

Mystery Upwelling

Into our briny city we bring potable supplies of anywhere from 75 to 100 million gallons a day. We also enjoy seasonal rains. Adding to those, water burbles up through our geologic substrate. While it is easy to see the reservoirs, aqueducts, and delivery trucks importing water, and natural to accept the rains and their contribution to the water tables, our unusual—though productive—springs and seeps have somehow evaded general notice. Unless you have walked Caselli Street or Pemberton Steps in the early morning quiet, you have probably never heard the babbling brook in the sewer. And if you have, you may have thought it the result of early risers showering. But it is, in fact, Dolores Creek.

Those San Franciscans with a more intimate sense of history talk about its creeks—Lobos, Islais, and Mission Creeks being the best known. These and other surface creeks and tributaries flowed unimpeded in the city's early decades. Spanning many centuries before that, five or six permanent villages were located along their banks. These are not seasonal creeks. The flowing surface waterways of San Francisco's past were year-round affairs, a detail that can be difficult to comprehend in a city which receives no rain for more than half of each year. In an article I wrote in 1994 about the "Wiggle," a stream-flattened valley favored by bicyclists intent on bypassing hills, I mistakenly implied that Sans Souci Creek flowed only in the wet seasons. I never received a single correction, despite the evidence presented (shortly after publication) by a construction hole left gaping all summer at Scott and Haight Streets, where fresh running water could always be seen.

What we forget, standing on impermeable pavement* is that water still exists beneath these streets, developments, and sandy lots. What once flowed in surface channels, though now buried in the ground or steered into sewer pipes, is still there somewhere. Tens of millions of gallons of fresh water each day (probably over three million just in the North Mission area) flow right below

---

*Very little rainwater permeates our largely paved city. Instead, it goes into the sewers that flow to the bay. Once a source of fresh replenishment to water tables in our soils, this resource could be renewed by recently developed, permeable types of pavement. The San Francisco Department of Public Works has resisted replacing current surfaces with this new type, saying that unexpected problems may arise with any new product.

our feet from artesian springs of potable water. 'Artesian' is the term for sources that rise above the water table to the surface due to their own hydrologic pressure, needing no pumping.

Adding yet another layer to the mystery, massive surges of groundwater, much of it potable, travel continuously just beneath us from related "subartesian" sources that even historically never came fully to the surface. We easily overlook these "creeks" since they have never come into view to receive formal names.

If people think about local groundwater they generally think of the Westside Basin aquifer, because it is visible where its water table meets the surface at Lake Merced. The Westside Basin gets its water from rain, irrigation runoff, and other local, seasonal sources descending through the sand, soil, and fractured rock. It needs the rain for replenishment. In contrast, the fresh spring waters indefatigably flowing on the eastern slopes of Twin Peaks are a wondrous geologic feature, of unknown origin and potentially great benefit to the city. This water comes in quantities and seasons unlikely to be associated with local rains. Further study is needed to determine its ultimate source.

Between the scores of true artesian springs and the city's underground flows fed by the same sources, San Francisco has, heading through our soils and sewers to the bay, enough water to supply many, or most, of our needs. With the Westside Basin rainwater aquifer added to these remarkable east slope sources, it appears that graywater recycling and treatment technology, along with conservation, could tip the balance to make meeting our entire municipal thirst feasible—relying only on local sources.

The Hayes River

Though ambling slowly, the mighty Hayes River is wide and voluminous, spreading through the alluvial sediments, bay muds, and landfill under the Civic Center and Downtown neighborhoods with a hydromorphology not unlike Florida's everglades. It broadsides Market Street, encountering a long concrete subway tunnel that interrupts its gait. So copious are the waters of the Hayes that, to protect their investment from damage, BART runs "dewatering" pumps day and night in the Powell Street BART station. Removing, each week, 2.5 million gallons of tested, high-quality, potable groundwater (into the sewer!) the transit agency keeps the Hayes from flooding the tracks.

The Hayes, then, is our nearest natural river, a dispersed underground flow that descends through Hayes Valley from "headwaters" (more precisely, hundreds of upwellings, springs, and seeps) in the area near Lone Mountain and the University of San Francisco, and also along the hillsides of Alamo Square. On average, the river is about fifteen feet below surface, and much deeper and wider than most surface rivers. It finally meets the surface South of Market, where it enters the bay beneath China Basin and the even-numbered piers. Originally, it came to the surface in a marsh at Mission and Seventh Streets. The extent of this slow fluid influx is such that hundreds of landowners along this waterway originally used private wells, built right into their foundations, to supply all their water needs.

A few buildings, such as the Olympic Club headquarters at 524 Post Street, and the California Automobile Association on Van Ness Avenue, still use Hayes water today. Many Civic Center buildings employ full-time pumping operations to keep their basements dry. The public fountains at United Nations Plaza and Fillmore Center are also fed by the waters of the Hayes.

The Hayes River still delivers quality, drinkable water to many areas. In the 1800s its wells, along with those tapping the Mission Creek water table, supplemented Lobos Creek in the Presidio to meet the needs of a growing city. Lobos Creek supplied San Francisco as the city's main Gold Rush water source from 1851 to 1895, through an enterprise named Mountain Lake Water Company.

Lobos Creek supplied San Francisco as the city's main Gold Rush water source from 1851 to 1895, running a flume around Black Point, seen here in the 1870s.

Misson Creek pictured here as it might have looked in the 1850s in an artist's rendering. The Centre Street Bridge in the left foreground is today's 16th Street.

Most of us go along unaware of these precious naturally flowing wonders, more concerned about what our guests wish to drink than with the specific source of the substance on which we depend. Even those of us devoted to environmental efforts usually overlook the native wellsprings of our coastal ridge formations.

More Than a Drop to Drink

We have found, much closer, one river and two creeks—Hayes, Mission, Lobos. Serving water to locals for ages, they were adopted by new Spanish- and English-speaking arrivals and then by the polyglot fortune hunters of the Gold Rush, all long before the Hetch Hetchy system was set up for its centralized dispensing of water and hydroelectric power. These local sources, something of a secret today, produced sufficient potable water to satisfy San Francisco's basic needs as it grew to a half million residents. Shortly thereafter, greed and political ambition began to change this landscape. But before we examine that shift, we should pause for some revisions in our own narrow perceptions of a city severed from nature.

On April 5, 1776, Juan Bautista de Anza's party rowed up Mission Creek from the bay to establish a mission. April 5 is the feast day of Our Lady of

Sorrows (Nuestra Señora de los Dolores)—thus the name Mission Dolores. The creek they entered wound through marshes to a tidal lagoon and then into a flowing freshwater lake, called Laguna de Manantial. The creek probably spanned a width of forty feet or more and, at 100 to 200 cubic feet per second, offered enough current to require real effort in the arms of the rowers. The water was sweet and excellent for drinking (as it still is today).

The first Spanish soldiers, coming also in 1776, set themselves up near the Golden Gate in time to keep Russian outposts from expanding down the coast of California. They took their water from El Polin Spring, which still flows from a small circle of stones in the Presidio. (Later the Presidio drank from Lobos Creek, which in its natural state flows out at Baker Beach.)

Newcomers settled in four districts at first, then later populations filtered in to connect those four. The town of Yerba Buena started on a cove near the current Bay Bridge anchorage, getting water from shallow wells.

And then, after the Gold Rush swelled Yerba Buena and the Mission with urban life, successful prospectors and financiers began building "country homes" around and beyond the Mission, near Islais Creek and its tributary, Precita Creek. Islais Creek today still flows from headwaters at McAteer High School through Glen Canyon, then in culverts beneath Interstate Highway 280 to the bay.

The combined water sources around Mission Creek, more than twice as voluminous as the Hayes River, flow directly from the steep sides of Twin Peaks through Upper Market neighborhoods. Unlike the Hayes, some flowed on the surface.

Mission Creek was navigable until 1874. By the early twentieth century, the lagoons and creeks of the Mission had been filled with trash and 1906 earthquake rubble, sold as private lots and built upon. But the water was still there, tapped by homes and businesses before the Hetch Hetchy system of subscribed and vended water superseded it. According to a 1913 survey of 700 San Francisco wells, Mission district wells produced more than 1.2 million gallons per day. The survey, one of the first projects of city Engineer Michael M. O'Shaughnessy, began the long process of replacing those wells with Hetch Hetchy Project water.

The springs that feed Mission Creek can still be seen and heard all along the inclines and alleys of Mount Olympus and upper Eureka Valley. At Clayton Street, where the main waterway's path crosses Market Street, permanently wet and mossy curbs attest to what was once a small cascade. New Century

Beverage (later Pepsi) at Seventeenth Street and Valencia where the police station now stands, supplied their bottling operations into the 1990s from free and potable waters flowing under their property. Atlas Home Laundry linen cleaning service, which was just replaced by a new development at Seventeenth and Hoff (between Mission and Valencia Streets), drew 10,000 gallons a day of groundwater before it closed.

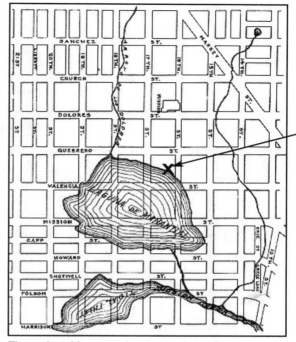

The earliest Mission padres began their efforts on a site that is now the corner of Albion and Camp Streets (X) in the Mission District (once the edge of the fresh lake, a bronze placard marks the spot today).

Mission Dolores is a lasting tribute to the abundance of this productive watershed. It was erected near the banks of a large lake fed by Dolores Creek (flowing approximately along Caselli and then Eighteenth Street). Another pond at Belcher Street (near Church and Market) supported an Ohlone village, from which it is likely that the builders of Mission Dolores were conscripted. That pond was fed by Sans Souci Creek from what is now called the Lower Haight. Below the pond, it flowed east down Fourteenth Street to meet the Mission Creek estuary at Fifteenth and Shotwell, where the ground is still sinking dramatically on the site of an oblong marshy inlet (see map above).

Power Struggle

Water is our right, but it is not a secured right. It is fraudulent for anyone to claim legitimate ownership of the air, the sea, or space itself. Yet we can see from historical events that these claims are inevitable. The prime example is land, which English courts of the sixteenth through eighteenth centuries allowed to be taken from the "commons" and converted into private property. Technological resources follow the same pattern. Where television receivers were once all that was needed by viewers of the public airwaves, cable TV giants have created a pay-to-view culture so entrenched that we risk water-cooler or schoolroom shame if we do not participate. It is sadly axiomatic, under our society's obsessively monetary value system, that land and nominal public space, as well as air, public airwaves, the Internet, and even knowledge itself, can be controlled by those charging for their use. So goes the story of water.

Examples from our own sordid town history indicate that these same resource struggles and abuses have permeated local politics for some time, dominating the agenda of power brokers here and in the state capital (occasionally reaching the federal level, with the unusual approval of a municipal reservoir in a national park). The record paints a less-than-rosy picture of San Francisco, past and present. Corruption, neglect, and simple bad policy led to our current predicament, in which private utilities have held lucrative sway over public decisions despite ongoing efforts—partly successful—to municipalize their services.

San Francisco's population grew quickly in the nineteenth century. Increased local demand prompted rivalries, exacerbated by boom-town greed. The first big shift from using only the wells and streams within our city limits was the tapping of surface water supplies from nearby counties. Under the control of speculator George Ensign, a small private company called Spring Valley Water was able to convince the state legislature to extend it rights of eminent domain. This legal power allowed Spring Valley to condemn and seize whole watersheds. In the 1860s the company built a system bringing water northward from Pilarcitos Creek on the slopes of Mount Montara in newly created San Mateo County. Ensign and his successors, notably Swiss engineer Hermann Schussler and the financiers William Ralston and William Sharon, managed to outwit a plan for city municipalization, gaining control of Alameda Creek in Sunol for the Spring Valley Water Company. Both of these creeks still supply our taps (making up 18 percent of Hetch Hetchy Project water).

Ralston and his partners launched a campaign to create large civic parks—green spaces from sandy lots—to leverage their property investments. In order to supply the necessary water, these private investors and their successors developed and zealously dominated a regional water system from 1858 until 1930.

The Spring Valley Water Company was reviled by the populace for its high prices, spotty quality, corruption, and imperial attitude, which intentionally mimicked ancient Rome's regional domination. Historian Gray Brechin described Spring Valley Water Company as "the state's most powerful monopoly and nearly as hated as the Southern Pacific Railroad would be later." Public outrage against Spring Valley for its abysmal water quality and service was first used to get public financing for the Hetch Hetchy Project in the 1910s. In 1932 the hated company was purchased by the city, in spite of an outcry over junk-bond bailout profits for investors.

Spring Valley does not employ EXACTLY this method; but it gets there just the same.

1889 cartoon from *The Wasp*, lampooning the mugging given San Francisco residents by the owner of Spring Valley Water Company and his bought-and-paid-for allies on the Board of Supervisors.

It would be a mistake to imagine that the ambitious dam and aqueduct project with the alliterative name is just about water. The dream of Hetch Hetchy, both capitalist and populist, was propelled in large part by changes in the technology of electricity. The 'teens saw the beginnings of an effort to electrify autocarriages, locomotives, factories, musical instruments, moving picture projectors, and the most magical wired invention of all, radio. It was in this frenzied context that, in 1912, Michael M. O'Shaughnessy was hired as city engineer to create the tunnels and overhead lines of the electric streetcars and develop the Hetch Hetchy system. One selling point of the expensive Hetch Hetchy system was certainly its water supply, but another of great significance was its promised "low-cost" generation of hydroelectric power. As with nuclear power promotion schemes in the latter half of the twentieth century, unrealistic "cheap energy" promises were made to justify large public investments in a system eventually to be controlled mostly by private hands.

Surging Demand, Tenuous Supply

Natural San Francisco is ready for a new look. We cannot, however, simply reclaim the pre-urban past. Circumstances have changed, both physically and politically, and a global struggle for water is brewing.

Most people on earth live in what we tend to call "developing countries." Per capita wealth in these places, depending how it is measured, is between one-eighth and one-hundredth of ours, and the disparity is growing. Meanwhile, the gap is encouraged and cultivated by companies whose shareholders and power brokers benefit. Global water management firms, like the locally based Bechtel Corporation* and Vice President Dick Cheney's friends at Halliburton, are carrying out further consolidation of their authority over supplies and delivery systems as water becomes more important to global markets.

A comparison of water demand and availability (accessible water) shows that whoever controls this resource can control human living conditions.

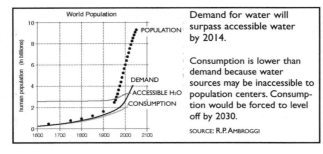

Demand for water will surpass accessible water by 2014.

Consumption is lower than demand because water sources may be inaccessible to population centers. Consumption would be forced to level off by 2030.

SOURCE: R. P. AMBROGGI

The oil-water comparison can be tempting. Although both are coveted by powerful interests, and both are waning resources relative to demand, there are two differences that rupture the parallel. First, water is needed for life. Second, water has a self-renewing cycle. These differences suggest that control of the delivery system and perceived rights are far more potent for water than for oil, where control of the actual substance is paramount.

All resources suffer from limitations on supply, even if we see them, at first, as limitless. We cannot expect to always have available that which we take

---

* In 1999, in a closed-door, single bidder process, Bolivia's government privatized the water supply of its third largest city, Cochabamba, by turning over all water rights, including the right to collect rain, to a Bechtel Corporation subsidiary. Immediate and extreme price increases sparked a popular uprising that was repressed violently by government troops. In April 2000 Bechtel was forced to leave. The next year, Bechtel filed a legal demand with the World Bank for $25 million against the Bolivian people, compensation for its lost opportunity to make future profits. In February 1996 and June 1997 bank officials made privatization a condition of hundreds of millions of dollars in loans and debt relief to Bolivia.

for granted today—not even those of us living in rich, selfish societies with unscrupulous military might. This is clearly true for water resources. Water supplies are diminishing in quality while under the strain of increased demand. Aquifers the world around are contaminated by unhealthy practices and neglect.

In Colorado, accidentally released plutonium from the former Rocky Flats nuclear bomb trigger factory has permanently destroyed the integrity of the groundwater supply. Water now being widely used for Denver area swimming pools and playground sprinklers has been shown to contain plutonium, deadly in minute doses.

San Francisco's water, too, could be irreparably contaminated by toxic waste from military and corporate malpractice. These extralegal institutions have bequeathed us the Southern Pacific railyard (Mission Bay Development), Hunters Point Shipyard, the Presidio, and other toxic sites, some recently catalogued by the *San Francisco Bayview* newspaper.

After nearly 6,000 years of innovations in urban living, humans are still tossing our waste casually over our collective shoulder into the absorbent land, streams, bays, and oceans when we can get away with it. To be fair, we are not really so casual. If we were simply leaving our waste where it fell, the way most organisms do, we might be better off. Instead, we carefully gather the fast-increasing and ever more poisonous discards of our "advanced" consumer culture and, often for a short-term profit, deposit them right into our most precious of all life-sustaining resources.

Where we don't actually throw our detritus and excrement into the life-giving waters, we amass them where the rain and aquifers can seep, percolate, and leach. This slightly delayed sludge of havoc will bring eventual disaster in the unforgiving rigors of species survival and ecological balance.

The city's Altamont landfill is monitored for toxic incursions into groundwater. But our local wetlands, water tables, ponds, and creeks that took in the refuse of the last 150 years will be harder to clean. The longer we wait, the more the polluting underground plumes expand. San Francisco has hundreds of sites where contamination of groundwater is already known. Some are being targeted for cleanup. We have yet to fully understand the effects of our past transgressions, but if we are to survive, we must make controlling this malignancy an immediate priority.

Until only a few decades ago, still ripe in the memories of our living elders, the bay was both the sewage system and the trash heap for every town along its shores. Ever since the first Gold Rush ship fell to pieces abandoned in the feculent San Francisco harbor, we have become accustomed to taking the easy way out of this mess. Or is it the easy way in?

Final Draft

Occasionally public entities set out to accomplish noble goals for the people. Such was apparently the case in the mid-1990s, when the Public Utility Commission (PUC) prepared a document called *San Francisco Groundwater Master Plan*. Published in 1997, it displays the label "Final" across its cover, but it may as well have been labeled "Dead in the Water."

It provides a thorough initial evaluation of San Francisco's groundwater resources, complete with goals and recommendations for action. The master plan's sensible starting goals have yet to be integrated into the daily activities of PUC and Public Works Department staff, let alone acknowledged as official policy:

- Protect and enhance groundwater quality
- Coordinate groundwater use
- Protect and conserve lakes and streams
- Improve ability to deliver water in emergencies
- Maximize groundwater use

Implementation and funding recommendations in the document are augmented by maps, diagrams, and charts showing water resources. Though the master plan does discuss the "long-term strategy" of capturing groundwater produced by dewatering operations, and shows how we might consistently capture 5 to 7 million more gallons a day from certain northern sites in the Westside Basin without serious detriment to water table levels, it falls short in its evaluation of subsurface water from artesian and subartesian sources. In other words, the plan, though potentially useful, falls far short of recognizing the remarkable geologic features of San Francisco's east slope watersheds.

All things geologic in San Francisco run in vast northwest-by-southeast patterns, a result of the tilted rock layers of a fault zone. Twin Peaks is composed of cherts and other dense materials of the Franciscan formation. Parallel to that and on its east side, a layer of softer serpentine runs from the Golden Gate to Hunters Point. It is at the juncture of these two layers that water emerges in artesian wells, springs, and wide underground flows.

The survey of wells contained in the PUC publication is not as exhaustive as

O'Shaughnessy's 1913 roster but the master plan does track some current usage. After predicting opportunities for construction site dewatering and identifying a couple of ongoing pump sites, the plan acknowledges that there are better uses for that water, now pumped directly into the downtown sewers. It neglects, however, to assess new well water possibilities in the eastern half of the city, despite affirming the high quality of the water involved.

Stone Soup

Within the precarious political and ecological context of our favorite precious liquid, we still face the practical challenge of supplying ourselves clean, tasty, potable water, here in San Francisco.

Despite a climate of low electoral confidence and even lower participation, there is a national movement to bring resource decisions out of the hands of officials who conspire with private interests to hide important political choices. Environmental mitigation programs have made it harder to fill and develop wetlands. Activists and other empowered citizens are taking action in record numbers, mainly as volunteers. *The Volunteer Monitor*, a national newsletter for thousands of watershed monitoring organizations, has tripled in size over the past decade. Quality of life gadflies have joined environmentalists to bring our lakes and streams back to health and visibility. There is ample reason for optimism.

Some of our optimism can be drawn from the power of recognizing past mistakes. Given all the high quality fresh water found within San Francisco's city limits, still sloshing in thousands of abandoned wells dotting flooded—if hid-

Shed on Islais Creek, c. 1870, near today's Glen Park BART station.

den—watersheds, why did we convert entirely to a system which requires that we pay "providers" for our water? We suffer a collective amnesia, crafted over the past century, preventing our recognition that water, like the air and sea, is right here for us to use, communally owned for no one's profit.

If we were to focus our abundant civic pride and technological prowess on the problem, we could make this city a model of self-sufficiency. Local water advocates must unite with the efforts recently taken up by municipal power advocates and decentralized electrical generation advocates. Our new Department of the Environment could assist in redirecting the PUC toward a "stone soup" of available sources for our water supply: conservation, recycled water (including greywater), rainwater, artesian and subartesian water, and surface water.

Surface water in particular deserves special attention. Not only should we be using local creek waters in our taps, we should be returning it to the land (not directly to the bay) either cleaned of our mess, or via active wastewater treatment marshes (doubling as wildlife sanctuaries) such as those developed in Bolinas and Arcata, California. The goals of using groundwater do not have to conflict with the goals of returning our surface streams to health.

I spent part of my childhood in Washington, D.C., where Rock Creek Park sets the standard for natural urban surface flows. Yet in the drier Bay Area, I had developed lower expectations. Then, in 1991, one of my students showed me the wonder of Strawberry Creek, daylighted by the Urban Creeks Council after seventy years in sewer culverts. Ever since that day— when my heart leapt upon first encounter with a restored surface creek— I have felt certain that similar rehabilitation projects are inevitable in San Francisco. Regenerating those waterways adds to the quality of our daily existence, the viability of the biosphere, and the momentum toward redress of past destruction.

The overhaul of obscured and corrupted natural systems through restoration of local lakes, creeks, wells, and springs is not just a dream. Thanks to neighbors implementing their vision of balance, Lake Merced now has a better chance to survive. The Presidio's Crissy Field wetlands restoration is a qualified success and has been an important experiment. South of the airport, reclamation of Bair Island wetlands, once considered an expansion area for Foster City, is well under way. Events—and even policies—are conspiring to bring in the next phase of water systems renewal. The daylighting of Islais Creek, which runs deep in the landfilled valley beneath the Glen Park BART station, is currently being promoted by hydrologists and activists at the Neighborhood Parks Council through a carefully drawn Glen Park Community Plan. Muralist Mona Caron has taken some of this vision and made it tangible in her mural at Church and Fifteenth Streets. In the context of a renewed city, she depicts what might be the Hayes River, brought into view as an urban waterway crossing beneath Market Street.

Creeks and falls that once tumbled year-round down the slopes of Twin Peaks still stream along, but are relegated to the storm sewers. Pumps on backup generators extract seepage from the basements of our civic buildings. Abandoned wells join the cisterns and neighborhood fire protection reservoirs in a network of underground water supplies awaiting an emergency.

The flow of hidden waters in San Francisco may be one key to the sustainability of the city. Yet, our leaders—and by that I mean our profit-and-loss leaders—still encourage us to spend public funds on private repair of quake-prone aqueducts and reservoirs, while obediently paying our redoubling utility bills. Urban dwellers, removed from a sense of nature, too often take water for granted and leave it to the experts. The time is ripe to make our connection to nature healthier.

The absence of these discussions during recent mayoral campaigns may temporarily reinforce their relegation to the realm of idealistic fantasies, but the politicos don't have the final say here. A hardier and truer solution is possible—and by embracing it we can induce local politicians to subscribe. We must integrate our most basic natural resource into our activist agenda, to succeed in the long-term challenges of political control and bioregional harmony.

Abundant local water is a resource we can use, along with solar and wind power, to create a fully decentralized infrastructure independent of the "marketplace." Will profiteering control these resources and determine our reaction (or inaction) in handling future shortages and past blunders? Or will we begin to work outside that system, as our own voluntary leaders?

We are ready to shift our outlook, our laws and our infrastructure using the guideposts of independence and self-reliance rather than financial reward. To create a sustainable, decentralized system, fortified against corporate vandalism, we must quickly move beyond the PUC's stagnant Groundwater Master Plan to implement a much grander vision. We can reclaim our water, decentralize its distribution, and divest PG&E of its control over our electricity, too. We can integrate our urban lives back into the web of nature. Imagine walking—or rowing—along a living creek through *that* San Francisco!

Thanks to Anna Sojourner and Beth Goldstein for inspiration.
Photos & Mission Creek art courtesy Greg Gaar collection. *Wasp* image courtesy Chris Carlsson.

Toward a Copyright-Free Zone?

Rick Prelinger

In the spirit of Weegee, the 1930s crime photographer, my friend Bill sleeps days and works the streets by night. Once a still photographer, now a video shooter, he monitors San Francisco police and fire radio and races to the scene of shootings, fires, and serious accidents. Other people's bad luck could be his good fortune; if he gets striking footage and beats the others to the TV stations, he'll get a sale. But most of his nights are spent waiting for something to happen.

It was just such a night a few months back. There had been a tragic shooting in the Western Addition and Bill was waiting for the body to be carried out (the "removal," as TV news assignment editors offhandedly call it). Biding his time, he idly panned his camera past a group of neighborhood bystanders waiting for the same reason. Suddenly the group erupted in protest. "Don't shoot us," they said. "No cameras. Copyright notice! Copyright notice!"

Their law was all wrong, but they certainly knew the C-word. Most of us do now. In the first years of the twenty-first century, copyright's gone mainstream. What happened? How did copyright quit being a specialized field for lawyers and a tiny group of people reprinting public domain works, and become an issue of mass concern?

One sure way to polarize people and motivate their intense interest is first to give them the ability to do something, whether it's smoking, late-night dancing, posting digital pictures of national scandals online, or downloading music, and then threaten them with fines and arrest for doing it. That's just what's happened around copyright. The Internet has given all of us the ability to produce, distribute, and share cultural and intellectual creations as never before, something quite threatening to a number of media companies who'd like to control the publishing process as they once did. New creative and distributive tools are challenging old-fashioned businesses to come up with new business models, but rather than innovating they enlist the services of the state to crack down on innovation. And when seniors and twelve-year-olds alike receive threatening letters from the RIAA, that's the kind of repression that makes news and breeds resistance.

As with the social revolutions of the 1960s and 1970s, San Francisco has become a key center in a geography of resistance to ruling ideas about the control of culture. Creators, scholars, activists, and geeks are critiquing copyright and associated issues from many different angles, and together they're propagating new and infectious ideas and projects that have already changed the way we interact with our cultures. This movement has heroes, but not real leaders; it's a diverse group moving in the same general direction. We define ourselves in space (San Francisco in opposition to New York and Los Angeles) and in time (your generational cohort generally determines what side you're on in the copyright wars).

As Lawrence Lessig puts it in his 2004 book *Free Culture*, "the battles that now rage regarding life on-line have fundamentally affected 'people who aren't online.'" Neither the information economy nor the cultural industries are controlled from San Francisco, but San Franciscans are resisting centralized cultural control and advancing a new vision of culture that's not based on virtual locks, fences, and gates. Like-minded on many issues, disagreeing on others, this group hews neither to classically progressive positions nor to *Wired* magazine-style techno-libertarianism. But reformists, radicals, and abolitionists all agree that current "intellectual property" laws and distribution practices need to evolve so that free speech and fair use can prevail over centralized control. And many believe that changing the way that culture is distributed can open the way to reconsidering how property is distributed.

Living where politics is just as much (if not more) about daily life than it is about elections, where artists and activists collaborate and switch roles, and where not everyone's been scared away from thinking in utopian terms, San Franciscans have a long record of challenging dominant thought on copyright and what lawyers like to call "intellectual property." San Francisco filmmakers, artists, writers, and musicians revel in a long-flourishing tradition of artistic appropriation, sampling, collage, and détournement. While some still believe in the myth of the lone creator, this town is where the idea of "one big remix" has legs. Collage and related practices continually resurface in new genres and generations, addressing not just bits of pieces of recycled content, but also questions of copyright, technology, and power.

It would take a whole book to credit even some of the people and groups who've worked with appropriation and collage in San Francisco, but here are just a few.

In text, the "language poets," who evolved as a group starting in the 1970s, frequently use recycled text, combining formalist concerns about language and poetics with an interest in power and how it's propagated and sustained through language. Many in this group, like Ron Silliman, Lyn Hejinian,

232

Steve Benson, and Carla Harryman resided in San Francisco, and now live in ubiquity via the Internet.

San Francisco's a center of found-footage filmmaking, a town where archaeological sensibilities, a dose of Dada, and a healthy disregard for copyright have given birth to some of the great works of cut-up and recycled cinema, including those of Bruce Conner, Craig Baldwin, and many others. Recycled cinema may be a passing fad elsewhere, but it's got legs in San Francisco, where no Dumpster containing old film is ignored for long and where archives such as Stephen Parr's Oddball Film and Video/San Francisco Media Archive and my own online collection at the Internet Archive give footage to artists and independents without charge.

In recent years the lowering costs of video production have made it possible for community-based and activist producers, many working collectively, to critique corporate and official media while freely appropriating its imagery. Whispered Media's *We Interrupt This Empire* (2003) shows San Francisco's response to the U.S. bombing and invasion of Iraq, using newly shot material, network TV coverage, feature film clips, and the sounds of police radio transmissions. Appropriated footage is used transformatively, forcing dominant media into confrontation with the critique that it generally does its best to escape. *The Fellowship of the Ring of Free Trade* (2002) and *The Lord of the Rings: The Twin Towers* (2004), two delightful examples of illegal art, are pseudonymously-created short films that use "revised" subtitles and skillful editing to prove that the blockbuster *Lord of the Rings* epics are in fact antiauthoritarian and antiglobalist parables. And recent outdoor screenings in Dolores Park associated with antiwar demonstrations have been multi-course feasts of appropriated imagery, propagating the idea that mass media images gain new value when remixed against their original intentions.

Disrespect for advertising, especially the outdoor variety, has long been a proud San Francisco tradition. From "Forest Dispenser" stickers on vending machines filled with ad-swollen newspapers to "updated" and "corrected" billboards along the Central Freeway, artists have done their best to associate corporate trademarks and ad campaigns with the less visible activities of the corporations they promote. The implication here for "intellectual property" law is that trademarks aren't sacrosanct, and appear in public subject to the same processes of commentary and critique as other speech.

San Francisco musicians and composers not only have historically played leading roles in working with found and appropriated material, but in engaging copyright laws as well. Negativland, a band from San Francisco and the Pacific Northwest, defended its fair use rights in a proceeding whose twists, turns, and lengthy duration make it one of the all-time great legal pranks. Countless DJs, hip-hop, electronic, and experimental musicians here (not to mention radio artists and activists) have explored the infinite permutations of remixing and sampling.

What ties together all these artists and activists who work in different genres is the acceptance that creation is a synthetic process, that the seeds of new work fall out of old, that culture doesn't form in isolation, and that performing and distributing work don't necessarily constitute billable events.

Assisting artists and geeks alike is a growing community of lawyers who seek to enable, rather than inhibit, an undammed cultural stream. Organizations like the Electronic Frontier Foundation, a San Francisco public-interest group dedicated to extending constitutional free-speech and fair-use rights online, work to defend and assert the rights of consumers and creators when these rights are threatened by aggressive rightsholders and agencies of government. EFF has also directly addressed issues of political empowerment and modernization, involving itself actively in the recent exposure of computerized voting machines and their disenfranchising potential. The Berkeley Center for Law and Technology (at UC Berkeley) and the Center for Internet and Society at Stanford function both as think tanks and as legal resources for people breaking new ground. Both centers have contributed time and talent to recent court challenges of overlong and overbroad copyright laws.

Stanford Law School also hosts Creative Commons, a new initiative that's affected over four million works in its first eighteen months of existence. Conceived by Eric Eldred, plaintiff in *Eldred v. Ashcroft*, a Supreme Court challenge to the Sonny Bono Copyright Term Extension Act, and chaired by legal scholar and San Francisco resident Lawrence Lessig, CC uses existing copyright law to give creators the opportunity to okay reuse of their work in advance. My new feature film, for instance, bears a CC license permitting anyone to reuse it freely for noncommercial purposes with attribution. Those wishing to copy or redistribute it within these limits don't have to ask special permission, and the online version of the film will show up in Web searches for films that have been cleared for reuse. CC is also working on realizing an idea that's been on many minds for several years—an "intellectual property preserve," resembling a national park for culture. Also known as an "IP conservancy," such an entity would contain donated cultural content and treat it as a shared, public resource, free for all to share and use. This model recalls the English common grazing lands before their enclosure by the oligarchy, and points to the possibility of adjusting the balance between private and public property.

San Francisco also hosts a community of archivists dedicated not simply to preserving past culture but also to making it available in new contexts. Pressure for archival access has influenced many archivists to reconsider the tenets of their profession, and San Francisco's Internet Archive, a nonprofit "Internet library" located in the Presidio, has played a leading role in expanding the definition of what archival access is and might be. Founder Brewster Kahle says that the Internet now gives us the ability to collect and preserve the world's cultural information and make it available to everyone at all times at miniscule cost. The archive collects Web pages and makes this ephemeral digital content available on the current Web through its Wayback Machine; hosts over 10,000 live music shows by consenting performers; makes the Prelinger Collection of almost 2,000 archival films available for free downloading, viewing, and reuse; and is involved in a project to digitize one million books and make them available online for free. Kahle, myself, and our organizations have also sought to reform copyright law via the courts—we recently filed *Kahle/Prelinger v. Ashcroft*, in which we assert that the practice of automatically renewing copyrights is unconstitutional. What unifies these activities is a sense that archivists must assert themselves to overcome obstacles to collecting and disseminating historical documents, whether they're paper, film, or digital, and that copyright law requires immediate reform if people are to have the ability to access and quote from these documents.

The Internet Archive was founded in 1996 to preserve ephemeral digital content on the net. But lately its functions have expanded: it's now a massive distributor of free and public domain music, movies, and books, and its activities point the way to a robust alternative economy of culture. The "model of plenty," as Lawrence Lessig puts it, a model based on gifting, sharing, and diverse nonfinancial rewards, now competes with the classic "model of scarcity." Enabled by the latest computer technology, the archive walks in the footprints of San Francisco's many utopians, imagining a world where culture and capital are no longer tightly bundled.

It's not simply artists that are focusing on alternative economies of creation. While most programmers labor in highly commercialized environments for financial gain, they often spend time creating free and open-source software as well. Open-source software is released to the world under a license that stipulates, among other conditions, that not only the original software code but any new code using it must remain available for free distribution. In other words, the free character of the original code "infects" new code that's written, thus building a body of free code available to all. Free code, such as the

Linux operating system and the Mozilla Web browser, constitutes a "commons" that's not owned or controlled by large corporations, and whose development isn't crippled for business reasons. The open-source and free software movements hark back to more traditional ways of creating socially useful goods and services; it's a remapping of the traditional gift economy into an efficient practice for sharing tools and ideas, granting attribution and fame, and enabling innovation without money changing hands. Though people all over the world develop and improve open-source and free software, there's a nexus of energy in San Francisco, and many of the most active contributors and theoreticians of the movements live here.

A growing community networking movement also contributes to realizing a "model of plenty" in San Francisco. The members of this movement seek to build a regional network infrastructure that isn't controlled by large telecom corporations. Using inexpensive wireless technology, they're building a free network on which they hope free culture will thrive. Anyone exploring the wireless networks in their neighborhood are increasingly likely to discover an SFLan node, to which they can hook up for free broadband Internet service. SFLan's self-description reads, "In many ways this is a return to the way the Internet used to be: You own your equipment, I own my equipment, and we connect to each other. Hence, we do not have to ask a large corporation what we can do with our network. If this works, we would like to spread this technology near and far."

Just as community wireless activists seek to establish parallel networks not under corporate control, bloggers seek to establish (and arguably already have built) a parallel mediasphere in which shared convictions, virtuosity of expression, and the esteem of one's peers govern what makes the news, rather than the decisions of highly paid editors and publishers. Though blogging isn't inherently about appropriation or reworking copyright, bloggers quote, recontextualize, slice and dice, comment and criticize up to and well beyond the narrow limits of fair use. A favorite indoor sport of the Bay Area, blogging is still young and disruptive, likely to pose a new set of challenges to conservative copyright law.

Brewster Kahle often jokes that "the Presidio should be a copyright-free zone." By this he doesn't mean that pirates should occupy the former army post, but rather that progress grows out of process. "We need areas to experiment," he says, "where the good ideas can be replicated, and where we can spend time going through and rejecting bad ones." He is, in other words, calling for a laboratory-type approach to issues of copyright and "intellectual property," where debate, the exchange of ideas and theories, and radically new practices all contribute to shaping a new and fairer consensus on the distribution of culture. If this is occurring anywhere today, it is in San Francisco.

If, as Lawrence Lessig says, online battles spread to the offline world, then the copyright wars have only just begun. In San Francisco, where we have a history of thinking about these issues earlier and more incisively than many others do, we can influence national consciousness on culture and copyright. More fundamentally: If, as many believe, reconsidering the ways we distribute culture can lead us to reconsidering how we distribute property, San Franciscans are again leading with a utopian wedge. Let us be a zone where a rich cultural commons and many models of plenty rule.

Digital Politics 101

What Does Information Want? *To Be Free!*
When Does It Want It? *Now!*

Annalee Newitz

nown equally for its unconventional culture and sprawling techno-
scientific industrial complex, the California coastal landmass stretching from George Lucas's LucasArts ranch in Sausalito down to the
Google campus in Mountain View is a hotbed of digital politics. Given the
social geography of the region, it's not surprising that Silicon Bay has
spawned a thriving population of radicals, inventors, and other malcontents
eager to challenge the status quo. But what is surprising, at least for people
involved in more conventional political movements, are the sorts of issues that
matter to geeks.

Activists and organizers in the community blend a weirdly socially responsible version of libertarianism with what can only be called market-mind-
ed socialism. Although it's hard to reduce digital politics to any single set of
concerns, often they are preoccupied with access to cultural resources—
whether those resources are pieces of art, frequency bands on the electro-
magnetic spectrum, information about government surveillance, or the
source code that makes up a piece of software.

But politics as such are rarely discussed among techies. Instead, geek activists
and community leaders in the Bay Area simply view themselves as particularly intrigued by making certain changes in the social order. Freedom may
be an ethical imperative, but it's also a form of community optimization. At
least, that's what many of the region's most ardent, wired organizers would
say. What follows are introductions to a few representatives from the politicized geek community who have inspired their fellow nerds to act up, speak
out, rethink received wisdom, and demand changes in the system.

The Hacker: Fyodor

After reading Fyodor Dostoevski's *Notes from the Underground* as a teenager,
Fyodor chose his online monicker and started to hack in earnest. Among
programmers, he is legendary for writing a software tool with the modest
name Nmap. Nmap is so widely known that it even made a cameo appearance in *Matrix Reloaded*, when hacker hero Trinity uses it to break into a

power plant computer and rescue the imperiled Neo. "I almost did a dance when I saw it up on screen," Fyodor told me with a grin.

Working from his home office in Mountain View, Fyodor spends his days doing what he loves best—programming, hacking, and socializing with fellow geeks online. Although hackers have gotten a bad rap in the media, Fyodor embodies the original meaning of the term, which he defines as "playing with computers and pushing hardware and software to its limits." He also values the hacker community he's helped create with Nmap—tens of thousands of Nmap users and developers subscribe to his email lists and offer him feedback on the constantly evolving tool. Fyodor makes money by licensing a commercial version of Nmap to corporations, but most people use his free software version of the program—anyone can use it and modify it as much as they like as long as they don't sell it.

"There are positive political/social/technological goals which keep me coding until the sun rises," Fyodor explained in an e-mail. "One of the goals has always been to promote free systems like Linux over Windows. Nmap is a way to give back to the the free software community that had given me Linux, gcc, emacs and so many other valuable programs."

But Nmap carries political risks as well. Some lawmakers would argue that using Nmap can be a criminal act—indeed, one user was brought up on criminal charges for scanning someone else's machine using Nmap (the case was eventually dismissed). What makes Nmap so dangerous? The program is a port scanner, which means it looks at ports—doorways between a computer and its network—to see whether the computer is open to receive information and, in some cases, what kinds of software that computer is currently running. While Nmap is generally used as a network diagnostic tool—essentially, to make sure you haven't left any ports open that might let in hostile code like worms or viruses—it can also be used for what Fyodor calls "network exploration."

You can use Nmap to roam the Internet, peering into people's ports at random, just to gather information about who has left their virtual windows open. Armed with this knowledge, it would be possible for a hacker to break into those computers through ports that their owners had unknowingly left in a vulnerable state. Using Nmap on the Internet is analogous to using a toolbox to take apart your car engine and see what makes it run. Car manufacturers, however, would rather that you go to a licensed repair facility if you're going to take your car apart. This essentially allows them to maintain control over your property even after you've bought it. Fyodor invented

Nmap to help people take back that kind of control from the companies and people who constrain the design and functionality of Internet public spaces.

"While it is true that Nmap can be used for negative purposes, those are overwhelmed by positive ones," said Fyodor. "I like to encourage network exploration and understanding. Like a lot of things, the Internet is even more fascinating and powerful when you understand and control how it works under the covers."

His position, which is held by many politicized software developers, can ultimately be understood as a kind of techno-populism. Fyodor wants Nmap to empower users, to help them fully understand the Internet rather than simply using it. Given how much information and personal data we entrust to corporations on the Internet, it's crucial that we have tools that allow us to explore this space and discover for ourselves how secure or insecure it is. The fact that Fyodor makes his tool available as free software helps advance his cause and allows thousands of other people to participate in making Nmap even more flexible and powerful. Fyodor and other Nmap users are pushing for what Princeton computer science professor Ed Felton calls "the freedom to tinker," the ability to take apart and explore the devices we use every day without corporate or government interference.

The Dork: Karen Marcelo

Karen Marcelo once told me that she'd gotten into building robots because she likes "to blow shit up." A former researcher at Xerox PARC, Karen has designed remote-controlled robotic creatures for Mark Pauline's monster robot performance troupe Survival Research Labs as well as for half-robot performer Stellarc. A longtime San Francisco resident who left the Philippines as a young adult, Karen once wrote a chunk of code that allowed a person in the U.S. to shoot a gun in Japan. Today, she is the organizer of a popular San Francisco nerd salon known as Dorkbot.

Dorkbot started in New York, but one of its most successful spinoff ventures has been San Francisco's version of the event, which is billed as "people doing strange things with electricity." Once a month, a group of programmers, artists, and hackers get together in a San Francisco art gallery to share their latest inventions. Usually there are two or three speakers, and the audience asks questions. Occasionally, Karen will host an "open dork," where anybody can get up on stage for a few minutes and talk about their work.

"Our politics are very anarchist and do-it-yourself," Karen explained to me over coffee. "We recently had a speaker who set up his radio transmitter to broadcast from a lunchbox, which is very illegal," she said. "We had a class on how to tap into the power lines and get electricity for yourself. Or how to set up antennae to get the Internet for free. Why pay some giant service provider when [local free wireless ISP] SFLan offers it for nothing? Also, we've done several sessions on how to generate your own media. Among the Dorkbot people, there's this idea that you can't rely on the press—you have to be your own media."

Karen says that what makes Dorkbot such a success is that it fosters community. "People meet here and then start projects together," she said, adding that the founders of Indymedia met through Dorkbot and that several of Matt Gonzalez's biggest supporters were also Dorks. "I'm not sure what Matt has in common with us, but there's clearly something," Karen mused. "I mean, we're not exactly environmentally sensitive—I have pictures of Mark [Pauline] standing in puddles of gasoline. And we frequently unplug pipes using M16s. That can't be good for the environment."

Nevertheless, the politics of Dorkbot clearly do share territory with grassroots, indie political campaigns. Liberating technology from its corporate context, Dorks want to turn castoff engines into art and invite ordinary citizens to infect the media with their own ideas about freedom. When electoral politics seem to be failing, and the media coverage of the war in Iraq features only the current Administration's point of view, it's easy to see why disgruntled techno-savvy citizens might want to cook up their own media culture in response.

The Activist: Ren Bucholz

After he finished up an undergraduate degree in media studies, Ren Bucholz came to work at the Electronic Frontier Foundation (EFF) as an activist. A nonprofit digital liberties think tank in San Francisco, EFF focuses on legal and policy issues around electronic privacy, free speech, and intellectual property. As the organization's Activism Coordinator, Ren—who describes himself as "a traditional liberal lefty"—runs outreach campaigns to educate the public on everything from the perils of electronic voting to the rights of people who are being sued by the Recording Industry Association of America (RIAA) for copyright infringement. He sends out action alerts on EFF's massive e-mail lists, works with other organizations on shared issues, and coordinates letter-writing campaigns. Of course, when you work on digital liberties, activism can take unusual forms: Ren described giving a speech in an online virtual world called *There*, where he handed out virtual EFF t-shirts that the avatars in the game could wear.

"What's fun and frustrating about the issues we work on is that a lot of the time we're the first to do it," Ren said. "We bear the burden of educating lawmakers and judges and the public about emerging issues and that is a huge job." But, he added, EFF has grown a lot in recent years because many issues that once seemed to touch only the lives of geeks are now mainstream concerns. "File sharing is a good example of that," Ren said. "Suddenly this issue is making national headlines, but EFF has been working on it for years. I could say the same thing about electronic wiretapping and searching people's e-mail." The USA-PATRIOT Act made Internet evesdropping—long a concern of EFF staff—into another hot-button issue.

Ren feels that the Bay Area has a strong digital activist community, but he pointed out that one of the best parts about his brand of activism is that it's so easy to engage in a national or international campaign without ever leaving your office. "Groups don't have to be in the Bay Area for us to work with them," he explained. "With the electronic voting issue, I have an affinity group with a representative from Working Assets, one from MoveOn, one from Verified Voting, and another from True Majority. We meet weekly via telephone, and when we aggregate our groups, we can reach about 2 million people across the nation with one e-mail."

According to Ren, there are really two kinds of digital activism. First, there's the technically enabled activism that allows him and his colleagues to reach millions of people with the click of one button. Usually this kind of activism involves getting traditional issues groups to have a strong Web presence and to communicate with their members or activists via e-mail. "Technically sophisticated activists can be more nimble and take instant feedback from their constituency," Ren noted. The other kind of digital activism is what EFF has been doing for years (along with technically enabled activism): dealing with issues where civil liberties and technology collide. Groups like the Electronic Privacy Information Center, Public Knowledge, and the Center for Democracy and Technology are other groups like EFF who focus on digital liberties. And this is where young activist leaders like Ren are most valuable.

Ren is helping the public understand that as new technologies evolve, it's important to keep tabs on how the government and corporations may use those technologies to manipulate citizens and consumers. E-voting, which has spawned both public protests and lawsuits in several states, is a prime example. Diebold, the manufacturer of e-voting machines adopted across

California and elsewhere, has funding from several individuals who are also major contributors to the Republican Party. The voting machine manufacturer is also notorious for altering the software on its voting machines without government oversight. Their machines have also been involved in several suspicious elections. EFF, with Ren's help, has been heavily involved in the activist campaigns to force voting machine manufacturers to provide voters with an auditable paper trail. If anything goes wrong with the software on the machines, a paper trail guarantees that voters can check to make sure their votes were registered correctly.

The Lawyer: Lawrence Lessig

Perhaps one of the most infamous geek activists of his day, Lawrence Lessig is a law professor at Stanford who has dedicated his life to changing the rules of intellectual property (IP) law. Like Fyodor, who believes everyone has the right to do what we choose with our computers, Larry thinks citizens should have the right to do what we like with public domain creative works.

Crucial to his argument is the idea that the public domain needs to be expanded. In 2002, he helped create a nonprofit organization called Creative Commons that offers authors alternative copyright licensing schemes that grant people the right to reproduce the copyrighted work as much as they like, or to use parts of it in their own work (CC licenses are popular with musicians who want other musicians to use their beats, for example). His work is particularly relevant in the computer age, when it is easy to use parts of other people's images, music, or movies in your own creative work to make something entirely new.

Larry also argues that copyright extensions have gone out of control, and that we need to cut back on the time that IP owners can keep copyrighted works out of the public domain. The more impoverished the public domain is, he argues, the more we deprive artists and scientists of the raw materials they need to make leaps forward in the artistic and intellectual realms. Taking as his premise that extended copyright terms and draconian punishments for infringement violate the First Amendment, Lessig has argued his cause in Washington D.C., in several books, and (memorably) before the Supreme Court in a suit to repeal the so-called Sonny Bono law, a copyright extension that brought the term of copyright up to 95 years (adding 20 years to the previous 75-year term). Although he lost the case, Larry has continued his fight to expand the public domain and challenge IP hoarders who have made copyright infringement a criminal offense.

In part as a result of Larry's tireless campaigning, IP reform has become one of the most crucial issues in digital politics. It touches on the natural antagonism between corporate interests and those of consumers, as well as the difficulties artists face as they attempt to work creatively in a medium where traditional notions of copyright infringement no longer make sense.

San Francisco–based public domain advocates such as Rick Prelinger (who maintains a vast digital archive of public domain films) and Brewster Kahle (who runs the Internet Archive, a facility that hosts historical "snapshots" of the Internet as well as Prelinger's archive, among others) have worked with Larry and Creative Commons to make sure the public has free access to creative works, and can reuse those works in their own media creations.

Another San Francisco nonprofit that has worked with Creative Commons is the Public Library of Science (PLoS), a group of biologists and science writers who are devoted to making the contents of scientific journals accessible to everyone. Currently, most medical and scientific journals are so expensive that it is impossible for people to conduct meaningful research unless they are part of a wealthy institution that can afford to license the content of these journals. PLoS wants scientific knowledge to enter the public domain as quickly as possible, so that medical advances don't depend on money, but simply on good research. They publish their own free, peer-reviewed biology journals online, and also work with other organizations to push large scientific journal IP holders like Reed-Elsevier to make the articles in their catalog freely available to everyone.

The Blogger: Danah Boyd

"Blogging is a political act in the feminist sense of the personal being political," Danah Boyd told me over the phone. In the background, I could hear her tapping on a keyboard. Danah is the consummate blogger in an era when blogs are fast becoming the twenty-first-century equivalent of soapboxes. And her Zephoria.org is the only blog in the world about blogging itself. Filled with Danah's observations about how online connections can be used to understand real-world social relationships, Zephoria is done in typical blog style: Danah posts an entry, often with pictures and links, and people who read her blog can comment on it. A graduate student at UC Berkeley, Danah uses her blog the way other academics might use a study group. Many of her fellow wired academics and analysts read Zephoria and post their latest findings there.

Recently she's grown more interested in social networking sites—which allow people to post a profile of themselves and link to other people they know, as well as groups they are interested in. Danah is fascinated by the way social networks allow people's social connections and political communities to be explicit. All you have to do is read somebody's profile to find out who all their friends and colleagues are.

"Of course you can figure out people's politics by reading what their blog is about," she said. "It becomes a political statement, a way of working through identity issues. That's why some of the most political blogs are involved with queer politics—because that's about participating in an identity."

Danah isn't terribly interested in overtly political blogs like Andrew Sullivan's. Her work centers on how bloggers and social networkers form webs of trust with other people they meet online and use those trust webs to explore their beliefs. Most bloggers say their sites are about what interests them on a personal level. But Danah has found that often political issues are so crucial to people's identities that their online presence becomes inseparable from their politics.

"I was fascinated by Friendster during the [anti-affirmative action] Proposition 54 campaign [in California]," she said. "People would put up "no on 54" pictures in their profiles or change their names to be "no on 54." But this wasn't something the site allowed them to do—they were breaking out of what the site permitted because it was so important to these people's identities. This was the kind of moment when politics are so much part of your identity that they become part of your profile on a social networking site." These are also the kinds of political actions that created such excitement around Howard Dean, which was the first blog-centric, tech-enabled presidential campaign.

Another aspect of social networking politics that intrigues Danah is the fact that putting so much personal information online can be dangerous. An employee at Microsoft was fired in 2003 for posting pictures in his blog that he'd taken on the Microsoft campus. The snapshots were of several Apple computers the company had bought in secret; the employee was fired simply for leaking the fact that Microsoft uses computers from other companies. EFF attorney Kevin Bankston, who is working with Danah on a white paper about surveillance and social networks, is concerned that the government may also use these sites for terrorist witch-hunts in which they place people under surveillance simply because their online profile and friendship network are defined as suspicious. "This is what scares me," Danah said. While blogs and networks enhance our ability to organize politically, they also make marginal groups more vulnerable to persecution.

The Journalist: Danny O'Brien

A British expat living in Silicon Valley, Danny O'Brien is famous for co-editing an e-mail newsletter called *Need to Know* (but generally referred to among its thousands of nerd readers as *NTK*). *NTK* charts the inside gossip, techno-politics, and pop culture obsessions of geeks who care about social issues.

Danny came to the States in 2000 in order to "track the decline of the dot.com boom" for the *London Sunday Times*. As an observer, he says he sees U.S. geek politics with a "very British eye." He is sometimes stunned by the liveliness of the grassroots activity here. "Britian has a more tightly knit political community," he said. "There's always a feeling that somebody in government will pay attention to your concerns, so there's little impetus to form long-lasting political movements or subcultures." But he sees the U.S. as having a very "thin and minimalist" mainstream culture that forces non-mainstream political groups to be more segregated and isolated—and, ultimately, far more organized.

"The Bay Area has a completely self-contained and self-sufficient geek culture," Danny explained. "I can live and breathe and die geek culture in the Valley and I'd never have to leave [computer superstore] Fry's—I could raise my kids in Fry's! They could buy motherboards at one end of the store, and sell them at the other. In the meantime, they'd live on frozen pizza." Famous for his politically pointed satire, Danny is also dead serious about the importance of this kind of geek isolationism. It can become a powerful organizational weapon when tech-related concerns go political.

Danny recalls one of the most interesting geek activist campaigns of the last several years: the protests over the arrest of Dmitry Sklyarov, a Russian programmer who was detained in a Silicon Valley jail for months because he'd come to the States to deliver a paper on a software tool he'd designed. Software corporation Adobe claimed his tool, which broke the (extremely weak) copy protection on Adobe eBooks, was in violation of the Digital Millenium Copyright Act (DMCA). Until Sklyarov's arrest, few people had realized that the DMCA had provisions that made it a criminal offense to design software that could be used to circumvent the copy protection measures used to keep people from pirating digital IP.

When the geek community heard that one of their own was being detained for building software—and that his only crime was that one part of his software could be used to pirate eBooks—they were instantly galvanized. "The impact of this geek self-sufficiency is politically very interesting. You have a long fermentation period, and then a burst of activity like the Sklyarov case," Danny recalled. "Within days of his arrest, there was a big protest, perfectly organized with t-shirts and banners and a website." Protesters marched outside the Adobe offices while the detained Russian geek got free legal representation from EFF attorneys. Adobe quickly dropped the charges, but the Justice Department pursued the case, and it took almost six months to get Sklyarov out of jail and back to his family in Russia. He is still facing charges in the U.S. if he ever returns.

"You have this instant organization in the geek community, which was originally there for handing out Linux distributions and then gets repurposed for political action," observed Danny. "Geeks know know how to plan a meetup because they've been working hard with their friends on how to build some fuckoff wifi thing—it's like a big cannon that they direct at something else."

The Future of Digital Politics

What's obvious, as of this writing, is that highly politicized digital subcultures won't be going away any time soon. As the developed world becomes more and more defined by information exchange, computer networks and other communications technologies will be crucial organs of propaganda and free speech. It will be incumbent upon citizens to understand something about how computers work if they are concerned about basic democratic issues like integrity in elections. Also, if they value their privacy, they'll have to learn about all the ways that their personal information gets circulated and revealed on the Internet. Fundamental, real-world issues like the right to vote and the right to privacy are now heavily mediated by digital machines.

While people in the United States and Europe are familiarizing themselves with weird new ideas like port scanning and electronic social networks, people in the developing world are just beginning to build out their digital infrastructures. Often, international groups like the World Intellectual Property Organization (WIPO) create treaties dealing with electronic IP and media regulation that are extremely disadvantageous for poorer countries. Today, it's simple for people in the developing world to get decent software because many countries have little or no penalties for copyright infringement. Want a copy of Microsoft XP in Russia? Just stroll down the street in Moscow and somebody will sell you a copy for a small chunk of cash. When I was in Cuba, a geek told me gleefully, "Windows is free software!"

Developed nations, the IP-holders of the world, are pushing developing countries to sign on to international treaties that will create an even greater rift between the digital haves and have-nots. While people in the Bay Area struggle to give people democratic access to software source code in voting machines, people across the world are fighting for access to digital content, as well as for devices that will allow them to use that content without paying exorbitant, developed-world prices for it. Our struggles go far beyond this rich stretch of land by the bay. Techno-utopians of the early 1990s used to say that the Internet would bring the world together in prosperity, but now we know their predictions were wrong. We're going to have to fight a lot harder than we ever imagined to reach that utopian *Star Trek* world where everybody lives in computer-enhanced peace and harmony. But every time somebody releases a new open-source tool, or liberates an idea or device from a large IP-holder, I have hope.

The Wave Of The Future

Lawrence Ferlinghetti

The old Spanish story of San Francisco as an island came true during the twenty-first century. The "island mentality" of early San Franciscans began in the nineteenth century when the town was founded by desperadoes, fortune seekers, gold-crazed miners, robber barons, castaway sailors, adventuresses, and outlaws from all over the world. The ones who struck it lucky and stayed prided themselves on being San Franciscans first and, secondly, citizens of the USA, more or less like Neapolitans who considered themselves Italians as an afterthought.

This attitude persisted into the twentieth century, until the imperial nationalism of the U.S. government, and the inroads of television, air travel, superhighways, and the Internet, began to make San Francisco more like the rest of Middle American corporate monoculture. Still, San Francisco remained somewhat apart in its spirit from the rest of Middle America (which some said began just east of Berkeley).

And a strange thing happened in the twenty-first century. A Green grassroots movement sprang up somewhat spontaneously, and at its center was a young Green Party member and cyclist with charisma whom people loved for his uncorrupted, uncompromised vision of a car-less green utopia for all races and creeds.

This movement that seemed to be "the wave of the future" went further than greening San Francisco. The new young politicos turned their sights on freeing themselves from the whole corrupt political and consumer culture that ruled America. And the logical way to free the island of San Francisco from the rest of the United States was to actually secede from it.

It seemed that this was not so outlandish a proposition. The old American Civil War had established that a state could not secede from the Union, but the idea that a part of one state could secede from that state—and thus from the Union—had never been tested.

Many forces coalesced in this liberation movement, including the reemergence of more popular alt-culture newspapers that "printed the news and raised hell" (as the *San Francisco Bay Guardian* put it), plus the revitalization of FM radio with many more programs like Amy Goodman and Juan Gonzalez's *Democracy Now*, as well as movement journalists infiltrating the newsrooms of the sold-out mainstream press. Hairy poets and rappers and stand-up performance artists, notorious for their devastating satires, added to the swelling tide.

Added to this was the growth of youth movements like the Bicycle Coalition that tied up rush-hour traffic all over the city every Friday night, with thousands of cyclists, not all young, streaming through main intersections, with no visible leaders to arrest. While the spread of indigenous farmers' markets and trade with independent Green farmers on the mainland made a self-sustaining economy a viable goal for the future.

Now, since the movement, in successive local elections, had managed to fill most of the positions on the city's Board of Supervisors with its own members, the coast was clear for revolutionary resolutions by the board, which was in total control of the city's politics, with much frustrated gnashing of teeth by Big Business and the Republican and Democratic machines.

And thus the first resolution to be passed almost unanimously was to declare that San Francisco proper was hereby seceding from the State of California and thus from the USA. And henceforth the city would pay no more state or federal taxes, and all the city's funds could go to improving the physical and cultural life of the city, including free citywide healthcare, free public transportation, and many other free social services.

And did not the state and federal powers with all their military might, immediately crush this rebellious city-state? Not at all. For in fact both the state and the federal government seemed totally delighted to be freed at last from this green thorn in its obese side, and most everybody lived most happily ever after.

"Jobs" Don't Work!

Chris Carlsson

With mind-numbing regularity, we are expected to trudge to the polls and cast votes for politicians who promise to pursue policies that will "fix the economy" and "create jobs." Predictably, nothing much changes. Why do we expect politicians and their policies to affect "the Economy," when the rest of the time we treat it more like the weather, something that gets "better" or "worse" according to events beyond anyone's control? The label "economy" is used to cloud in abstraction specific choices made by specific people that shape the rest of our lives for better or more usually, for worse. By framing our own daily lives of work within the abstract framework of "the Economy" we disconnect ourselves from a deciding, subjective role in determining our own activity and instead leave ourselves as unaware and relatively helpless pawns of forces beyond our knowledge or control. "The Economy" becomes a mystifying category, full of nonsensical and inexplicable categories that only experts can decipher; it is our era's religion, an explanatory framework that offers fictional and strangely "natural" explanations for what are simple (albeit confusing), observable relations between human beings. Politicians and economists who claim they will fix "the Economy" are playing the role of contemporary priests in the Church— they and they alone are competent to communicate with the higher power that ultimately controls our lives.

This underlies the emptiness of our democracy. Clearly there is little democracy in our lives when it comes to "the Economy." Our much-vaunted "freedom of choice" supposedly allows us to "choose" any jobs we want. By this "free choice" we exercise our tiny influence over the giant "invisible hand" of the market. But as we all know, most of us are only "free" to take one shitty job or another (or several!). In taking a job, no one asks for our ideas about what kind of work the enterprise *should* do, how the company impacts the environment locally and beyond, or what quality standards our work should meet. We have no say over who works there or how hiring is decided. In fact, on the job we lose most of the basic rights we take for granted as citizens in a democracy, including freedom of speech, freedom of assembly, freedom from search and seizure, freedom from random drug testing, right to due process, trial by peers, and so forth. On the job we are wage-slaves—if we depend on our wage, our condition can easily be construed as a version of slavery "with a human face."

Curious, then, that people across the political spectrum, especially "progressives," are so ready to demand "jobs" without a murmur of qualification or criticism (at best, the demand is qualified as being for "good jobs"). Most jobs today are a waste of time at best, if they aren't actually pernicious. As a social mechanism for allocating tasks that keep us all alive, "the Economy" and its foundation on "jobs" could hardly be *less* efficient, less fair, or a bigger waste of time and resources. One of the most glaring failures of the so-called free market is the well-paid elevation of patently useless and/or dangerous activities and the unpaid denigration of vital human tasks. Juxtapose bankers and weapons designers to child care workers and nursing home employees, for example. Even within ostensibly useful human work, for example, doctors and nurses, at least half of their work time is spent fulfilling the parasitic, useless demands of insurers and the bureaucracies of business, instead of providing the medical care that so many can no longer afford.

San Francisco's current economy is awash in the inflated equity of a housing market unmoored from historic values. This has greatly rewarded the lucky fraction that owns at the expense of the majority of renters. Meanwhile people work in offices, restaurants, stores, and hotels where real wages are stagnant or actually falling. In a city with a dozen major hospitals and tens of thousands of medical workers, at least a quarter of the residents are uninsured and prone to destitution through catastrophic illness or injury. A construction boom fueled by the dot.com frenzy, sustained after the frenzy's collapse by the spiraling inflation in real estate and long-term infrastructure programs of the city (San Francisco airport, BART, and MUNI expansions, Bay Bridge retrofit, Moscone Convention Center expansion, Transbay Terminal) is also helping to keep economic collapse at bay for the moment.

But all the signs for a major reckoning are before us: Unsustainable debts (government, corporate, and individual); absurd investment in useless office towers and unneeded hotels and shopping centers; stagnant or falling incomes and savings; soaring rates of illness and unmeasured workplace injuries; radically increasing homeless population; food programs serving more meals than ever—the list goes on.

In the face of the one of the most severe impending economic collapses in history, the recent mayoral campaign managed to avoid facing the catastrophe. No one wants to vote for a gloom-and-doom naysayer, so neither candidate offered a frankly pessimistic view of the city's near and medium-term future. Gavin Newsom's winning campaign featured dozens of detailed position papers that offered warmed-over platitudes about private-public partnerships, eliminating waste, and improving government efficiency.

Matt Gonzalez's "progressive" approach to "the Economy" failed to break with the basic categories and assumptions of all mainstream politicians. Gonzalez himself cannot be blamed, since nobody could get elected at this point by staking out a radical rejection of the capitalist organization of life. Progressives skate between the impossibility of thoroughly rejecting the framework of business, wage-labor and taxes imposed by capitalism, and the sheer impotence of policies they can actually promote and implement if elected.

Some of Gonzalez's rhetoric pointed to a deeper understanding of San Francisco's municipal economics when he intelligently attacked the laissez-faire boom and bust "mono-crop" attitude of previous regimes, especially Willie Brown's. But finally, between Gonzalez and Newsom, San Francisco's public debate remained thoroughly stuck in a reactive and self-defeating logic that defers to the initiative of capital and the world market when it comes to determining what San Franciscans are to do with our physical and mental resources.

Gonzalez promised to "put San Franciscans first" in his platform. To do this he proposed to develop an economic policy that has at its heart "the creation and retention of jobs, held by San Franciscans, which pay enough to afford the cost of living in San Francisco." Contrary to the open courting of business and "private-public collaborations" by Newsom (a patently empty strategy that he is still pursuing as mayor), Gonzalez at least clearly acknowledged that San Francisco "cannot simply follow the economic agenda of businesses but must meet the economic needs of its residents." It sounded vaguely promising, but since he lost the election, there was no chance to see this rhetoric translated into concrete actions.

In his campaign literature there were already plenty of reasons to be skeptical. Accepting the limits of a municipality's dependence on tax revenue and such revenue's source in capitalist business led him to assert the consequential tautology "jobs generate tax revenue." Accompanying this apparent "fact" Gonzalez also endorsed the notion that a city government must make equal priorities of retaining existing businesses as attracting new ones, precisely to solidify the "necessity" of tax revenue. The only way out of this conundrum is to identify the city's wealth not in taxes but where it is actually created: labor. San Franciscans are multitalented and resourceful but thousands of residents are wasting themselves at dumb jobs that no one ought to do (banking, real estate, insurance, advertising, military, and so on). What if all that talent were directed to solving problems and radically improving our lives?

Gonzalez deserves credit for suggesting that economic development has goals beyond *itself:* it should sustain communities, strengthen public education, the arts, and "community-based development initiatives," and ensure that existing communities are not destroyed by it. But after some simple reforms to reinforce local hiring and restructure the payroll tax, he jumped with both feet back into the abyss of government subordination to business when he stated "The primary challenge facing the next Mayor of San Francisco is securing sustainable employment opportunities for San Franciscans. The key responsibility of the city in securing such employment opportunities is insuring that the city's "human infrastructure" is so skilled that businesses will compete with each other to employ them . . . As Mayor, I will focus on unifying San Francisco's educational infrastructure, and along with business and community leaders, devise and implement an integrated program aimed at offering San Franciscans the education we need to compete in a 21st century economy."

Not even three months later the newspapers were filled with reports of "outsourcing," the increasing transfer of the Bay Area's much vaunted high-tech and service sector expertise to India, China, and other low-wage, high-skilled areas. These new boom zones have been knit together precisely by the globalization spearheaded by San Francisco–based multinationals (Standard Oil of California, now Chevron-Texaco, Pacific Bell, now SBC, Southern Pacific Railroad, now merged into Union Pacific, and Bank of America have all fled, though Bechtel, Levi's, The Gap, Wells Fargo, and PG&E are still homegrown, world-spanning engines of economic exploitation and environmental devastation). "Competing" in the twenty-first century means lowering wages and giving tax breaks, creating conditions for the maximum profitability of business. If lower costs and bigger tax "incentives" are offered somewhere else, most jobs these days are pretty easily moved.

Primary education in San Francisco, not to mention the rest of the U.S., is abysmal. The destruction of public education corresponds to a destruction of skilled work and a reduced need for intelligence at work. (To say nothing of the problems created by thoughtful, critical citizens!) Beyond some thousands of programmers and the skilled trades, most jobs are easily learned in a day or two, and most workers are easily replaced—skills are much less important these days than attitude. And even if you have great skills and a Mormonesque enthusiasm for your job, chances are the company will move or restructure or change its focus to increase profitability—leaving you out of work and wondering what to do next. In those increasingly rare examples of stable companies that provide decent, steady wages, and benefits, there's still a total absence of self-management or worker participation in determining *what the company does,* what its ecological impact is, how it connects to subcontractors and suppliers and *their* practices, and so on.

In 1991, former police chief Frank Jordan was elected mayor. As soon as he took office, he began trumpeting the northeast Mission district as a new "industrial zone" (Northeast Mission Industrial Zone, or NEMIZ) for the emerging biotech sector. This chimerical planning never really took hold due to neighborhood objections and an indifferent business community. The NEMIZ eventually filled up with the short-lived "Audio Alley" and other dot.com startups, only to empty out again after the dot.com bubble burst. Meanwhile, a mile eastward a whole "new neighborhood" (anchored by a forty-two-acre parcel for the biomedical campus of the University of California) called Mission Bay was started during Willie Brown's regime. Again, the assumption is that by investing public money in a fancy new campus and giving incentives to the developer (Catellus Corporation, a spinoff of the former Southern Pacific Railroad real estate division—"owners" of a real estate empire spanning the west, gained through corrupt land grants provided by the federal government in the nineteenth century as an "incentive" to build the railroads!), jobs and housing will be created. For over a decade, San Francisco has been waiting for the biotech ship to come in.

But that ship is just another in a long line of Potemkin-village promises of so-called "good jobs":

> On bad days Toby said he worked as a "pipette bitch." With no interests other than computers, a few select hormones, and science fiction novels, Toby was perfectly poised to work as a low-level researcher in yet another lab where the muckety-mucks studied genetic tagging. And so that's where he found himself most days, holding his trusty pipette over a box of clear gel attached to some electrodes . . . Usually he thought about nothing at all. He didn't achieve a Zen-like state of pipette-mediated calm. There was no enlightenment. He simply immersed his entire consciousness in the tiny movements of his body, the precise measurements and procedures . . . After almost a year of unbroken routine . . . Toby realized he could spend an entire 24-hour period without ever having a single, extended thought . . . he didn't have the kinds of multilayered or complex ideas he used to have back when he was hacking hormone pathways in graduate school.
>
> Here he was, a hypereducated twentysomething, his whole life before him, and his supposedly professional middle-class job had turned his brain into nothing more than basal ganglia . . . according to all the usual news sources, his job was hot. Supposedly Toby was at the center of an economic revolution in biotech.

The most-wanted jobs of the new millennium were in genomics; cities like San Francisco were developing vast office parks full of proto-wet lab spaces and special cold rooms for all the code-crunching clusters . . . Toby [felt] like he worked at McDonald's: The plastic gloves were practically the same. But more important, there was an almost unbridgeable gulf between what he actually did for a living and the hype about it. Reading the papers was like looking at one of those glossy ads suggesting that women kicked off welfare would have great futures if they just took jobs at fast-food restaurants. Look at our shiny kitchens! Full of happy people in hair nets and gloves making toasty burgers and crispy fries! Fast food is at the center of the restaurant economy! Just like biotech. *

This pattern of exaggerated expectations attached to what are quickly discovered to be boring, routine, mind-numbing jobs is all too common, and yet rarely reported with such clarity and wit. Another place to find compelling accounts is among the "Tales of Toil" featured from 1981–1994 in San Francisco's *Processed World* magazine (full disclosure: I was a participating collective member). From word processing to desktop publishing and web design, jobs in new technologies paid relatively well until the field filled with thousands of people following the false promise of "good jobs," only to find that high pay rates had disappeared. Irrespective of the pay, the crucial issue of content—of what we do, why, for whom or what, and usually how—is never confronted. And with almost no exceptions, the creative component of any job is what disappears soonest, replaced by management-controlled pacing, productivity demands, routinization, and bureaucratization.

Gonzalez's program might, at best, have opened up new avenues to change the relationship between the city and the work that is done in it. But if public monies were invested in training citizens to become so skilled and desirable as workers, we would still have to question which world economy we are getting prepared for. And just how this training would make San Francisco workers so well-paid (that is, expensive for their employers) that they could afford to live here! Everything going on in economic development—locally, nationally, or internationally—indicates the key trends continue to be lower wages and higher productivity (that is, longer hours, harder work).

A real alternative is called for. Tens of thousands have been meeting in the World Social Forum for the past five years, most recently in Mumbai, India. While participants have reported frustration at the absence of concrete alternatives, many representatives of cities from around the world are confronting the same problems that faced our progressive mayoral campaign.

---

* Annalee Newitz, "Techsploitation: Pipette Bitch Blues," *San Francisco Bay Guardian*, February 18, 2004.

And clearly the answers require a break with the dynamics of a world economy that pits city against city, country against country, human against human. The role of government, so diminished as the power of corporations has grown unchecked during the past quarter century, requires revision. Limiting local government to public spending on infrastructure and training for the benefit of private business is clearly self-defeating. Limiting local economics to a system in which private capital employs people as wage-laborers is to guarantee that the logic that imprisons us in a suicidal and degrading system will only grow stronger.

With my tongue only partly in cheek, I propose that San Francisco take the lead in visionary urban tranformation. "Jobs" as we know them are an obsolete way of organizing life. I propose a complete rethinking of what municipal government does, no longer "governing" so much as facilitating, allowing us to grow together, to begin building a life outside and against the Economy. If we are nearing a collapse in housing and other asset bubbles fueled by the insane expansion of credit, as it seems we are, then visionary politicians and citizens need to start redesigning the role of local government *now*, while we still have time and resources and before the coming depression and collapse begins. Not entirely seriously, but not altogether frivolously either, I propose the following New Department of Public Commons for a New Municipality, all of which can and should be integrated into our public education system for children and the continuing education of adults. A casual examination will reveal that there is a lot of work to do! But not the kind that generates private profits and sales.

Department of Public Commons

Overall, the city must focus its efforts on an economic strategy that grows the commonwealth and steadily shrinks the private sector. This is a program of decommodification, reframing work as a shared adventure in shaping and extending the quality of our lives.

A. **DIVISION OF PUBLIC SPACE** In charge of plazas, parks, and common lands, and their expansion, maintenance, and programming, this division would administer public libraries, tool and technology libraries, and public workshops, amply stocked with materials recycled from existing stocks. It would also begin the process of converting many streets into gardens and parklands (see "H" below).

B. DIVISION OF AGRICULTURE With the goal of San Francisco feeding itself as much as possible, it will expand community gardens, urban farming, and aquaculture projects, working with the Division of Public Space to reappropriate the vast acreage dedicated to moving and parking cars. Relationships will be cultivated between existing slow-food restaurants, local farmers, and local markets to create an unprecedented abundance of outstanding, healthy, tasty food, eliminating hunger and radically reducing dependence on fast-food outlets.

C. DIVISION OF AQUIFER AND LIQUEFACTION MANAGEMENT (AND DECONSTRUCTION) Irresponsible building patterns on historic mudflats and landfill should be removed *before* the next big quake; plans will be made for how to manage collapsing streets and buildings and how to reuse areas prone to liquefaction. Expanded use of existing aquifer will promote local self-reliance and reduce current dependence on quake-vulnerable aqueducts.

D. DIVISION OF CREEKS AND WETLANDS Working with the three previous divisions to open streets to make creeks visible, restore wetlands, and establish areas for aquaculture, farming, fishing, and recreation.

E. DIVISION OF HIGHEST-EVER TIDES AND SEAWALL CONSTRUCTION Preparation is needed for rising sea levels and catastrophic high tides from global warming. Technologies to protect the city from inevitable flooding should be explored now. Also, San Francisco's strong technology-savvy population can take the lead in developing techniques for adapting existing transportation and structures to widespread flooding.

F. DIVISION OF WORK REDUCTION Most work done in this culture is a waste of time, if it's not actually dangerous and counterproductive. This division will facilitate the creative reappropriation of our time and talents, redirecting our work (which is inherently *social* after all) toward socially determined needs and desires (see "I" below).

G. DIVISION OF CO-OPS AND COLLECTIVES Businesses will be encouraged to convert themselves from private ownership to worker-owned and -run co-ops and collectives. As much as possible, such enterprises should be encouraged to contribute to the commonwealth without measurement or pay . . . from each according to their abilities and to each according to their needs and desires.

H. DIVISION OF RECYCLING AND REUSE This important division will be responsible for innovation in more than just recycling garbage, but also in spawning whole industries to rehabilitate and reuse the discarded junk of the twentieth century. *Long-term goal: Stop importing new junk!*

I. DIVISION OF CRACKPOT REALISM Thousands of techies, artists, and tinkerers live in San Francisco. Already this city has served as world HQ for rapacious exploitation of huge swaths of the planet. It's time to make it up. Technology transfer of global-warming-reducing technologies: energy efficient transit, shelter, appliances, and communications. Reengineering technologies to last at least twenty-five years with minimum maintenance and energy use (see "J" following). (Bechtel engineers, for example, should be encouraged to direct their own time and creativity towards projects of social importance—something *useful* for a change!)

J. DIVISION OF NO HOME IS A CASTLE Housing is one of the most intractable problems facing any social transformation toward equality. A focused effort will be made to raise everyone's dwellings to a shared standard of space, safety, comfort, and beauty. Land trusts will be established to remove all land from the market, and housing will be owned and controlled by those who live in it. Reengineering every dwelling to be as self-sufficient as possible in water, power, and waste management (fertilizer manufacturing for "B" above).

K. DIVISION OF FREE MOBILITY

• First on the agenda will be the creation of a Bicycle Library with a fleet of 5,000 yellow bicycles. A municipal contest will be held annually for bike design and local manufacture with local materials.

• To support the Bike Library—a network of 100 bike huts and repair shacks will maintain the publicly owned fleet of bikes.

• The Panhandle will be expanded and extended on converted streets in dozens of directions to crisscross the city with greenways. The DFM, with the Division of Creeks and Wetlands and the Division of Public Space, will build green corridors along the natural terrain of creeks and shorelines, with meandering bike and multiuse paths.

- Public transit will be free, with radical expansion of routes for full city coverage. Rapid development and adoption of new transit technologies based on wind, solar, biofuels, and magnetic, "frictionless" tracks will revolutionize energy use.

L. DIVISION OF PUBLIC MEMORY

- Publicly owned and produced media will be expanded, and multiple daily newssheets and Web sites advanced, with independent editorial boards elected by districts.

- There will be oral history collection booths, and the Living Archive of San Francisco history will be available online and at a new city museum. Satellite museums in every neighborhood, where techniques of oral history collection and digitizing of archival materials is shared and learned, will reduce social amnesia.

- Public history forums will be held regularly throughout the city, debating various points of view on how life has changed over the years in San Francisco.

M. THE JAMES BROWN MEMORIAL DIVISION OF FEELING (GOOD)

- Everyone will have free comprehensive health care—state-of-the-art preventive care covering medical, dental and mental for all. San Francisco is a town overrun with care practitioners of widely differing quality and philosophy. A clearinghouse and licensing system will help residents get what they need.

- We will encourage the public declaration of desires, whatever they may be.

- Fear abatement will get top priority with programs to help people overcome fear of others, fear of disapproval, fear of speaking out, fear of not owning enough, fear of losing possessions.

- There will be a vigorous program of shame and guilt reduction.

N. DIVISION OF PUBLIC ART This division will involve itself in all urban projects, ensuring a high level of artistic participation in urban design, food preparation, historical presentation, and transportation design. Sculptures, paintings, multimedia installations, soundscapes, and new art experiments will fill the city, eliminating the visual blight of advertising in favor of art.

CONTRIBUTORS

D.S. BLACK is a ghostmodern writer and entropologist based in the Mission District of San Francisco. His series *The World At My Feet* is more than twenty years in the making. E-mail him at chaote@gmail.com

IAIN A. BOAL is currently Director of the Environmental Politics Colloquium at the Institute of International Studies, UC Berkeley. He is associated with *Retort*, a gathering of council communists based in the Bay Area. The Retort pamphlet, *Afflicted Powers*, will be published by Verso Books in the spring of 2004.

STEVEN BODZIN is a freelance writer who has lived in San Francisco since 1991. His service in the Civil War won him a silver star. He frequently translates Phoenician papyri for the National Museum of Kyrgyzstan, which equips him well to interpret local politics.

CHRIS CARLSSON was one of the founders, editors and frequent contributors to the San Francisco magazine *Processed World*. He is a founding participant of Critical Mass and is one of the creators of the urban history CD-ROM *Shaping San Francisco*. He has edited three books, *Bad Attitude: The Processed World Anthology* (Verso: 1990), *Reclaiming San Francisco: History, Politics, Culture* (City Lights: 1998, coedited with James Brook and Nancy J. Peters) and *Critical Mass: Bicycling's Defiant Celebration* (AK Press: 2002). His first novel, *After the Deluge*, will be published in autumn 2004. ccarlsson@shapingsf.org.

MONA CARON is a San Francisco-based illustrator and muralist. Her work can be seen at www.monacaron.com.

HUGH D'ANDRADE is a San Francisco-based artist and agitator. You can read more of his writings and see his work on his Web site: www.hughillustration.com.

LAWRENCE FERLINGHETTI's latest book of poetry is *Americus, Book I*, which he describes as "part documentary, part public pillow-talk, part personal epic —a descant, a canto unsung, a banal history, a true fiction, lyric and political."

BIANCA HENRY grew up in public housing in the Bayview–Hunters Point district. She organizes with Family Rights and Dignity of the Coalition On Homelessness.

KEITH HENNESSY, activist, performance artist, circus director, citizen. Raised in Canada, lived in San Francisco since 1982, with intermittant years working and living in Europe.

ERICK LYLE is the editor of the punk/crime-based *Scam* magazine and the coeditor of the irregularly published 6th-Street newspaper, *The Turd-Filled Donut*. He is currently the drummer or guitar player for too many bands to mention here.

QUINTIN MECKE was one of the original founders of SOMAD and he has worked extensively in the South of Market neighborhood on land use and community development for the past several years. He is a former Coro fellow and also served on the Elections Task Force on Redistricting for the City and County of San Francisco.

ALEJANDRO MURGUÍA is a longtime literary activist, editor, translator and author. His books include *The Medicine of Memory*, University of Texas Press and *This War Called Love*, City Lights Books, winner of the American Book Award. He teaches at San Francisco State University.

ANNALEE NEWITZ (www.techsploitation.com) writes about the social impact of technology for publications like *Wired, Salon.com,* and the *San Francisco Bay Guardian*. She also pens a nationally syndicated column called *Techsploitation* and works as a policy analyst at the Electronic Frontier Foundation.

JOEL POMERANTZ wears many galoshes. Self-educated in liberal arts, he has spent decades self-unemployed on nonprofit projects in journalism, transportation, food, housing, health, wilderness education, and public art. Joel gives culture, ecology, and history tours of San Francisco. www.bok.net/jig.

RICK PRELINGER (www.prelinger.com) is a moving image archivist, filmmaker, and partner (with Megan Prelinger) in an appropriation-friendly library located South of Market.

MICHAEL RAUNER is a San Francisco-based artist and photographer who has worked in several local nonprofit art organizations over the past decade. He has exhibited work nationally and has artwork in private and public collections, including the SF MOMA and the Bancroft Library. He can be reached at www.michaelrphotography.com

DAVID ROSEN is convener/executive producer of "Digital Independence," a forum on creativity, technology and democracy [www.digitalindies.com]. He is author of *Off-Hollywood: The Making and Marketing of Independent Films* (Grove Press), commissioned by Sundance Institute & Independent Feature Project, and has written for *The Hollywood Reporter, Red Herring, San Francisco Focus*, and other publications. He is managing director of the Media and Technology Group, a consulting firm. [www.mediandtechgrp.com]

MARLENA SONN is working her way through a suite of interesting professions: a former merchandiser for underground musical acts, rock journalist, photo editor, and dominatrix, she plans on a few more before her tell-all memoir. She lives and writes in North Beach, San Francisco. E-mail: toughunderfire@yahoo.com.

ALLI STARR is the founder of Dancers Without Borders and Cultural Links/Art in Action Camp and is a cofounder of Art and Revolution street theater movement. She is also the founder of the Bay Area's eleven-year-old Radical Performance Fest. Starr teaches movement theater, antiracism, and contemporary political arts history workshops, with students and activists across the country.

DR. AHIMSA PORTER SUMCHAI is the Health and Environmental Science Editor of the *San Francisco Bayview* newspaper and chair of the radiological subcommittee of the Hunters Point Shipyard Restoration Advisory Board. A former physician specialist with the San Francisco Department of Public Health, Dr. Sumchai founded childrens' clinics in community centers and public housing projects in the southeast and southwest communities of San Francisco and served as an emergency physician for the San Francisco Giants at Candlestick Park for ten seasons.

MATTILDA, a.k.a. **MATT BERNSTEIN SYCAMORE**, is the author of *Pulling Taffy*, and the editor of *That's Revolting! Queer Strategies for Resisting Assimilation, Dangerous Families: Queer Writing on Surviving*, and *Tricks and Treats: Sex Workers Write about Their Clients*. Mattilda is an instigator of Gay Shame: A Virus in the System, a radical queer activist group that fights the monster of assimilation.

MICHELLE TEA is the author of three memoirs, most recently *The Chelsea Whistle*, as well as a collection of poetry, *The Beautiful*, and the graphic novel *Rent Girl*, a collaboration with artist Laurenn McCubbinn. She has edited anthologies, and writes for publications including *The Believer* and the *San Francisco Bay Guardian*.

JAMES TRACY is a longtime housing organizer in San Francisco. He has written for *Race, Poverty and the Environment, Left Turn*, and *Contemporary Justice Review*.

MICHAEL "MED-O" WHITSON is a writer, activist, saxophonist, and community-based arts builder. He has co-directed San Francisco's 848 Community Space since 1992. med-o@848.com.

JOSH WILSON, a San Francisco resident, is one of the founders of Independent Arts and Media (www.artsandmedia.net/), a nonprofit group promoting free speech and strong communities.

INDEX

268

269

CITY LIGHTS PUBLICATIONS

Alberti, Rafael. CONCERNING THE ANGELS
Alcalay, Ammiel, ed. KEYS TO THE GARDEN: New Israeli Writing
Alcalay, Ammiel. MEMORIES OF OUR FUTURE: Selected Essays 1982-1999
Allen, Roberta. AMAZON DREAM
Amat, Nuria. QUEEN COCAINE
Angulo, Jaime de. INDIANS IN OVERALLS
Artaud, Antonin. ARTAUD ANTHOLOGY
Barker, Molly. SECRET LANGUAGE
Bataille, Georges. EROTISM: Death and Sensuality
Bataille, Georges. THE IMPOSSIBLE
Bataille, Georges. STORY OF THE EYE
Bataille, Georges. THE TEARS OF EROS
Baudelaire, Charles. TWENTY PROSE POEMS
Blanco, Alberto. DAWN OF THE SENSES: Selected Poems
Blechman, Max. REVOLUTIONARY ROMANTICISM
Bowles, Paul. A HUNDRED CAMELS IN THE COURTYARD
Borde, Raymond & E. Chaumeton, eds. PANORAMA OF AMERICAN FILM NOIR (1941-1953)
Bramly, Serge. MACUMBA: The Teachings of Maria-José, Mother of the Gods
Brecht, Bertolt. STORIES OF MR. KEUNER
Breton, André. ANTHOLOGY OF BLACK HUMOR
Brook, James, Chris Carlsson, Nancy J. Peters eds. RECLAIMING SAN FRANCISCO:
    History Politics Culture
Brown, Rebecca. ANNIE OAKLEY'S GIRL
Brown, Rebecca. THE DOGS
Brown, Rebecca. THE END OF YOUTH
Brown, Rebecca. THE TERRIBLE GIRLS
Bukowski, Charles. THE MOST BEAUTIFUL WOMAN IN TOWN
Bukowski, Charles. NOTES OF A DIRTY OLD MAN
Bukowski, Charles. TALES OF ORDINARY MADNESS
Burbach, R. and B. Clarke, eds. SEPTEMBER 11 AND THE U.S. WAR
Burroughs, William S. THE BURROUGHS FILE
Burroughs, William S. THE YAGE LETTERS
Campana, Dino. ORPHIC SONGS
Carlsson, Chris, ed. SAN FRANCISCO: THE POLITICAL EDGE (A CL Foundation publication)
Cernuda, Luis. WRITTEN IN WATER: Collected Prose Poems
Cassady, Neal. THE FIRST THIRD
Chin, Sara. BELOW THE LINE
Churchill, Ward. FANTASIES OF THE MASTER RACE: Literature, Cinema and
    the Colonization of American Indians
Churchill, Ward. A LITTLE MATTER OF GENOCIDE: Holocaust and Denial in America,
    1492 to the Present
Churchill, Ward. KILL THE INDIAN, SAVE THE MAN: The Genocidal Impact of
    American Indian Residential Schools
Churchill, Ward. PERVERSIONS OF JUSTICE: Indigenous Peoples and Angloamerican Law
Churchill, Ward. STRUGGLE FOR THE LAND: Native North American Resistance to Genocide,
    Ecocide and Colonization
Cliff, Michelle. FREE ENTERPRISE: A Novel of Mary Ellen Pleasant
Cohen, Jonathan. APART FROM FREUD: Notes for a Rational Psychoanalysis
Corso, Gregory. GASOLINE
Cortázar, Julio. SAVE TWILIGHT

Cuadros, Gil. CITY OF GOD
Daumal, René. THE POWERS OF THE WORD
David-Neel, Alexandra. SECRET ORAL TEACHINGS IN TIBETAN BUDDHIST SECTS
Deleuze, Gilles. SPINOZA: Practical Philosophy
Dick, Leslie. KICKING
Dick, Leslie. WITHOUT FALLING
di Prima, Diane. PIECES OF A SONG: Selected Poems
Doolittle, Hilda (H.D.). NOTES ON THOUGHT & VISION
Ducornet, Rikki. ENTERING FIRE
Ducornet, Rikki. THE MONSTROUS AND THE MARVELOUS
Dunbar-Ortiz, Roxanne. OUTLAW WOMAN: A Memoir of the War Years, 1960-1975
Eberhardt, Isabelle. DEPARTURES: Selected Writings
Eberhardt, Isabelle. THE OBLIVION SEEKERS
Eidus, Janice. THE CELIBACY CLUB
Eidus, Janice. URBAN BLISS
Eidus, Janice. VITO LOVES GERALDINE
Fenollosa, Ernest. THE CHINESE WRITTEN CHARACTER AS A MEDIUM FOR POETRY
Ferlinghetti, L. ed. CITY LIGHTS POCKET POETS ANTHOLOGY
Ferlinghetti, Lawrence. LIFE STUDIES, LIFE STORIES: Drawings
Ferlinghetti, Lawrence. PICTURES OF THE GONE WORLD'
Ferlinghetti, Lawrence. SAN FRANCISCO POEMS (A CL Foundation publication)
Finley, Karen. SHOCK TREATMENT
Franzen, Cola, tr. POEMS OF ARAB ANDALUSIA
Frym, Gloria. DISTANCE NO OBJECT
García Lorca, Federico. POEM OF THE DEEP SONG
Garon, Paul. BLUES & THE POETIC SPIRIT
Gil de Biedma, Jaime. LONGING: SELECTED POEMS
Ginsberg, Allen. THE FALL OF AMERICA
Ginsberg, Allen. HOWL & OTHER POEMS
Ginsberg, Allen. KADDISH & OTHER POEMS
Ginsberg, Allen. MIND BREATHS
Ginsberg, Allen. PLANET NEWS
Ginsberg, Allen. PLUTONIAN ODE
Ginsberg, Allen. REALITY SANDWICHES
Glave, Thomas. WHOSE SONG? And Other Stories
Goethe, J. W. von. TALES FOR TRANSFORMATION
Gómez-Peña, Guillermo. THE NEW WORLD BORDER
Gómez-Peña, Guillermo, Enrique Chagoya, Felicia Rice. CODEX ESPANGLIENSIS
Goytisolo, Juan. LANDSCAPES OF WAR
Goytisolo. Juan. THE MARX FAMILY SAGA
Goytisolo, Juan. STATE OF SIEGE
Guillén, Jorge. HORSES IN THE AIR AND OTHER POEMS
Hagedorn, Jessica. DANGER AND BEAUTY
Hammond, Paul. CONSTELLATIONS OF MIRÓ, BRETON
Hammond, Paul. THE SHADOW AND ITS SHADOW: Surrealist Writings on Cinema
Harryman, Carla. THERE NEVER WAS A ROSE WITHOUT A THORN
Higman, Perry, tr. LOVE POEMS FROM SPAIN AND SPANISH AMERICA
Hinojosa, Francisco. HECTIC ETHICS
Hirschman, Jack. FRONT LINES
Jenkins, Edith. AGAINST A FIELD SINISTER
Jensen, Robert. CITIZENS OF THE EMPIRE: The Struggle to Claim Our Humanity
Jonquet, Thierry. MYGALE

274

Pessoa, Fernando. POEMS OF FERNANDO PESSOA
Poe, Edgar Allan. THE UNKNOWN POE
Ponte, Antonio José. IN THE COLD OF THE MALECÓN
Ponte, Antonio José. TALES FROM THE CUBAN EMPIRE
Prévert, Jacques. PAROLES
Purdy, James. GARMENTS THE LIVING WEAR
Rachlin, Nahid. THE HEART'S DESIRE
Rachlin, Nahid. MARRIED TO A STRANGER
Rachlin, Nahid. VEILS: SHORT STORIES
Rey Rosa, Rodrigo. THE BEGGAR'S KNIFE
Rey Rosa, Rodrigo. DUST ON HER TONGUE
Rigaud, Milo. SECRETS OF VOODOO
Rodríguez, Artemio and Herrera, Juan Felipe. LOTERIA CARDS AND FORTUNE POEMS
Ross, Dorien. RETURNING TO A
Ruy Sánchez, Alberto. MOGADOR
Saadawi, Nawal El. MEMOIRS OF A WOMAN DOCTOR
Sawyer-Lauçanno, Christopher. THE CONTINUAL PILGRIMAGE: American
    Writers in Paris 1944-1960
Sawyer-Lauçanno, Christopher, tr. THE DESTRUCTION OF THE JAGUAR
Schelling, Andrew, tr. CANE GROVES OF NARMADA RIVER: Erotic Poems from Old India
Scholder, Amy, ed. CRITICAL CONDITION: Women on the Edge of Violence
Schuhl, Jean-Jacques. INGRID CAVEN: A Novel
Serge, Victor. RESISTANCE
Shelach, Oz. PICNIC GROUNDS
Shepard, Sam. FOOL FOR LOVE & THE SAD LAMENT OF PECOS BILL
Shepard, Sam. MOTEL CHRONICLES
Sikelianos, Eleni. THE BOOK OF JON
Solnit, David, ed. GLOBALIZE LIBERATION: How to Uproot the System and Build a Better World
Solnit, Rebecca. SECRET EXHIBITION: Six California Artists
Swartz, Mark. INSTANT KARMA
Tabucchi, Antonio. DREAMS OF DREAMS and THE LAST THREE DAYS OF FERNANDO PESSOA
Ulin, David, ed. ANOTHER CITY: Writings from Los Angeles
Ullman, Ellen. CLOSE TO THE MACHINE: Technophilia and Its Discontents
Valaoritis, Nanos. MY AFTERLIFE GUARANTEED
VandenBroeck, André. BREAKING THROUGH
Vega, Janine Pommy. TRACKING THE SERPENT
Veltri, George. NICE BOY
Waldman, Anne. FAST SPEAKING WOMAN
Wilson, John. INK ON PAPER
Wilson, Peter Lamborn. PLOUGHING THE CLOUDS
Wilson, Peter Lamborn. SACRED DRIFT
Wolverton, Terry. INSURGENT MUSE: Life and Art at the Woman's Building
Wynne, John. THE OTHER WORLD
Zamora, Daisy. RIVERBED OF MEMORY

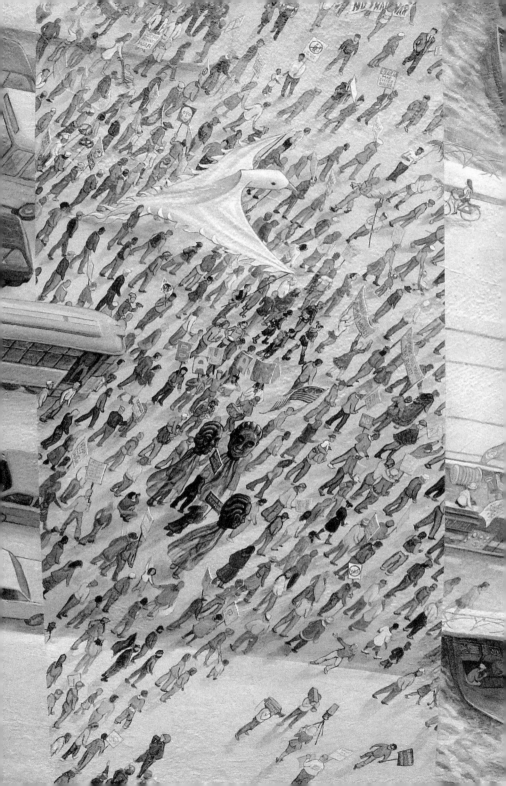